1 ADAPTAB

Being adaptable helps you to embrace chan... g ready for potential opportunities and handling setbac...

2 CRITICAL THINKING

Knowing how to think and work smarter, being more resourceful, creative and collaborative really gets you places. We've got amazing brains – get yours truly working for you.

3 EMPATHY

Never has empathy been so important. Nurturing all your relationships, understanding where other people are coming from and experiencing how effective it is to live in the present will have an immediate and tangible effect.

4 INTEGRITY

Trust, values, principles and honesty are valuable in a world of constant change. Integrity helps you to make decisions and set direction for your life as well as making you stand out.

5 OPTIMISM

Happiness is right at your fingertips every day. No matter what life throws at you, you can respond with positive action and achieve different outcomes as a result.

6 BEING PROACTIVE

Respond rather than react to whatever is going on around you. Be the captain of your own ship in life through small every day steps.

7 RESILIENCE

Know how to bounce back from disappointment, rejection and setbacks. Equip yourself with a strong support network and look after yourself. Resilience has never been so vital.

Praise for *7 Skills for the Future*

'It has been a delight to work with Emma Sue; she has so much passion for what she does. Her workshop and book are excellent and fit particularly well with our core company values - definitely seven key skills we need for our future!'

Tanya Zuchowski, Learning and Development Manager, CMS Cameron McKenna Nabarro Olswang LLP

'This book is an essential read for technology leaders transforming their people at pace, and for sale individuals with a growth mind-set, especially in high growth organisations.'

Rob Johnson, FInstLM. Sr Director, ServiceNow

'A great CV might open a door, but these seven skills will determine your future success and happiness. This gem of a book will help you to develop these essential work and life skills.'

Dr Lisa Day, Director of Studies Online MBA, University of Liverpool

'Emma Sue Prince exemplifies someone who has learnt to bounce back from adversity. Her timely and practical analysis of important life skills shows us how she did it.'

Virginia Isaac, President, Career Development Institute 2015–2017; Chief Executive, the Inspiring Futures Foundation

'Life is too important to live it without some guidance; this book is THE guidance all of us need to flourish in work and beyond.'

Dr. Sarah Mercer, Professor of Language Teaching, University of Graz, Austria

'Emma Sue is a consummate professional in the world of soft skills and emotional intelligence and is highly regarded as a leading authority. In this captivating read, Emma Sue openly shares details of her own incredible journey into the realms of self-awareness and developing these crucial skills, and why mastering them is so critical to achieving your own excellence.'

Hardeep Rai, Founder and CEO, Kaleidoscope Investments

'Although we are born with these seven skills, it is never too late to improve the way we use them in life and work. Everyone should buy this book and keep it by their bedside for reference. This way each of us can continually increase our happiness, success and well-being.'

Mark Swindell, Founder and CEO, Rock Rail

'It has been a delight to work with Emma Sue. She has so much passion for what she does. Her workshop and book are excellent and fit particularly well with our core company value definitely seven key skills we need for our future!'

Tanya Zuchowski, Learning and Development Manager, CMS Cameron McKenna Nabarro Olswang LLP

Pearson

At Pearson, we have a simple mission: to help people
make more of their lives through learning.

We combine innovative learning technology with trusted
content and educational expertise to provide engaging
and effective learning experiences that serve people
wherever and whenever they are learning.

From classroom to boardroom, our curriculum materials, digital
learning tools and testing programmes help to educate millions
of people worldwide – more than any other private enterprise.

Every day our work helps learning flourish, and
wherever learning flourishes, so do people.

To learn more, please visit us at **www.pearson.com/uk**

EMMA SUE PRINCE

7 SKILLS FOR THE FUTURE

Adaptability, critical thinking, empathy, integrity, optimism, being proactive, resilience

Pearson

Harlow, England • London • New York • Boston • San Francisco • Toronto • Sydney
Dubai • Singapore • Hong Kong • Tokyo • Seoul • Taipei • New Delhi
Cape Town • São Paulo • Mexico City • Madrid • Amsterdam • Munich • Paris • Milan

PEARSON EDUCATION LIMITED
KAO Two
KAO Park
Harlow
CM17 9NA
United Kingdom
Tel: +44 (0)1279 623623
Web: www.pearson.com/uk

First published 2013 (print and electronic)
Second edition published 2019 (print and electronic)

ISBN: 978-1-292-25916-1 (print)
       978-1-292-25918-5 (PDF)
       978-1-292-25919-2 (ePub)

British Library Cataloguing-in-Publication Data
A catalogue record for the print edition is available from the British Library

Library of Congress Cataloging-in-Publication Data
A catalog record for the print edition is available from the Library of Congress

10 9 8 7 6 5 4 3 2 1
24 23 22 21 20 19

Cover design by Madras

Print edition typeset in 10/14 Plantin MT Pro
Printed by Ashford Colour Press Ltd, Gosport

NOTE THAT ANY PAGE CROSS REFERENCES REFER TO THE PRINT EDITION

*This book is dedicated to my husband
Nick, without whom, writing it would
not have been possible.*

   *It is also dedicated to my Golden
Retriever Oscar who taught me the
real meaning of empathy and who
spent most of his time at my feet whilst
I was writing the second edition.*

Contents

About the author

 **Emma Sue Prince** is a specialist in experiential learning and believes strongly that this methodology is key to developing life skills and soft skills as it is the only way to develop self-awareness, upon which all behavioural change is based. She delivers powerful workshops in this regard and does so with many different target groups including 'closed' groups such as Muslim communities in Bangladesh and North Africa and diverse groups in the UK including lawyers, doctors, software engineers and many others. She also trains trainers to facilitate using the same methodology. Her successful approach lies in working totally in the moment with a group and with what emerges from that group. She is passionate about a group developing their own context for skills such as empathy, adaptability and being proactive. In this way real and powerful learning outcomes emerge from which strategies, progression and ideas can be defined.

Emma Sue is committed to supporting young people and an adapted version of her workshops are also run with secondary schools, youth offending teams and with young people who are not in education, training or employment.

Emma Sue works in emerging and developing countries as well as in the UK training trainers, designing materials and providing consultancy on employability skills.

Her work has taken her all over the world and has given her a leading reputation in the field.

She is the director of Unimenta – www.unimenta.com - a free membership website for trainers and for anyone interested in soft skills. Her website provides resource and support for trainers and lots of tips and support on developing the 7 skills for everyone.

Emma Sue believes passionately in the principles and concepts she writes about and tries to apply them in all she does.

Author's acknowledgements

7 Skills for the Future reflects experiences, contributions and insights, not just from my own life and all the wonderful research that is out there but also from a number of people along the way. In particular, I am very grateful to:

Nick English, my husband, who supports everything I do, who loves me and accepts me and has made my life so very much happier. Without a happy and stable home and family life it would be quite challenging to write a book! My children and my wider family enrich my life and give me so many opportunities to practise the 7 skills each and every day.

The editing and publishing team at Pearson Business who are such a great group of people to work with and who make the whole process of writing and producing a book a delight and joy.

I work with a lovely group of trainers and associates who are supportive, encouraging, hard-working and very talented, and without whom I could not have produced this second edition. These people stick with me through thick and thin and embrace all 7 skills in their life and work:

Idorenyin (Rhian) Fowler-Utip, a very talented trainer, whom I first met whilst working on a skills project in Tanzania and who now leads on all of our projects with young people, Chris Dudley, an incredible life coach who dedicates his work to the 7 skills and to helping people fulfil their true potential, Julie Cooper, another amazing trainer, coach as well as an author in her own right, Alison Rood, the sanest digital project manager I know – her calm and peaceful spirit is a shining light in that hectic world!, Andrew

Search, a colleague from my Cranfield MBA days who has offered me encouragement, kindness and laughter so many times, Hardeep Rai who has been a treasured friend, kindred spirit and sounding board for many years, Kate King who is 100% committed to working with disadvantaged young people and making a real difference in their lives, Jacinta Hargadon, a passionate personal development coach who has worked with most leading bluechip companies and is a source of support and wisdom, Andrea Giraldez, a simply delightful trainer and educator who has the skill of bringing out the best in people, Gabriela Weglowska who is passionate about diversity and cultural intelligence and embodies that passion in all her work.

I am very thankful to have the most wonderful Caroline Skydemore working for me. Caroline has great ideas, marketing flair, social media savvy and website genius. She's also mum to three young children whom she home-educates.

I would also like to thank each and every one of our workshop participants all over the world. They are the ones who have demonstrated just how important these 7 skills are and they make our work so worthwhile and in many ways, this book is for them.

Publisher's acknowledgements

Photo Credit:

x **David Morgan:** Image courtesy of David Morgan

Text Credits:

2 **Leo Tolstoy:** Leo Tolstoy, As quoted in The Artist's Way at Work : Riding the Dragon (1999) by Mark A. Bryan with Julia Cameron and Catherine A. Allen, p. 160 **10 Price waterhouse Coopers:** Workforce of the future: The competing forces shaping 2030 **17 Price waterhouse Coopers:** Workforce of the future: The competing forces shaping 2030 **35 Alison Rood:** Alison Rood, Digital Project Manager **40 Charles Darwin:** Charles Darwin **48 Paul Lutus:** Paul Lutus **55 LinkedIn Corporation:** 2018 Workplace Learning Report **60 Chris Dudley:** Chris Dudley, Life Coach and Founder of The Coach Collective. **64 Robert Shea:** Robert Shea **67 Jon Wilkerson:** Jon Wilkerson (www.jonwilkerson.com) **80 William Bruce Cameron:** William Bruce Cameron **89 Linda Elder:** By Linda Elder, September, 2007 **88 Philosophical Library:** A. E. Mander Logic for the Millions **92 The New York Times:** Lazlo Bock, Senior Vice President of People Operations at Google, Interviewed by Thomas L. Friedman, How to Get a Job at Google, Feb. 22, 2014, https://www.nytimes.com/2014/02/23/opinion/sunday/friedman-how-to-get-a-job-at-google.html. The New York Times **90 Foundation for Critical Thinking:** Critical Thinking in Every Domain of Knowledge and Belief , Richard Paul, Director of Research and Professional Development at the Center for Critical Thinking, Chair of the National Council for Excellence in Critical Thinking **94 Todd Rose:** Todd Rose **124 Brené Brown:**

Brené Brown, "I thought it was just me (but it isn't) (2008) **131 Goleman:** Goleman **133 Carl Rogers:** Carl Rogers **162 Alan K. Simpson:** Alan K. Simpson **169 U.S. Department of Justices:** 'Perspective Leadership Moments', FBI Law Enforcement Bulletin (October 2011). **176 Association for Manufacturing Excellence:** Park, D. and Huge, E. (July 1998) 'The Best Companies Have the Most Integrity', Association for Manufacturing Excellence **182 BIBLICA:** Luke 16:10 New International Version **198 Winston Churchill:** Winston Churchill **207 Hodder & Stoughton:** Seligman, M. (2011) Flourish: A New Understanding of Happiness and Well-Being and How to Achieve Them. Nicholas Brealey Publishing **208** Oprah Winfrey: Oprah Winfrey **221 Jo Marchant:** Jo Marchant PhD, science journalist and author **236 Milton Berle:** Milton Berle **241 Hachette UK:** John C. Maxwell(2008).Today Matters: 12 Daily Practices to Guarantee Tomorrow's Success,Hachette UK **247** Elsevier: Grant, A.M. and Ashford, S.J. (2008) 'The dynamics of proactivity at work,' Research in Organizational Behaviour, 28, 3–34 **254 Taylor & Francis Group:** Dweck, C.S. (1999) Self-Theories: Their Role in Motivation, Personality,and Development. The Psychology Press **254 Mango Media Inc:** Covey, S. (2004) The 7 Habits of Highly Effective People: Personal Workbook. Simon & Schuster **272 Winston Churchill:** Winston Churchill **281 W. Sams, St James's Street and Sherwood and Co:** 831 May, The Royal Lady's Magazine, and Archives of the Court of James's,Volume 1, Facts and Scraps by A Bookworm, Start Page 330, Quote Page 331, Published by W. Sams, St James's Street and Sherwood and Co., London. **285 Centre for Confidence and Well-Being:** Centre for Confidence and Well-Being,2006 **290 Robert F. Kennedy:** Robert F. Kennedy **313 George Bernard Shaw:** George Bernard Shaw **316 John O'Donohue:** John O'Donohue **318 Audrey Hepburn:** Audrey Hepburn **319 Anthony de Mello:** Anthony de Mello.

Foreword

To be part of the launch of the second edition of The Advantage (now re named "Seven skills for the future") by Emma Sue Prince is an unexpected privilege. I first stumbled upon Emma Sue's book at a workshop organised by the Health Education East of England. This workshop was designed to support internationally qualified doctors who were struggling to get to grips with the nuts and bolts of working in the NHS and living in the UK. Emma Sue's team were delivering sessions on mindfulness, empathy and resilience. Her book was a revelation and opened up some interesting discussions at the workshop.

In medicine and indeed other professions, we are hurtling through life, grappling with a complex, demanding and stressful existence. The tectonic plates of technology advances can be exhausting and overwhelming. There is generally a feeling of an ever-increasing pressure to do better, live longer, be healthier, earn more and be more successful.

This well researched book is a fountain of inspiration for anyone aiming for success, happiness and wellbeing in their lives.

Whist reading Emma Sue's book, I was reminded of my late brother, Dr Rakesh Sinha's book, 'Anatomy of Success' where he discusses the field of Anthropomaximology . This is all about human beings reaching their full potential. Emma Sue gives us an easy recipe to tap into that potential in ourselves and overcome the fallibility and fragility that is involved in being human.

Emma Sue gives us a mental toolkit, the seven soft skills distilled into a compass to point us towards the true North. These are appealing because they are comprehensive, simple and logical. These non- technical skills do not demand a paradigm shift or a seismic change in mind set because Emma Sue argues that we do not have to be genetically gifted with these qualities; they are all learned skills. Throughout the book Emma Sue uses her own background as well as her extensive work in training and personal development to contextualise the skills and there are numerous easy exercises to try out. Each chapter ends with a compelling vignette of the lives of real people. This brings home the key principles underpinning these deepest human qualities.

Emma Sue paints a succinct analysis of the world as it is today and its projected future; then narrows it down to the here and now at an individual level. What is illuminating are the numerous reference to in how to apply and use these skills in everyday life. I particularly like her take on Resilience that can help healthcare professionals adopt a different vantage point to learn to recover from and cope with setbacks and life events.

There is a Japanese concept "Ikigai" meaning a reason for being. It is the intersection of what you love, what you are good at and what the world needs. By applying Emma Sue's seven skills, anyone can bridge the gap between being ordinary and extraordinary and move a step closer to achieving Ikigai. After all, as Halford Luccock said 'no one can whistle a symphony; it takes an orchestra to play it'! Thus a deep engagement with all the seven key skills and adapting Emma Sue's blueprint gives us all the capability to stay one step ahead!

Dr Ratna Makker FRCA, MA (Med Ed) AOME

Consultant Anaesthetist

Clinical Tutor, FPD

Introduction

The seven skills of adaptability, critical thinking, empathy, integrity, optimism, being proactive and resilience tap directly into people's sense of control and autonomy about their own lives. These skills are in you and within every one of us.

Developing these skills puts you back into the driving seat of your own life, enabling you to be happier, find and do work you love and have a true sense of purpose.

You will:

- Radically increase your self-awareness
- Know what to do and say in any situation you find yourself in
- Be able to get ready to do the work you truly love
- Understand how to live your life with purpose and passion
- Have happier and more fulfilling personal relationships
- Be equipped for the workplace of the future

I wrote *The Advantage*, now retitled as *7 Skills for the Future*, because I know with utmost certainty that each of the seven skills I describe have contributed to the success of my own life. I only really became aware of this through writing this text. Being **adaptable** makes the difference between being ordinary and extraordinary. Being adaptable helps you deal with change with grace and ease. The right **critical thinking** skills mean you'll be creative, resourceful and smart in an age of information overload and ambiguity. Living with **empathy** is crucial for having and nurturing a healthy, clear and meaningful relationship, not only with yourself but with others too. You need **integrity** to live a life aligned to values, accountability and making the right choices. **Optimism** and using positive psychology principles helps you create and live the life you want to lead. If you're **proactive,** grab opportunities and understand how to respond to what's around you, rather than react, you will succeed. All of this requires **resilience** and strength, not least because we need to get better at failing and at persevering through setbacks and rejection.

Since this text was first published in 2013, there have been many studies and links around the importance of resilience, empathy, mindfulness, critical thinking, creativity, being adaptable and flexible, having integrity and values and being proactive and optimistic. These aren't just skills for now – they are skills that are needed more than ever because the world is changing even faster than it ever has been.

Many of the tools and approaches in the first edition have become very topical – for example, practising mindfulness, the important of brain neuroplasticity, resilience and building strong networks, practicing self-care and nurturing oneself, going out of our comfort zones, life-long learning, reinventing ourselves several times in our lives and using new skills consistently.

My life experiences have not been easy, but I know my life is and has been rich, exciting, wonderful and challenging, and will continue to be. From a young age I had to learn to be self-reliant, adopting a survivor attitude for coping with mental health issues in my family, major childhood moves to Germany and the USA with a lot of disruption to my schooling. During this time, I also experienced sexual abuse and I left home at 16 with no qualifications and no family support. This led to several (perhaps inevitable) difficult years in my late teens and early twenties, which included single parenting, divorce, severe financial hardship and the loss of my mother in a violent road accident. By the age of 25 I had been through what some people might experience in twice that time and what many people perhaps never experience. It took me a long time to confront and handle the subsequent emotions, blame and bad relationship decisions I made. It took me even longer to embrace my experiences and make them part of who I am today.

Whether I am adaptable and resilient naturally, or as a result of my early life experiences, I have certainly never shied away from taking on challenges and taking risks. I was always determined to make the very best of things. I made lots of mistakes and I still do. I didn't want to struggle financially. This was a priority for me and so I made sure I got the education I needed and it turned out I was good at making money. I've had to be proactive in creating a life that made sense for me and didn't mean being stuck in a rut or following a predictable life trajectory as a result of my early experiences. Getting the education I missed was so important to me that my early career included working in a cheese shop, coffee house, several restaurants and bars and often working two or sometimes three jobs to make ends meet. All of this gave me some very useful skills and a strong work ethic.

Throughout my life, I've always been optimistic. I now know that there is a strong link between being proactive, optimistic and resilient. Critical thinking helped me to be creative and resourceful when it came to working out what I needed in order to be where I wanted to be as well as to question my own assumptions and limiting beliefs about what I could and could not achieve.

I've been through the whole self-help movement, reading dozens of books and doing hundreds of different exercises. Some helped, some didn't. What really helped me through the most difficult times was a hard-nosed therapist who urged me to get up and make the most of my life, skills and potential. To even begin to do that I had to build empathy skills and develop integrity and these both could only come from and start with ME. Hard work? Yes, but worth it.

Such therapists and counsellors are very rare. However, I know that *7 Skills for the Future* gives you a shortcut to some of the lessons I learned.

Where have these skills brought me? Career-wise my work has evolved over the years and has included teaching, lecturing, training, research, qualification design, building my own consultancy business, designing training programmes, supporting disadvantaged young people, volunteering, serving on charity boards and being a trustee. All of this has meant creativity, taking risks and recognising and grabbing opportunities. My work has allowed me to travel widely to countries where there is extraordinary poverty and social issues, for which insight I am extremely grateful. I'm passionate about training, improving skills and developing people. The bulk of my work now is in helping people to develop self-awareness around these seven skills. Together with my team of licensed trainers, we run experiential learning workshops with diverse groups – from junior doctors to corporate lawyers, from young offenders and young people in pupil referral units to graduates, from employees in software development to middle management and senior leaders in major companies.

All, without exception, express the need for and a desire to work with these seven skills.

I am now happily married to the love of my life and I have a wonderful family. I live within a community where I can be active and contribute. I have fantastic work–life balance. Life is good. Actually it's brilliant. But it always has been, really.

We each have our own stories and our own experiences. We each can develop and become the very best of ourselves and live a life with meaning, purpose and real happiness. I'm still working on it and I use these skills every single day of my life. I also fall short of them each day too. I'm always learning.

I know these seven skills make a difference and I want you to experience this difference too.

So why not you, why not now?

'Everyone thinks of changing the world,
but no one thinks of changing himself.'

Leo Tolstoy

THE WORLD WE ARE LIVING IN

We are all aware of how the world has changed incredibly in recent years. That's not stopping any time soon. We are living in times of unprecedented change, complexity and competition. Big step changes and advances in technology, globalisation, economic uncertainty, the shifting workplace and changing social dynamics present us all with challenges and opportunities never before experienced. And everything happens so fast. On an individual level, we are faced with a huge overload of information, a lack of work–life balance and a lot of uncertainty when it comes to jobs and security. Technology has given us tools to have much more freedom in our lives. We have unlimited choice as consumers, we order food that arrives in minutes, we have access to billions of people all over the world and yet. . .

I don't believe we are very well-equipped when it comes to navigating our way through. We do not develop the skills we need to thrive in today's world from school, university or employer. We have all the information and knowledge we could possibly need at our fingertips and are, in many ways, so much better off than previous generations, yet there is a real lack of effectiveness when it comes to living our lives with purpose, passion and happiness. At the same time, the ability and the capacity to do just that are at our fingertips and right in front of us!

So what are the skills that are going to help us to be truly effective in our lives? Not just in the workplace but also at home and with our loved ones? Not just when we are starting our careers but throughout our lives as we change and move through different phases of it?

It is the soft skills that underpin successful, effective and happy people. For me, these kinds of skills are personal competences that make THE difference, help each and every one of us cope better with extraordinary change and challenges and make the most of the opportunities that are coming and that are already here. They are the skills that enable us to live truly happier lives as a result.

Your knowledge and technical skills may get you the job interview, but it's your soft skills that will get you the job, give you the tenacity and perseverance to set up your own business, take risks and embrace change in the midst of uncertainty. It is also your soft skills that will help you exploit better the many tools we now have to connect, to make money, work remotely and do our jobs better in a way that suits us individually.

It is up to each of us to develop stronger personal skills that help us to work well, reach our potential, be financially secure, have a fulfilling relationship and family life. It is up to each of us to contribute to society and life with the best of ourselves that we have to offer. That means being willing to step up to the table and take on personal responsibility for developing the competences and skills we need not only to survive in the world we now live in but also to thrive in it.

> It is the soft skills that underpin successful, effective and happy people.

What's great is that the skills we need today can all be developed and strengthened. You already have them and this text shows you just why these skills are important both now and in the future. You'll find out how you can develop these skills, how to use and apply them and be truly successful and effective as a result.

It's all about you

We live in a world where it is often easier to place blame than to take responsibility, especially when there is so much uncertainty around us. But whatever the circumstance we may find ourselves in, we can feel empowered and in control – each of us has untapped potential and strengths that we probably are not using to the full. What better way to discover these than a world and situation that challenges you like never before? Another way of looking at the times we now live in is to view them as an exciting era of opportunity and change. Difficult and challenging – yes. Impossible to rise above and succeed? Not necessarily, especially if you look from within for your strength, resource and security.

It can feel like there is a lot of negativity out there. In his book *Global Trends,* Adrian Done stated that we're living in a world with a highly uncertain economic outlook and with living conditions worsening for millions because of past failures and not dealing with what was 'foreseeable and actionable'. But we can also choose to look at this as an opportunity for each of us to rise up to the challenge, to actually take responsibility, to become and be the very best of ourselves. We need to start relying more on ourselves and on our inner resources.

In the past we didn't necessarily *need* to be **resilient** or **optimistic** – two of the key personal competences we need to have now. The speed and pressure of our lives combined with uncertainty mean that we need to be so much better at bouncing back from rejection and disappointment. Cultivating and nurturing optimism in ourselves is part of being resilient but also equips you with a different and much more resourceful way of thinking and approaching challenges and setbacks. Your capacity to use optimism impacts how you live your life, the choices you make and the directions you take.

New skills for the world we now live in

The idea of personal competences and soft skills is nothing new. Some 20 years ago, there was a recognition that people entering the workforce lacked key skills such as oral communication, collaboration, work ethic, self-discipline, written communication and problem solving; these have loosely become known as 'twenty-first-century skills'.[1] In my consultancy work around the world, I have come across these kinds of skills being labelled anything from soft and interpersonal skills to key skills, core skills, generic skills, employability skills and life skills. When you start to unpick this further, the list of such skills can include anything and everything from how well we communicate and manage conflict to the extent we seek to be collaborative, creative and curious. There has long been confusion and ambiguity around what to call these skills as well as what they actually are!

And although such skills are also firmly on most government agendas, they are still lacking across all levels of the workplace, from top to bottom. Why is this?

In the past ten years or so, society, the way we interact and communicate with each other as well as world and, economic events have, quite simply, made these skills *feel* less relevant and urgent. Skills like written communication and problem solving are impacted by the fast rise in the use of various technologies. Schools and universities do not explicitly teach us to be creative, curious and collaborative, although there are probably many opportunities to do so. Even when it comes to understanding how to work well in a team, there is no obvious way to raise awareness of individual contributions. This would require the teacher to facilitate self-reflection on a consistent basis and make the time to do this after group projects.

Technology and how we use that technology to communicate actually requires even stronger interpersonal skills. We have not been strengthening our ability to focus, communicate and collaborate and we are now weakening this ability significantly, each and every day. We need to slow down. Speed, whether because of fast thinking and actions or technology, is making us bad communicators – we listen poorly to others and figure out where they are headed after the first few words and then interrupt. Executive function is a set of mental skills that help you get things done and they are controlled by an area of the brain called the frontal lobe. Executive function means to focus, ignore distractions, remember and use new information, action planning, revising the plan and inhibiting fast impulsive thoughts and actions. We certainly have the brain capacity and ability to use these skills, yet the way we manage and use technology can impact these skills adversely. Habitual use of smartphones can have a negative and lasting impact on our natural ability to focus, manage emotions, think, remember and pay attention.[1] On the opposite side of the spectrum and rather ironically, for those who have weaknesses in executive function, assisted technology can be a huge asset in strengthening these skills too![2]

Empathy will be a key skill to harness and develop for all our relationships, whether offline or online because part of developing empathy is becoming more present and in the moment. Regular practice of being present and mindful has a significant impact on strengthening our ability to focus and manage distractions.

When looking to the future – let's name a year – 2030 – most studies traditionally focus on job losses and automation of jobs. This leads to fear and greater uncertainty. It is possible to choose a different outlook – one of excitement and opportunity instead. Employment in 2030 includes a whole host of skills we are more than able to grow and nurture. According to the Future of Skills 2030 Pearson and Nesta study[3], employment in 2030 will require skills such as:

> these skills make THE difference
>
> They are ADAPTABILITY, CRITICAL THINKING, EMPATHY, INTEGRITY, BEING PROACTIVE OPTIMISM and RESILIENCE

- **Judgement and decision making** – being good at weighing up relative costs and benefits of something and choosing the most effective and efficient solution

- **Originality** – coming up with unusual or clever ideas about topics or situations and being able to develop creative ways to solve a problem

- **Learning strategies** – getting to grips with the implications of new information for both current and future problem-solving and decision making
- **Fluency of ideas** – being able to come up with lots and lots of ideas about a topic – nothing to do with quality here, just quantity!
- **Active learning** – being able to find and use appropriate strategies for learning and teaching new skills and competences

'So what should we tell our children? That to stay ahead, you need to focus on your ability to continuously adapt, engage with others in that process, and most importantly retain your core sense of identity and values. For students, it's not just about acquiring knowledge, but about how to learn. For the rest of us, we should remember that intellectual complacency is not our friend and that learning – not just new things but new ways of thinking – is a life-long endeavour.'

Blair Sheppard

Global Leader, Strategy and Leadership Development, PwC[4]

When I look at this list, it is easy to link these skills with being adaptable, optimistic, resilient and proactive. Critical thinking is also key and empathy and integrity are the icing on the cake, strengthening each and every one of your relationships. And remember, this is not just about work – these seven skills also have a major impact on your well-being and overall happiness.

Key drivers of change

Let's take a closer look at some of the most important trends and changes in the world we live in and why it is these seven key personal competences and skills that we now need to nurture and develop throughout our lives.

Technology

Advances in technology have completely transformed the world we are living in. We live in a connected world – we are online more and more and globalisation means we are competing, not just locally, but internationally too. When it comes to the workforce, what sorts of skills are needed? We shouldn't necessarily be fixated on how automatable or not an occupation is but focus on skills – skills are something we can ALL do something about. We KNOW the future will look different to the past.

Technology is a key factor behind why our soft/interpersonal skills are in need of help both at work and in our personal lives. Why? There are two reasons, which are closely related:

1. We now spend an increasing amount of time interacting with an electronic screen, as well as being bombarded with a sheer overload of information, messages and data. This means that key interpersonal skills, which are best developed face to face and through experimentation and repetition, are simply being ignored.

2. All this time spent 'online' impacts our ability to focus attention, concentrate and listen – key elements of effective communication. Just think of a typical evening at home, 'relaxing': chances are you're probably watching a film while chatting to someone, checking something on the Internet, answering email and texting. You think you're multi-tasking, but your brain is actually becoming less able to focus efficiently. What you are really doing is simply shifting from one task to the other and dividing your attention. Or think about when you are trying to complete an important work project. Your ability to focus and block out distraction and even the quality of your work is directly impacted by how you manage your technology.

In terms of the technology itself, products are developed and become outdated far more quickly than before. Technical, detailed knowledge of, say, an iPad is obsolete in less than two years compared with, for example, a car of the 1950s. Back then, an engineer could repair engines successfully over decades with the same knowledge. Today, we

Consider this

I experienced this recently when I caught myself in the bad habit of taking my iPad to bed, planning to read my latest book download. However, despite telling myself not to, I got distracted and ended up checking email, Twitter and Facebook. This didn't help me to relax, so my sleep was disrupted. This is a very easy habit to fall into, and much harder to break. In fact, breaking it for me has meant removing the apps from my device completely. Even now there are times when I still break this habit and pay the price through poor sleep and a restless night.

have to work much harder to keep ahead of changes. It is also true that technology can amplify human performance in some jobs as well as provide opportunities for completely new jobs and sectors. Because of greater connectivity, it is becoming easier to enable 'intelligence' to be embedded into everything – from our cities, to all the products we use and even to our bodies. Peer-to-peer platforms change the way industries are run and owned. The sharing economy brings opportunities for new ways of doing business or 'disrupting' traditional models. Automation is just one of a number of technology trends – such as biotechnology, nanotechnology and the Internet of Things – that will have profound implications for the composition of the workforce.

Internet use and global connectivity is rising, largely due to more affordable smartphones and data plans in developing and emerging economies. The number of people around the world who can access the Internet is growing by large percentages every year and will continue to do so.

We use online platforms as daily communication tools, whether as individuals, professionals or businesses. For many, life without the Internet is unthinkable now.

If you think things have changed beyond all recognition in the last twenty, ten or even five years in terms of technology and social media, this will only increase. There'll be further incremental changes of existing technologies – how would wireless energy transfer Avatar-style robotics or anti-ageing drugs impact *your* life, for example? Technology familiar to us now will continue to evolve and change further. For example, I used to have a discussion forum on my website but in only a short space of time, this became an outdated way of sharing information and discussions, given the fast explosion of social media platforms and other ways to connect.

We all need to embrace the new and keep moving and learning. Generally, these changes will be incremental so you hardly notice them on a day-to-day basis. This makes it even more important to make sure your own efforts to manage and understand technological change are constant and part of your daily life. It's not going to be enough to say to yourself, 'I think I'll learn something new today'. It's dangerous to ignore the potential for further development. Things are changing every day!

It is a fact that many companies go under as result of not being able to adapt to new ways of doing things, but statistics show that even more new companies are created through innovation and the ability to innovate quickly or disrupt an existing industry. Technology can open up lots of new opportunities to new players with the right focus and determination.

> your soft skills become even more important with each new technological advance

A simple example of how the necessary competences needed in a particular sector are changing is the advent of 3D printing. 3D printing can now create a single item as cheaply as mass-producing thousands. Prototypes can be made quickly and cheaply. Right now it is difficult to predict the long-term impact of 3D printing, but economists say it will impact the world as profoundly as the factory once did. Therefore, it makes sense that those businesses or individuals that grab and act on opportunities within the 3D printing sector will likely thrive, though they will take some risks, in the short term, to do so.

Societies, businesses and individuals open-minded enough to embrace such technology are certainly more likely to flourish because it's now easier and cheaper to produce new prototypes and get new products to market. This is a further reason to become more adaptable, as you need this skill to cope with all of these changes. You must be able to think the unthinkable and thrive in spite of it. **Adaptability** is a key competence in today's world. It's also key in terms of how you view your ability to learn and change throughout your life.

On an individual level, all of this calls us to move forward with confidence, determination and optimism – all qualities we have inside ourselves already.

The workplace

The way we work is constantly evolving and changing. Traditional organisational structures have been fading for some time, and even the 'office', our place of work, is changing. Our tools and technologies shape the kinds of social, economic and political organisations we inhabit. These changes will mean that we need to rise to the following kinds of challenges:

- **Being more in control of our work and careers.** Job security doesn't really exist anymore in the way we like to think of it. The CEO and founder of LinkedIn, Reid Hoffman, says in his book *The Start-up of You* that we are natural entrepreneurs and it is the entrepreneurial way of thinking that will help us in this new era. We need to rediscover these instincts. He speaks of work and career being a predictable 'escalator' – of following a specific path of education, work experience, training, job and promotions. Now this escalator is 'jammed' at every point. We need to, and have to, find ways to 'unjam' this escalator. Being **proactive,** another key skill, takes on a whole new meaning.

- **Working flexibly, smartly and autonomously, collaborating virtually across different time zones and**

geographies. Our face-to-face interpersonal skills need to be replicated in how we communicate virtually over the Internet and email, and cross-culturally. **Empathy** helps us work more effectively as team members and leaders both online and offline, because it supercharges our ability to understand.

- **Becoming far better and more efficient at working with data.** Whether running a business or managing our individual health and finances, our work and personal lives will increasingly demand abilities to interact with data, see patterns in data, make data-based decisions and use data to design desired outcomes. New media technologies are bringing about a transformation in the way we communicate. This will require us to really step up our **critical thinking skills** as we know them. We also need critical thinking to be able to apply logic and reasoning so we can work out the strengths and weaknesses of alternative solutions, conclusions or approaches to problems. This key skill is also instrumental in managing and processing the overload of information we are exposed to online.

- **Shifting demographics** mean we'll all likely be working way past the traditional retirement age so it's important that you are doing work that you enjoy, that you are skilled at and that enables you to keep reinventing yourself. There are many exciting opportunities, but they also mean shedding our traditional view of work and career as we think of them now.

Everything in the workplace tends to be performance-based and short-term which changes the 'rules'. No job is secure. We need new skills for the new economy. We need to be adapting all the time and we'll stay young and agile by doing so.

changes in the workplace mean opportunities for work–life balance, new business and portfolio careers and working to your strengths

Globalisation

Global labour markets are becoming more and more integrated. The West no longer holds a monopoly on job creation, innovation and political power. The economic and political orbit has tilted towards the BRICS countries (Brazil, Russia, India, China and South Africa) and it's a trend that shows no sign of stopping, despite economic dip and imbalance between the BRICS countries themselves.

We're all familiar with the example of the call centre in India. Outsourcing like this has led to loss of jobs in IT, customer service and software development in the West, but this isn't the end of the BRICS countries' development. Emerging markets are now also climbing the social scale – going far beyond embracing low-paid manufacturing jobs towards higher-end research and development roles, innovation and design. India has over 200 million graduates, and UK and US universities are capitalising on this by expanding overseas. Many UK universities, as well as private independent schools, are opening more and more campuses abroad, specifically in India and China where there is 40 per cent of the graduate talent pipeline.[5] Many more are providing transnational education (TNE) in Malaysia, China and Singapore.[6] India has set up 14 research and innovation-themed universities in collaboration with US institutions. This is significant as, in the UK, the higher education market is still considered to be only at the beginning of globalisation.[7]

Competition for jobs is ever more ferocious in the globalised marketplace. Jobs will be increasingly polarised between well-paid, highly technical and professional jobs and service-type jobs in retail, leisure, health and hospitality, which are less well paid. However, this globalisation will also create opportunities for diverse cultures to work with each other, and individuals with this capacity will be at a competitive advantage.[8]

There will be buoyant demand for many existing professional occupations reflecting a growing demand for service industries. Public sector employment is also likely to grow. What's important to remember here is that it is not so much our actual jobs that will necessarily dramatically change in the future, but rather the skills and abilities for how we conduct our work. There will be an increasingly strong emphasis on interpersonal skills and higher cognitive thinking skills as well as essential human skills that cannot be automated.

Consider this

By 2030, the UN projects that 4.9 billion people will be urban dwellers and, by 2050, the world's urban population will have increased by some 72 per cent. Already some of the world's largest cities have a GDP larger than many mid-sized countries, making cities an important agent for job creation.

The BRICS economies are growing and with this comes political power.[9] If you're not involved with these countries in some way, you are likely to be in an ever-shrinking pond, even more reason to up your skills. Despite recent economic turmoil and social changes, BRICS will still continue to be potential powerhouses that drive world economy. The USA is the world's biggest debtor and China its largest creditor. If current trends persist, China will be the world's second largest economy by 2025 with India not far behind.

There are lots of opportunities within our changing geopolitical landscape – medium-sized rising powers such as Brazil, Indonesia and Turkey are redefining their roles regionally and internationally, creating new forums to resolve

you need to take initiative, be flexible, and why not learn another foreign language?

geopolitical issues. There will be a greater need for collaboration within business and society. The rapidly developing nations, particularly those with a large working-age population, that embrace a business ethos, attract investment and improve their education system will gain the most. Emerging nations face the biggest challenge as technology increases the gulf with the developed world; unemployment and migration will continue to be rampant without significant, sustained investment.

Within such a changing and dynamic geopolitical landscape, individuals who are well informed, prepared to be flexible in the face of change and prepared to adapt will have the best chance to prosper. This also opens up space for new entrepreneurs to address market needs across the globe and disrupt existing industries. In developed nations, this can maintain the current standard of living, and in emerging nations, it can lift people out of poverty.[10] It also means that people will become more mobile and be more open to working and living in different countries.

Demographic changes

The current demographic changes we are experiencing are going to have a significant impact on how we live and work and they also have a ripple effect on healthcare, finance, housing and education. With a few regional exceptions, the world's population is ageing, putting pressure on business, social institutions and economies.

We are living longer, are generally healthier and we are also expected to work for longer. Retiring on full pension at age 65 or younger is already a thing of the past for the majority and, in the future, working until you are into your seventies and even eighties will not be that unusual. Increasing global lifespans mean that young people may face competition from more skilled and experienced older people. At current trends worldwide, there will be only four potential workers per each 65+-year-old by 2050.[11] What this means is that if we were to continue to expect to retire at around the age of 65, there wouldn't be any sustainable form of financial support. This is something we need to accept, especially in the West. It is a sobering fact that means we simply have no alternative but to adapt and embrace the new future that is here. The rising millennial population also have different ways of consuming and divergent work behaviours. Millennials born between 1980 and 2000 are the first to come of age after the arrival of digital technology and they have heightened expectations of immediacy, participation and transparency. They also have a different attitude to risk and confidence and often want different things when it comes to success, money and lifestyle.

Young people everywhere need to develop these seven skills too, to grab opportunities and build new businesses and ways of working. And, surely also, the old can work with the young? We may see a big comeback of good old-fashioned mentoring as we move steadily towards a five-generation workforce for the first time in history. I also think it is important generally to encourage older people, wherever they are, to be willing to continue to make valuable contributions to business, economy and society beyond the traditional retirement threshold.

Businesses that manage to retain the experience and valuable knowledge of a senior workforce, while at the same time capturing the vitality of a young diverse workforce, will be the ones who excel in this scenario.

Consider this

Whatever your age, you could be working till you are much older so that makes it even more important to be doing something that you really love and that plays to your strengths, and to recognise that what you do will change and evolve also. All the more incentive for you to increase your personal skills and competencies and look inward for the resources that you will need to cope. Each of us has the resources to not just cope but to shine. We all have far more capacity than we think to be resilient, proactive and adaptable!

Personally, I have no expectation of 'retiring' because I see my work as bound up intrinsically with my strengths and what I contribute to the world. Indeed, I see my work in phases of reinventing myself, drawing on all the experience and skills I've gained over the years and becoming better and better at what I do. People in midlife career need to keep being innovative, changing in readiness for the next part of their career, not only because of working longer but also because the way they work or where they work might change. What you've been doing for the last ten years or so may not sustain the next part of your career. Individually, we need to keep an open mind on our expectations in later life. We're all in for a longer life anyway, so we need to find ways of making this healthy, contented and fulfilling rather than the opposite, or anticipating the opposite. A fair bit of this is linked to **resilience** too where it is vital to look after yourself, build strong networks, find a sense of purpose and get really good at embracing change. And luckily, anyone can learn to be more resilient.

The best opportunities will be for the savvy who make a valuable contribution to society and business. They'll be in constant demand everywhere. Emerging and developing economies will provide entrepreneurial activities, career development and personal growth for value-adders. Making sure you are in that pool means commitment to education and life-long learning as well as a focus on your self-awareness.

Health

We know we are going to live for longer. Living longer is not necessarily great if those extra years are spent suffering from poor health. It is much more important to live longer lives in *better* states of health. Part of developing personal competences and skills is an increasing awareness and responsibility for our own health. And it's proven that, if you are stronger physically, you are more likely to be resilient mentally too.

The general nature of our health problems is changing as a combined result of global ageing, urbanisation, globalised lifestyle changes, accelerated worldwide transmission of communicable diseases and the higher burden of chronic disorders. In high-income countries, 70 per cent of all deaths are among people over 70 and this elderly population are more likely to suffer from multiple chronic conditions as they get older. In the West, we are likely to see a return to younger members of the family increasingly caring for the elderly, as the healthcare system will not be able to support the level of care required and the costs of such care are likely to rise. So cultivating a sense of looking after ourselves will ensure those older years are spent living more healthily. This means embracing a different way of living that is more flexible. Most children born today are likely to live a multistage life with a variety of careers and transitions.

Our health and our lifestyles are linked to our inner resources and skills. For example, it is proven that if you want to build psychological resilience, starting with the body and building physical strength can drive this forward significantly. If we develop our ability to be **optimistic,** it is well known that those with optimism live longer and more healthily. And we also need optimism to face our lives and our futures with determination and vigour.

There are some practical and really simple things we can do to strengthen our health and to live longer and better ranging from making time to relax and recharge (away from technology), the food we choose to eat, getting daily exercise and sufficient sleep. I said they are simple – they may not be easy though! These simple things need to take on as much importance in our lives as work and our endless 'to-do' lists. They are the key to achieving more balance.

Many of the skills we need to strengthen have their roots in neuroscience and our brains. For example, it is now proven that we can develop what's known as our 'working memory' and that this actually gets stronger with age. Why is this important? Our working memory is like a mental jotting pad that enables us to adapt and change our behaviour. Knowing that this improves with age, as opposed to declining (as traditionally thought) is a breakthrough and turns our view of ageing on its head. It also has significant impact on our **critical thinking** skills.

Likewise, strengthening the body through Yoga, Pilates, exercise and meditation has a strong impact on our mental capacity and practices like mindfulness and meditation are linked with our ability to demonstrate **empathy,** another key competence and one that we are hard-wired to have. Strengthening our bodies in this way has a positive effect on our ability to be resilient and proactive too and helps us become better at focusing and being present.

> meditation, yoga and mindfulness are becoming more and more popular as ways to help build resilience and empathy skills

Education

In the West, we seem to be overeducating without providing essential skills. Our young people are finishing education without the skills they need to be employable. The number of young people leaving school and college with serious shortfalls in their employability skills is still high, according to the CBI/EDI Education and Skills Survey 2017.[12] The top weaknesses in both school-leavers and graduates alike are communication, team working, problem solving and self-management. This is also reflected in global surveys too. There is a widespread weakness in core workplace skills among existing employees, with literacy and numeracy topping the list. Some 775 million adults worldwide can't read or manage a bank account – that is a whopping 16 per cent of the global population.

Students in developed countries are still being stuffed with too many complex things, given where their lives are likely to go. They tend to be 'overqualified' and, these days, a university degree does not guarantee you a job nor does it equip you with employability and essential soft skills. Perhaps that has not traditionally been the function of a university degree but where and how can young people develop these sorts of skills? Economic pressures to work are also pushing younger and younger children into full-time day care or nursery education, which in turn produces an overload of 'learning'. Generally, education in the West and in emerging markets now starts too young and goes on for too long. Education systems are still not aligned to the labour market despite a growing understanding of the necessity to have this. There is the potential threat of steady and systemic youth unemployment which already exists in some countries. Even if jobs are available, individuals without appropriate training and support are unlikely to possess the required skill set. Governments need to engage with businesses more to determine what they really want and need and these requirements need to be included in education. This is starting to happen but there is still a long way to go.

Often, the focus is on teachers, schools, classroom size, funding, government and parents rather than placing any responsibility onto young people themselves. However, this approach allows it to be OK for individuals not to be responsible for their actions because the root cause of failure to achieve is believed to lie not in an individual but in the situation or external factors. This kind of thinking only feeds into a blame culture. What I do know with certainty is that it is possible for young people to develop these skills without an expensive education or training, or necessarily waiting until they are employed.

Generally, having young people study and specialise through university is a good and positive thing as long as they **These skills are at your fingertips.** can put this into practice; it needs to be for a purpose, otherwise a degree in a humanity is a luxury few can afford unless they intend to go into further training such as accountancy, teaching or law. However, even these professions are now fast-tracking undergraduates and school-leavers with good results, without necessarily demanding a degree first. Graduates who are generalists no longer automatically step into a well-paid job and haven't for quite some time now. In Germany, young people can learn one of 350 skilled trades through their vocational schools. Teenagers not bound for university apply for three-year programmes combining classroom learning with practical experience within companies, which have fully bought into the scheme. A massive two-thirds of schoolchildren in Germany undertake apprenticeships, and the cost is shared between the company and the government and generally positively regarded in German society. The result is superior German quality in everything, from haircuts to waitressing! Of course, there has been wide criticism of this system and Germany has been accused of not producing enough graduates, but in our current economy isn't this dual system starting to look more attractive?[13] In the UK, vocational training has long been seen as less attractive because of a belief that it is somehow second-best to an academic education, although this perception is starting to change now. More recently, Germany brought their apprenticeship model to the USA via Volkswagen with great success.[14] These sorts of programmes are gaining in popularity and will likely continue to do so. In the UK, the apprenticeship degree combining university study with on-the-job training is gaining momentum too.

Case study

As part of the new podcast series for this second edition, I interviewed the amazing Virginia Isaac who has held a number of positions in education and outside of it too. The extract below is from a talk she gave to Year 10 and 11 students in 2018 and which she very kindly shared with me:

'When I first started my job as Chief Executive of Inspiring Futures, I sat next to one of my favourite "careers gurus" – someone called Tony Watts. He asked me about myself and

I gave him a quick run down of all the different things that I had done in my life. He agreed that it was not so much a career ladder as career crazy paving. I then said that no careers adviser could have told me what I should – or would – do because I had done so many different things. Tony was unfazed. "Virginia", he said "you are an example of 'Planned Happenstance". What on earth is that I asked? Yes, qualifications are important but a career can go "wide" as well as "deep". Tony observed that I was an example of someone who had built up a whole host of different – transferable skills –

Adaptability

Flexibility

Optimism and enthusiasm

Preparedness to take risks

Strong interpersonal skills

Judgement

Resilience

Critical thinking

One could go on. The fact remains that all skills (soft and hard) are important and can be applied to a wide variety of different roles. Picking up the knowledge/expertise is often the easy bit; having the skills to apply it is a different matter.

So, I want to leave you with these thoughts –

We might live to 100 years so don't worry about having everything all at once. There will be plenty of time to try different things, dip in and out of the jobs market, have children if you want and travel the world (if you want). No doubt you will need to work until well into your 70s – do everything you can to ensure that you choose things that suit you and that you are happy with.

> *It's not just about having plenty of "me time", it's also about finding things that are socially useful so that you feel that you are putting something back – not just taking. Some of you might want to make lots of money; others might want to stay at home, looking after children and being a pillar of your local community – there is no one right answer.*
>
> *There are many forms of success; some are more difficult to attain than others. DO try and get your qualifications; DO pick up lots of skills as you go along; identify what they are and clearly articulate them; DO get as much experience as you can – try different things – even if things don't work out – it will make you stronger.'*

There is a clear need for lifelong learning. Our modern world is complex and it certainly does not allow for any stagnation of thinking once you have a degree or only if you have a degree. There is always more knowledge to be gained. Martin Seligman, in his book *Flourish,* says that all young people now need to learn both workplace skills and the skills of well-being and positive psychology. He says that if you were to ask parents what they want for their children, they would probably tell you that they want their children to be happy, confident, balanced, kind, healthy and loving. Schools teach achievement, thinking skills, success, literacy, test-taking and discipline. Seligman argues that what is important is to build character strengths such as honesty, loyalty, perseverance, creativity, kindness, wisdom, courage and fairness as well. It is possible that some schools do embrace this, but this is not generally the case in mainstream education and building these sorts of character strengths need to be given far greater importance and support.

We now need appropriate and useful theoretical knowledge, together with practical skills, social values and employability skills. This includes finding ways to recognise and build awareness of life skills that we develop outside of education and through exposure to different life experiences, opportunities and risks that we decide to take. The teaching of values, lifelong skills, literacy and numeracy will remain essential to equip future generations.

Making it happen

Much of traditional self-help says that if you want to improve your life, you first have to change how you think through using tools such as positive visualisation and affirmations, as well as just generally thinking positively. This will, in turn, have an impact on your emotions and how you feel, following which, your behaviour and outcomes will change. In principle, some of this sounds perfectly reasonable, but in practice, these methods are ineffective. Affirmation and visualisation are achieved through using relaxation techniques and cultivating self-belief but do not give any focus on dealing with the setbacks, sheer effort and hard work that go with striving towards any goal or behaviour change.

Yet change IS possible. Decades of research shows that there is indeed a simple but highly effective way to transform how you think and feel through focusing first on how you are behaving.[15] By using and applying the seven skills of adaptability, critical thinking, empathy, integrity, being proactive, optimism and resilience outlined in this text, you will start to tap into and develop your inner resources that enable you to do this.

Exciting times ahead

We are experiencing a change revolution. On every level. We have a real opportunity now, more than ever before, to become 'better versions' of ourselves and truly reach our full potential. And we can. Each of us really does possess the resources and capability within to develop the key personal skills and competences that we need. We need to be much more present and aware in our own lives and be proactive in how we live, work and the choices we make. Each day presents an opportunity to learn more, do more, be more, grow more. Each day provides ample opportunities to practise and strengthen these seven skills if we are open enough to spot these.

We are entering a new era. We CAN do more with less. Eighty per cent of effect and impact comes from 20 per cent of action. It's important to focus on the small, incremental things you can do and not to be overwhelmed by the thought of having to suddenly develop a whole set of new skills. Trying to work on everything at the same time wastes effort and resources and progress will be limited. Taking small steps and acting on that most important 20 per cent is what will make the difference and this text will show you how to do that.

Let's take a closer look at the seven skills that are going to help you succeed, get or create that job, find your true strengths and fulfil your potential.

1 **Adaptability:** It's more important than ever to be flexible, adaptable and agile, with plenty of resourcefulness and creativity to help you respond effectively to challenges and grab new opportunities. Why? Because things now change at a far greater speed and pace than ever before. Change is with us and it's constant. Being adaptable means you are far more able to handle uncertainty and risk without feeling overly vulnerable.

2 **Critical thinking:** Your attitude needs to be more open than ever. Critical thinking is raw material for twenty-first century success! To challenge assumptions, we have to be able to look at things from different angles, think outside the box, collaborate with others, clarify goals and find solutions. Problem-solving skills have never been so crucial. Being able to handle huge amounts of data effectively and come up with lots of creative ideas requires us to really sharpen our brains. You must be brave enough to challenge

conventional approaches and be adaptable to changing situations and circumstances. Experiment when you can, or you'll be stuck.

3 **Empathy:** This is the ability and capacity to really understand what someone else is experiencing and to walk a mile in their shoes. In other words: social perceptiveness. Why is empathy important? Because without it you will never have strong listening skills or the ability to respect others and really value your relationships. Everything you do is now more visible than ever. Managing and nurturing all your relationships well is a key skill and competence requiring focus and effort. You may not always get it right but building your empathy muscles will help you get it right most of the time.

4 **Integrity:** As the speed of life has accelerated, so has the number of people who are neglecting to do the things that are expected of them, such as being on time for appointments, returning calls and completing projects on time. These may seem like small things but they are not! Trust, values, principles and honesty are the name of the game now, as is authenticity. You must consistently behave in ways that are in line with your values. Throughout periods of intense change, be consistent – a harbour in the storm. Integrity will also guide you to making the decisions that are right for you and your life.

5 **Optimism:** Knowing how to develop and keep a positive attitude, no matter what life throws at you is vital for being happy. The world is not divided into pessimists and optimists after all. We each have the capacity to be optimistic and passionate about life if we can just learn to breathe, relax and lean into being happy.

You have the ability to generate and radiate good will and positive energy wherever you go and this will get you far. It's even more important in the absence of certainty, to be able to influence and inspire others around you as well as yourself.

6 **Proactivity:** You probably will have to reinvent yourself a number of times throughout your life and work and that is exciting too! You are more likely to end up working for yourself, have a portfolio career or start your own business. At the very least, you'll be changing jobs and roles a number of times. Being proactive is also about acting in the face of procrastination and responding, rather than reacting, to what is going on around you. More than anything, it is about choosing to put your energy into the things you can control rather than those that you cannot.

7 **Resilience:** Dealing with ambiguity, coping with stress and overcoming set-backs can be emotionally draining, psychologically demanding and intellectually challenging. Resilience helps you to bounce back and respond at your best and you will have higher levels of emotional stability. Through different points in our lives, we are faced with stress, sometimes traumatic. How we negotiate this stress has a big impact on our overall mental and physical well-being.

You already have these skills within you. If I were to ask you to reflect on your life experiences thus far, you would be able to identify many times when you have used and have applied each or all of these skills. What we tend to do less is focus on **strengthening** them and that is done day-to-day in small reflective steps. Doing so will develop your capacity and ability to thrive and be happy, do meaningful work and live a life full of purpose and happiness. Why not you and why not now?

Each section of this text focuses in detail on one of these skills. Backed up by the latest and ongoing research, I help you to understand what each skill looks like, why we need it and why it's important.

Each skill can be developed in different ways and it's important to understand how much of that is down to your own character and personality and how much is related to life circumstances.

The focus is on giving you practical and easy ways to develop these skills.

- You will be equipped to deal gracefully and effectively with information overload.
- You'll have strategies to respond well to change.
- You'll thrive despite uncertain work options and an uncertain future.
- You'll know how to get work–life balance right.
- You'll get better at taking risks, making decisions, working collaboratively and having great ideas.

Each skill ends with practical tips and exercises and a 'day in the life of' case study that takes you through someone's day, holding up a magnifying glass to that particular skill and how it makes a difference. If we can get into the habit of building and nurturing all seven skills in our day-to-day lives, we will soon notice big differences to the choices we make, happiness levels and our relationships with others. Each chapter includes links to longer worksheets and exercises that you can download directly from my website. Visit https://unimenta.com/seven-skills/

Since this book was first published, I have designed experiential learning workshops specifically to raise awareness of these seven skills. These are run with all sorts of people from all walks of life through my company and group of licensed trainers. We know that self-awareness is the cornerstone of all behavioural change and that these seven skills are ones that are strengthened day-to-day throughout life. Workshops like this deliver powerful learning, yet we do not vary any of the exercises that we use! They are the same for every single group – from NHS doctors to corporate lawyers and from graduates to HR teams and disadvantaged young people. What changes is how each group contextualises the skills for themselves and how WE work with what emerges from individuals. This enables each workshop participant to experience change, self-growth and have some immediate strategies in place from which to continue.

A corporate law firm case study

As I walked into the smart corporate training room, my heart sank slightly. It was set up like a board room with little space to move, designed for participants to sit passively while they endured Power Point and, perhaps at the most a role-play or two.

This was also a pilot workshop – everything rested on whether participants would respond favourably. Our workshops are experiential, energetic and exposing and I knew immediately that this methodology would be new for this group.

'This is for me?' – one of them exclaimed when she noticed that each person had a learning journal and a book. 'Oh wow, thank you!' – she was overjoyed as was the next participant.

Throughout the day, the group were engaged and a delight to work with. They work incredibly long hours and although they do receive lots of training, I think this may have been their first experience of focusing on their own self-awareness.

The firm had been through a recent merger and this was raised during the **adaptability** session – the feelings that can arise when change like this happens and how to best deal with it and handle it well. The exercise also raised immediate awareness of participants' willingness (or lack of) to go out of their comfort zone and to actively seek opportunities to be in the *stretch* or *learning* 'zone'.

'Perhaps I am not as adaptable as I thought I was and this made me think more about the impact of this in my life'.

A key part of each exercise we do is for participants to identify easy ways to flex their skills – to develop their adaptability, empathy and optimism skills through small day-to-day actions and awareness.

Empathy – one of the hardest skills to practise. Yet lawyers need this skill, as do we all, to have strong relationships, to understand clients and to win new business. This part of the day focused on active listening skills and using mindfulness to be present, to breath and to give attention.

We are naturally hardwired to be empathetic but it is a challenge to use this skill because to do so requires us to move away from our own perspective and to pay attention and be in the moment more rather than coming at things from our own ego and issues.

In the afternoon, we used some **comedy improvisation exercises** to raise awareness of using spontaneity, not prejudging, being flexible and present and handling life and challenges with a positive attitude – things that relate to all seven skills. This also brought up insights around how we can become emotionally affected by someone else's behaviour.

Optimism is a skill that really can be developed regardless of whether you see yourself as 'glass half empty' or 'glass half full'. If anything, optimism is a choice we can make on a daily basis. Cultivating an attitude of gratitude each day by recording what we are grateful for is a simple but hugely effective way to build optimism. We also used an exercise to help take personal emotions out of any situation or circumstance and leading to the understanding that WE decide how we want to respond in any given situation.

Outcomes

All participants found the day extremely useful, and this is what some of them said in their feedback:

1 *What did you enjoy most about the day?*

   - The positive message, energy, enjoyable group activities and engaging trainer.

- The soft skills I learned today are things I will carry with me for the rest of my life.
- It was very practical in an easy way – so things that can be implemented in normal life, fairly effortlessly but make a big difference.

2 *To what extent do you feel you learned some useful techniques to help you? (5 stars being the highest and 1 star the lowest)*

90 per cent of respondents scored 5 stars, and 10 per cent scored 4 stars.

3 *What are the most important techniques/tips you feel your learned?*

- Focus on deep listening, motivational 'YES', reconsidering inherent beliefs and assumptions about situations
- Mindfulness, body language and improvisation as well as the need to be stretched and to seek out those opportunities
- Active listening – really listening
- ABCDE technique, gratitude and power posing

It was such a privilege for me to work with this wonderful group. I really wasn't quite sure what to expect. We now run regular workshops with this law firm and others to raise awareness of the seven soft skills.

Find out more about our workshops here: https://unimenta.com/advantage-workshop/

Case study – Digital Project Management and the Seven Skills

My name is Alison Rood and I work in digital project management. I attended a workshop on developing the seven skills a few years ago. I have since found myself using the skills repeatedly in my work:

Why do you need all seven skills for a go-live deployment?

From time to time I have been asked by a client to sit with them during a 'go-live'.

'A go-live' - is the time when you the digital project manager (DPM) and your team (UX, designers, backend and frontend developers, sysadmins and testers) are ready to deploy, for example a new/updated website or an ecommerce integration project with third parties to the public online. In this particular instance, the team and I were ready to deploy a membership platform and administration portal, connected to a customer relationship management platform.

Why did I need all seven soft skills?. . .

Firstly, the team and I had thoroughly reviewed the go-live procedure, setting out a step-by-step plan including a roll-back plan, and ensuring everyone was clear about their roles and responsibilities during the deploy, including a backup team if required. I did this for many reasons, but mainly because anything can happen during a go-live that simply cannot be predicted. However, if you have a framework, you have a point of reference which is visible to everyone and this provides people reassurance and clarity during times of ambiguity and potential chaos. This allowed me to be more **adaptable and proactive** when dealing with the situation in the moment, providing me the breathing space to

think critically, so that I could analyse and assess the situation objectively; during a period of extreme pressure.

Being optimistic during times of pressure, will stand you in good stead for a successful delivery. Optimists evaluate a situation from different perspectives, they size up the situation accurately and if there are problems, face them, seek solutions and take action.

For this deployment, I was onsite with the client and so working remotely with the team; one of the key skills required was **empathy.** As a DPM, it is imperative you develop and nurture rapport with your team including the client; it is also imperative to get buy-in from the team at the start of the project and maintain it to the end (go-live). Demonstrating respect and valuing the relationships you have with the team, both individually and as a whole, helps to create an environment of mutual respect and honesty. **Integrity** has a huge impact on others being able to trust you. The way to build this into project delivery is by keeping commitments you have made to the team at the start.
Be emotionally honest and open, don't withhold information and be receptive to input from others. Actively listen, acknowledge and seek to understand their points of view or concerns. This continuity helps to build trust and stronger relationships all of which are vital for go-live.

During most live deployments, I have found that you are required to demonstrate a high level of **resilience.** This can take time to build up and starts with looking after yourself, this includes sleep, food, and exercise. Personally, I have found meditation and getting involved in creative activities such as painting beneficial. In short, any form of self-care which feeds the mind, body, and soul. Just as you have to create an environment for your team to thrive in you need to do the same for yourself.

> Demonstrating and honing these seven soft skills helps you contextualise a situation at work which in turn keeps people focussed on the task at hand, allowing you to be fully present and in the moment. One of the greatest gifts of a DPM is the opportunity to ensure both your team and client know someone is there to hold their hand and reassure them everything is going to be ok.
>
> Alison Rood, Digital Project Manager

These seven skills help you both at work and in your personal life – there is no doubt about that. Time and time again we see people benefiting both personally and professionally in our workshops. Because the focus is on awareness-raising, they leave the workshops knowing that they have the tools and tips to help them continue to develop. Because our methodology is experiential, our workshops are high impact meaning that participants retain the learning long after attending.

You may or may not attend one of our workshops – right now you have chosen to read this book and I thank you.

I know it will help you to sharpen your own self-awareness no matter your background, what kind of work you do, what kind of person you are. I promise that if you use some of the tips and exercises described in each chapter, you will notice a positive difference. I have seen this happen with hundreds of people all over the world.

If you want to focus more on your own awareness of these seven skills, please visit https://unimenta.com/seven-skills/ where you can sign up for free daily tips for each skill and also access online exercises, curated video clips, articles and downloadable worksheets.

If you are interested in attending one of our workshops or would like us to run one in your company, find out more here: https://unimenta.com/advantage-workshop/

Interested in learning more?

I've put together some extra resources here:

The Future of Skills, Employment in 2030 by Pearson https://futureskills.pearson.com/research/assets/pdfs/media-pack.pdf

Brown, A. (2017) *Emergent Strategy. Shaping Change, Changing Worlds.* A.K. Press.

Chatterjee, R. Dr (2018) *The 4 Pillar Plan, How to Relax, Eat, Move, Sleep – Your Way to a Healthier Life.* Penguin.

Done, A. (2012) *Global Trends, Facing up to a Changing World.* Palgrave Macmillan.

Gladwell, M. (2009) *Outliers: The Story of Success.* Penguin.

Haig, M. (2018) *Notes on a Nervous Planet.* Canongate.

Hoffman, R. and Casnocha, B. (2012) *The Start-up of You: Adapt to the Future, Invest in Yourself, and Transform Your Career.* Random House Business Books.

Pang, Soojung, K.A. (2018) *Rest: Why You Get More Done When You Work Less.* Penguin Life.

Seligman, M. (2011) *Flourish, A New Understanding of Happiness and Wellbeing and How to Achieve Them.* Heinemann.

Sinha, Rajesh Dr (2016) *The Anatomy of Success, Management Lessons from a Surgeon.* Harper Collins.

'It is not the strongest of the species that survives, nor the most intelligent that survives. It is the one that is the most adaptable to change.'

Charles Darwin

Chapter 1

ADAPTABILITY

Adaptability is an attractive quality. We all like to think of ourselves as being flexible and adaptable, a team player, 'going with the flow'. It means that we are not rigid or stuck and that we are open to change and challenges. I think if you were to ask most people if they consider themselves to be open and adaptable, they would tell you 'yes'. If you truly are adaptable, then you are more likely to handle change with grace and ease, not be thrown by the unexpected and be a lot happier. Yet most of us are actually a lot more resistant to change than we might perceive ourselves to be.

What is adaptability?

Adaptability can be defined as the ability to change (or be changed) to fit altered or unexpected circumstances. Every one of us has the basic capability to be adaptable; without this being hard-wired in us, we would not be able to function in the world. Throughout our lives we adapt, and indeed we have to. We adapt to school, to new environments, to work, to relationships, to learning and developing. Even though it is natural to resist change because we don't want to let go, our capacity to adapt is probably also greater than we think. That's because it's a basic survival skill – the ability to adapt smarter or faster than any current situation is what has allowed humans to flourish and consistently make progress since caveman days.

Adaptability is more than being flexible – it is about being open to things, even outside our comfort zone, and not expressing pre--conceived judgements such as 'I could never do that' or 'That will be too hard for me'. Sometimes we say these things only to ourselves rather than openly and what we tell ourselves has a powerful impact on our brains.

We equally cannot afford to think we know everything either! Something new will come along and blow that out of the water, whether it is a new technology, a new process or a new plan. Adaptability is about continually developing more of what we are truly capable of and living up to our potential. This is critical for our skills now and in the future. Unfortunately, it is also something we may well talk ourselves out of more than we think we do.

Change is difficult because we want to stay inside our comfort zone and we will naturally resist anything that requires us to step out of it. Therefore, a conscious effort is needed to do this for those of us less open to change, and even for those of us who are. Our comfort zones are, quite simply, as small or as big as we make them. We make our comfort zone bigger by engaging in more activities, tasks, thoughts and experiences that lie outside of it. The bigger our comfort zone, the more adaptable we will be! The comfort zone is where everything is easy and nothing risky ever happens. Equally nothing great or exciting happens there either. Just outside your comfort zone is the 'stretch zone' where learning and growth happen. This is the place which can feel a little uncomfortable because you might be stretching yourself in new and different ways but you're still able to manage. It's not easy but not impossibly hard either. However, if you go too far in this direction, you'll reach the panic zone which is not a good place to be, as the name might suggest. Learning and growth can't happen here because we are so far out of the comfort zone that we find ourselves in fight or flight mode.

your comfort zone is the key to how adaptable you are. Make it bigger and your ability to adapt soars

The stretch zone is the best place to be and one of the most effective ways to increase your ability to be adaptable is to ensure you are spending plenty of time there.

Here are some ideas to practise getting into your 'stretch zone' more regularly. Download the exercise here: https://unimenta.com/adaptability/

Adaptability enables us continually to work towards and fulfil our individual potential and to not necessarily stop once we've reached a certain level or point in our career and life. This is probably a good thing, given that we are all going to be living and working for longer. Life-long learning is a key skill to cultivate and adaptability feeds directly into this. You may need to reinvent yourself more than once in your career or life stages and even enjoy the opportunity to do so.

The more opportunities there are (or that we are presented with) that invite us to adapt successfully, the better! Doesn't this mean embracing change rather than our natural first reaction, which is to resist it? Adaptability in our world today means a whole bunch of things:

- keeping calm in the face of difficulties
- embracing uncertainty
- persisting in the face of difficulties
- taking on new challenges at short notice
- saying 'YES' to challenges
- dealing with changing priorities and workloads
- improvising
- bouncing back from setbacks and showing a positive attitude
- keeping an open mind
- seeing the bigger picture
- coping well with the unexpected.

Adaptability is all of these, and more. And the best way to build adaptability is to simply train ourselves to become more open to change and uncertainty. Being able to look honestly at this list and have an understanding of where you might find some of these harder than others requires reflection and self-awareness.

When we intentionally put ourselves in situations that are (just) outside our comfort zone, there is no doubt that we grow and that our comfort zone becomes bigger. Being adaptable can lead to tangible results in our work but can also make us feel much happier as we discover what we are truly capable of being or doing and as we fulfil more and more of our human potential. By contrast, not taking advantage of opportunities to live in our "stretch zone" makes our comfort zone smaller as does thinking that once we have reached a certain point we don't need to keep stretching and growing. If anything, the larger your comfort zone becomes, the more you have to work at getting yourself into stretch as what once may have seemed scary is no longer. A few years ago I had the opportunity to travel to Bangladesh for work – this put me firmly in my stretch zone and was a great thing to do. However, earlier on in my career this possibility would have seemed quite out of reach to me. This year I am actively learning some new skills such as how to make chocolate bars, podcasts for this book and create mosaics – for me these are new challenges that lie in my stretch zone. Next year, who knows! What I do know is that I will continually seek out opportunities, big and small, to widen my comfort zone and hopefully, after reading this chapter or coming along to one of our workshops, you will too!

Why adaptability is a must-have skill

It's now more important than ever to be flexible and agile, with plenty of resourcefulness and creativity to respond effectively to challenges and grab new opportunities. Why? Because things now change at a far greater speed and pace than ever before and will continue to do so. Change is with us, it seems constant and, as we have seen in recent years, so are disappointment and difficult times. The ability to bounce back, reassess and adapt is a top one. Yet, when change is imposed from the outside, whether that is through world and economic events or through personal changes or even just something new and unexpected, this can create stress which means we can actually become less adaptable and flexible and start

Try this

Pick four words that describe when you are most comfortable, for example, when are you most comfortable in your day-to-day activities and when are you most comfortable at work – what words would describe this for you?

_____

_____

_____

Can you think of a situation where you have remained in your comfort zone?

_____

_____

_____

What is it that kept you in your comfort zone?

_____

_____

_____

What would have been the benefits if you had stepped out (of your comfort zone)?

_____

_____

_____

to exhibit behaviours that are counter-productive to achieving results. According to Ken Buch, Senior Consultant with Managing Concepts Inc., people in the midst of change tend to experience heightened stress levels on a day-to-day basis but at the same time they are expected to function even more productively. He says that these stress hormones remain in the body for extended periods and actually need to be depleted for people to remain functional and adaptable to change.[1] So, sometimes the difficulty in being adaptable can, quite simply, be a physical reaction. Certainly if you operate in your stretch zone, sometimes you will physically feel a surge of adrenalin and excitement. What isn't so good are the fight or flight physical responses of a racing heart, shallow breathing and sweaty palms leaving you sometimes literally paralysed with fear.

> *'And the most successful people are those who accept, and adapt to constant change. This adaptability requires a degree of flexibility and humility many people can't manage.'*
>
> Paul Lutus

Consider this

Adaptable people see opportunity where others see failure.

To adapt is to grow, to change and to change you must forego what you once believed to be 'right', classify it as 'wrong', and then adopt what you now believe to be the new 'right' and be aware that this is an evolving, ongoing process and does not remain static. If you don't grow, you stagnate. This is something that not only individuals but organisations struggle with – habits that *have* defined their success in the past rather than questioning whether those same habits will *continue* defining success in the future. Chances are, they won't. If they did, then Blockbuster, Borders, and every other company that failed to adapt to a 'new right' (i.e. new reality) would still be in business.

Here are some key reasons why being adaptable is so important for you *now*:

- **Advances in technology mean that we have got to keep learning and evolving,** otherwise we will be left behind. It's easy to be closed to social media surges, constantly changing devices and the demands that technology makes of us. Some of this is simple fear. But adaptability means being open to all and any changes that come into our lives, even embracing them and then learning how to manage them. Steep learning curves only get steeper if you don't even attempt the ascent!

- **Remote work teams and telecommuting are fast becoming everyday.** We need to learn how to adapt to communicating and working effectively in these environments. Companies need to embrace cultural diversity, and cultural intelligence requires all of us to be far more adaptable than we currently are. Surprisingly, even large multinationals still struggle with global diversity and adapting to different cultures.

- **Multiple generations in the workplace and at home** mean that we need to embrace different attitudes, ways of working and living. We are becoming less insular and more community-focused. This is often imposed on us more than anything else, but is also a good thing. The truth is, our lifestyles have made us quite insular and self-focused. That is all being challenged and changed which might also have great positive benefits.

- **We need to embrace innovation.** There are many opportunities out there for those able to embrace and grab them. These opportunities will go to those who are flexible and adaptable enough to navigate their way. Opportunities happen by taking action and by being open enough in the first place to spot them. That might mean learning something new or being willing to try out things we have never done before.

- **Many people are struggling with major changes to their lifestyles and work** perhaps for economic reasons: being made redundant or not being able to find work easily. Changes such as living with parents for far longer than we'd like to, or suddenly finding ourselves without work but with many more years ahead of us where we want, and need, to work can seem daunting though they need not be.

There's probably no other time in recent history where adaptability has been more important than it is right now!

What sort of things make a person adaptable? These four skills are important:

1 **Intellectual flexibility** – this means keeping an open mind, being able to integrate new information smoothly and easily and switch easily from detail to the big picture. You may prefer the big picture or you may prefer detail and you need to be willing to strengthen both areas and move quickly from one to the other. This is why I bake or, more recently, make chocolates. I'm naturally more a 'big picture' person but learning to bake has trained me to become more detail-oriented.

2 **Being receptive** – especially to change! Being able to respond to change with positivity and being willing to try out new ways of doing something or looking at something. Being willing to override any initial resistance that may well be a very natural first response. Again, you can teach yourself to be more receptive – simply by practising acceptance and saying 'yes' to change.

3 **Creativity** – actively seeking out new things and not being afraid to experiment or improvise. That can mean tapping into intuition and not second-guessing yourself. We are all probably a lot more creative than we think!

4 **Communication style** – which can be adjusted to suit different contexts or situations. This means being much more aware of your own communication style and preference and being aware of which communication styles to adopt in different situations, even if these differ from your own natural style.

All of these can be learned. Both nature and nurture affect our ability to be adaptable. Remember, adaptability has been present within the human race for millions of years. We all have this innately. Anything that hinders adaptability has been learned (see 'What makes being adaptable challenging?', later in this chapter) and so we may well have to *unlearn* some of this to get back in touch with our inner flexibility and natural openness.

Being adaptable is very important for a healthy and happy life. Everyone faces hurdles and setbacks, personally and professionally. Those who are adaptable get better at dealing with those tough moments throughout their lives by paying attention to their natural response, then changing it when necessary. Like all seven skills, it is down to building your self-awareness.

Consider this

It's important to build adaptability incrementally. You'll be surprised by just how resistant to change you are! Next time you take part in a class or group event, try sitting in a different seat. Next time you go out to dinner, try a different food. Say 'yes' rather than 'no'. Your initial reaction definitely will be to not want to!

An example of being adaptable at work

Let's say you are asked to take on a new project that you know will stretch your skills or to give a presentation at short notice or to prepare for a meeting you do not even really want to go to. These are all situations where your natural response might be to avoid it, to fear it or to feel annoyed by it. Try instead to see such events (or indeed any change or uncertainty at work) as an opportunity to practise becoming more adaptable. How do you do this?

Other skills in this text will definitely help you here – like being proactive and optimistic so this is why it's important to strengthen all seven. With adaptability most of the time it is about adopting a lovely 'yes' attitude, getting yourself into stretch zone and working out strategies for how you will shine within each of those:

1   **A new project that will stretch your skills:** Say 'Yes' with enthusiasm and then commit to the new project with all your heart. Learn

everything you can and get ready to take instruction and learn the skills you might need. Relax – be aware when you are tensing up (that's just your body wanting to go into 'fight' or 'flight' mode). Allow yourself to become excited about the new challenge too. List all the ways in which you will develop and grow. Trust yourself that you can rise to the challenge and you most certainly will.

2 **Give a presentation at short notice:** Obviously say 'yes'! Take action and research your topic, find some great images and tap into who your audience is and what they might be expecting. Presentations can be stressful and certainly put most people into stretch but the more often you do them, the easier they become and the bonus impact is a huge confidence boost. Keep things simple. If you have already given a lot of presentations, then do something different this time – add an activity or a joke, if appropriate or be a little more dramatic than you might normally be.

3 **Prepare for a meeting you don't want to go to** Say 'yes' – think about who will be there and choose to see this as a great opportunity to get to know them better and to shine. Hone your active listening skills – meetings are such a great vehicle to do this – so that means when you're at the meeting no tuning out, no looking at your phone but listening with intent. I promise you that if we all just upped our listening skills at meetings we would always know what to say and come up with great ideas. Surprise yourself by doing just that. And if you have an idea to contribute, share it.

How being adaptable helps us at work

We are surrounded by ambiguity, and today's workplace is full of changes, uncertainty and complexity. This is all being driven by changing workflow, processes, different kinds of internal reporting structures as well as the market environment and the impact of technology, labour mobility and economics. So it is that the rules of how to succeed in this environment are changing too. The three examples I have given above could all be within this context and so there may be elements that are unknown and new. Perhaps the meeting is all about looking at a new way of reporting results, for example. The meeting may include other people you do not get on with that well or who are even toxic in some way. Your choices here are to avoid the meeting and justify why you are doing so and to view the potential changes as something to dread. Or you can choose to approach it in a different way as I've described above. It will need to be a conscious choice that you make.

Businesses and people who are unable to or, more likely, do not want to adapt will go the way of the dinosaur and will quietly be replaced by those who know how to and want to adapt to 'new school' challenges or embrace it as necessary to do. Our environment craves people who are flexible and adaptable and who are, as a result, great to work with too.

Try this reflection exercise to help raise awareness of your own adaptability skills. You can download it here: https://unimenta.com/adaptability/

Consider this

Large businesses often struggle most with being adaptable and responding fast because there are so many layers of the organisation. Freelancer? Portfolio career or small business? You are in a unique position to be adaptable each and every day and you need to be.

If you are adaptable, you will be perceived as being effective, optimistic, supportive and proactively seeking solutions. If you are not adaptable, you could easily be perceived as being overwhelmed, resistant, stuck and resentful. Even if you aren't! I know how I'd rather be perceived.

In his book *Adaptability: The Art of Winning in an Age of Uncertainty*, strategy and innovation expert Max Mckeown argues that adaptability is now a threshold requirement for business survival because, as the pace of change quickens, companies are finding it harder and harder to keep up. He says the most successful adaptors are curious and they know that stability is actually a dangerous illusion. Did you know that Twitter was, in fact, a 'plan B' produced by a struggling software company during an ad hoc brainstorm in a playground of all places? Drawing on creativity and even on failure (because of trying different approaches) can lead to innovation, new ideas and success. In fact becoming more adaptable can often include risk taking and making mistakes – once we can adopt the view that there are no 'wrong' decisions, only different decision consequences, taking risks and being willing to make mistakes becomes much easier.

Case study

Blockbuster was a very successful movie-rental chain. Yet it filed for bankruptcy just 6 years after achieving $6 billion dollars in revenue. Why? Because of a failure to adapt.

The retail stores had a huge selection of movies and new releases with 9000 stores. It had a strong brand with 100 per cent recognition and a customer-friendly experience where you could also buy popcorn and snacks to go with your rental. Most of its profits, though, actually came from late fees if you did not return your rented movie on time. I remember those days well!

Meanwhile, Netflix began its fledgling DVD-by-mail service and later its streaming/online service. Blockbuster was complacent then as it was still earning billions of dollars using its current model. So this made the company late to the game when technology shifted and companies like Apple and Amazon started offering streaming services. Blockbuster would also have had to radically change its business model from bricks-and-mortar to a completely new way of functioning which, at the time, was unknown and would have meant significant risk-taking and change. By the time Blockbuster did decide to innovate, it was simply too late and the company went bust very fast.

According to the 2018 Workplace Learning Report from LinkedIn Learning,[2] 'In the age of automation, adaptability rules'. Being flexible enough to handle a changing working environment and feeling confident in the workplace of the future means not being afraid of change or uncomfortable with uncertainty and feeling comfortable and secure that you will find ways of handling it. A fear response will have you wanting to keep things as they were because you don't think you will be able to cope with the new. This is so whether you are Blockbuster or an individual. We need to cultivate a tolerance for ambiguity – maybe not knowing the answers but knowing how to find them and trusting ourselves that we will find them.

Adaptability is a key skill that organisations as a whole need to develop and nurture. Anne Loehr, leadership coach to large corporates, with a successful chameleon career herself, says: 'This means organisational leaders need to embody adaptability as individuals and then embed it into the foundations of the company culture. That in turn means allowing employees to make mistakes, be creative and contribute at all levels.'

In today's environment, when surrounded by highly intelligent and specialist-knowledge workers, trading on our old knowledge and skills, relying too much on our titles as a definition of our work and what we do and believing in job security are not going to work. We need to adapt by continually evolving and reinventing ourselves. It means continuing to grow and transform and, in a way, become better versions of ourselves. This applies to every level in an organisation,

Top tip

Ask different questions

The questions you usually ask will get you the sort of answers you usually get, which is not so helpful when you need new ideas. For a twist, try asking a new question.

Most of us naturally ask questions that narrow and push to a solution. If something is complex and uncertain, though, that might lead to getting overly attached to a solution that may not be relevant any more.

Push yourself to ask questions like: 'What is most surprising in this situation?' 'What is at the edges of what seems possible today?' 'What data am I ignoring because I don't happen to like what they tell me?'

Different questions open you up to new possibilities and create a more flexible, agile mindset.

and to each of us, regardless of what our job is, always looking for which areas we need to develop and nurture – both within ourselves as individuals and within the organisations where we work or lead.

We ourselves have to take on far more responsibility for this. That can mean working harder to create our own career paths and new opportunities. If the job for life is long gone, then being able to adapt and define our own job roles is even more important. Employers today count adaptability as a key skill and it is often ranked as the highest, along with communication skills, interpersonal skills and a strong work ethic. In any job, in any company, you have to adapt to that company's culture and be able to 'fit in'. If you are working for yourself, you need to constantly adapt to changing market needs, try out different approaches and become used to handling rejection and criticism.

People who are adaptable tend to be both flexible and versatile. Research shows that most people view themselves as being more flexible and adaptable than they really are. That's because we *aspire* to being flexible, open and adaptable as they are attractive traits. The Emotional Competence Inventory is a scientifically reliable test often used by employers during assessment panels.[3] It looks at different aspects of emotional intelligence and measures adaptability on four scales: openness to new ideas, adaptation to situations, handling of unexpected demands and adapting or changing strategy. Employers using this can start to gauge how adaptable an individual really might be, as opposed to their self-perception.

Top tip

Try holding back on forming an opinion and instead actively listen to the person you have might have written off as a lost cause; for example, the group of people at work who seem so different from you that you don't even know their names, or even the one who has seemed close to you but now seems annoying. Keep asking yourself, 'In what ways could I be wrong or missing something?'

Working across different cultures in the workplace also makes demands of our adaptability skills. We need to be willing to accept and work with cultural differences and, the more adaptable we are, the easier that will be to do. But think about mental scripts (see later in this chapter) and we come smack up against possible prejudice and assumptions and not being as open as we might think we are to other cultures. Again, we all like to think that we are, but it's not necessarily the case deeper down.

you are very likely to perceive yourself as more adaptable and flexible than you really are

What makes being adaptable challenging?

Even though we are hardwired to be adaptable, we are also naturally resistant to change and this can stand in the way of being open to new experiences and opportunities. We also naturally fear rejection, so that is why we may shy away from doing something new or going out of our comfort zone for fear of being rejected. Remember this type of fear can be deeply embedded and is not necessarily rational.

Our mental scripts

One barrier to being adaptable is to do with the way our brain processes any new information. It creates what is known as 'behavioural scripts' which are mental models that automate our actions.[4] An example is how our brains might build a behavioural script for riding a bike. Through practice, this behaviour becomes entrenched and automatic until we can do it without thinking. Our brains will have lots of these scripts, from driving a car, speaking our mother tongue to even cooking a favourite dish. These scripts extend to other experiences and ways of doing things that we have learned. The scripts help us to be more efficient. They influence not only our actions but also what we see and believe. Just as these mental scripts help our brains to 'file away' a set of learned actions such as driving or

---

Try this

Open your mind

An open mind allows fresh ideas to come in and can help you with your plans and goals because answers, ideas and solutions simply come more quickly to an open mind. It can help you see opportunities others might miss, discount or neglect. How to have an open mind? Challenge any limiting beliefs, become more aware of your own 'mental scripts' and challenge your own 'rut' thinking – if your way of responding to something is comforting, inviting and familiar, try changing it and see what happens!

You can try this out any time simply by noticing how you are responding to something or noticing how you are feeling in a particular situation or with a particular person.

speaking our mother tongue, they also mean we file away learned and set ways of responding to something or behaving in a certain way and this may or may not be positive. If they are negative ways of responding to something, then these types of mental scripts can take a lot of effort to override and 'relearn', but this becomes easier the more self-aware you are and the more you realise that you can 'throw away' mental scripts and train yourself to learn new ones whenever you like.

Adaptability is linked to youth and vitality. As we get older, we develop more mental scripts, which can really challenge our ability to adapt to anything new. So by developing your adaptability skills, you are tapping into agility, youth and new energy!

Our brain's efficiency to file away learned behaviours and actions carries a downside. Mental scripts can cause us to ignore the reality of a situation and dismiss any signals or new information because our brains already 'know what to do'. Mental scripts may also result in clinging stubbornly to the notion that 'this is how we have always done it', refusing to understand and accept the realities of a new situation. Henry Plotkin, a psychologist at University College in London, states that 'We have a tendency to believe that whatever has worked in the past will continue to do so. That means that if something has worked well we'll do it gain or keep doing it and whatever didn't work, we'll tend to simply avoid.'

Our mental scripts can make us rigid and unresponsive to change, as can work or other stress.

Mental scripts can also be linked to limiting beliefs. Limiting beliefs are the internal thoughts that inhibit what we are willing to commit to or do. Many of our limiting beliefs have been held for a long time, and once a limiting belief has been created, we often construct our lives to avoid breaching that belief. Sounds crazy but it's what we do! If we believe we're not confident, we'll avoid activities that push us out of our comfort zone. If we believe we can't be happy, we will seek out opportunities to evidence that our lives are bad. Here's the key with a limiting belief, they have power because we give them power and they increase their control because we actively seek situations and make decisions that create memories of our limiting belief being correct.

Our propensity to being adaptable can also be challenged if we feel we are in competition with others and/or experiencing discontent or discomfort with a situation – usually this can also be traced back

Consider this

'If limiting beliefs are just statements we make to our self, why are they so difficult to overcome or simply ignore? There are a few reasons. Firstly, you've been running this pattern of behaviour for a long time and your brain is good at it and has learned it very efficiently. Secondly, when your brain locates the limiting belief it also connects to any past decisions and memories of this belief in action. Therefore, your brain is potentially calling on thousands of memories of times you've said no to something because you're simply not confident. Add to this a whole host of memories of remaining inside your confidence comfort zone and we have a firmly cemented approach to a variety of events. Finally, if you just remove the limiting belief you haven't provided the brain an alternative action. When something triggers your unconscious brain to hit the confidence check button it fires to the old program, finds nothing there and becomes confused, in this state of confusion it digs deeper and finds the final thread of a connection to the old limiting belief and creates the same action all over again. Here's the key, once you've removed a limiting belief, you need to replace it with a new belief, so that when the brain is triggered it finds the new behaviour. Prepare to get excited . . . once you do the new behaviour your brain adds in to the mix a new decision and a new memory, making this new approach a little more powerful than it was before.' – Chris Dudley, Life Coach and Founder of The Coach Collective.

to fear or our mental scripts. What's important is to start to understand that our mental scripts and learned behaviours and beliefs can impact what we choose to do and cause us to be inflexible and not adaptable at all, however much we like to think that we are!

You undo limiting beliefs by asking them questions and breaking them down, gaining a greater understanding of why they exist and what purpose they serve. If you'd like to try this out, we have a great exercise to help you do that. You can download it here: https://unimenta.com/adaptability/

Finding opportunity

There are always opportunities for us to test our adaptability skills but some of us may not actively seek these opportunities, and this in itself can be a barrier. If we have few opportunities growing up, to travel or try new things, then we may be even more resistant to this later in life. One of the reasons I wanted to start taking my then-five-year-old son with me on some of my business trips to far-flung places, and the reason I've always strongly encouraged my daughter to travel widely, is because many of these trips have opened my eyes on so many different levels and have often challenged my reference norms and what I didn't know were set ways of doing things in that particular culture. I have been fortunate enough to travel to places I would never have visited on holiday, or otherwise. I suppose one could also argue that maybe I would not have travelled to so many places others perceive as being unusual or high-risk, had I not been exposed to so much travel and moving when I was younger. One of the reasons I am so adaptable is because I know I **can** adapt, having experienced different schools, different countries and having had to plunge in and learn a new language and make new friends. It's created a kind of fearlessness, which I now feel very fortunate to have and is why I feel so fortunate to be able to continue travelling as an adult.

As a society in the West, we've become far more protective of our children. They are ferried about everywhere by car, do not play in

---

Try this

Travel more

If you can afford to do so, take yourself and your family on an adventure! Even if you can't travel abroad, consider visiting different parts of your city or country where you perhaps would not normally consider going. Or go camping and try cooking and sleeping outdoors. Travel really does broaden your horizons.

---

the streets and any travel is likely to be to holiday resorts far removed from the country's real culture. In the UK, most of our children do not even learn a foreign language! I can remember well other parents' horror that I actively encouraged my daughter to navigate her way alone around the London Underground system at the age of 12. It meant that when she was a teenager, she was the one others relied on for getting around independently. None of her friends had any experience of using public transport independently.

Top tip

If you are a parent, experiment with giving your children or teenagers more freedom and independence – they just might surprise you!

Is this overprotectiveness making our kids less adaptable and less equipped for what the world and life will throw their way? Does it make them less willing to seek out opportunities to stretch their comfort zones? Quite possibly.

Consider this

Even just doing something completely out of your normal day-to-day routine is incredibly good for you and builds your skills of adaptability. So, whether it's travel or just taking a different route to work, if you're doing this kind of thing consistently then, believe me, you will become more adaptable. What is one small thing you could try today or tomorrow to flex your adaptability skills? On our workshops, we encourage participants to think of things. Have a look at the list below for some ideas.

Here are some easy things to try which can help develop your adaptability skills. Go through this list and find something you could do today, tomorrow or next week:

- Approach someone you don't know that well (or normally might not approach) and – compliment them!
- Send someone a gift for no reason
- Make a new recipe you've never tried before
- Ask for constructive feedback/criticism from a colleague
- Reconnect with someone from your past
- Eat something you've never eaten before
- Learn a new skill or find out more about it
- Take on a new challenge at work
- Have that difficult conversation
- **What else?**

  _____

  _____

  _____

Fear

Fear is probably the biggest barrier to being adaptable. Fear of rejection, of failure, of circumstances, fear of change, fear, fear, fear. This fear causes stress which creates physical responses that can actually prevent us from being flexible and open. It's as if those parts of ourselves simply shut down. This is why the expansion of our comfort zone is *so* crucial, because the more we experience that we can, and do, adapt, the more flexible and open we will be.

How to become more adaptable

'Individuals who cultivate a variety of skills seem brighter, more energetic and more adaptable than those who know how to do one thing only.'

Robert Shea, American author and journalist

By learning how to be more adaptable, we also become better equipped to respond when faced with a life crisis and this in turn helps us to become more resilient. Resilient people often use these events as an opportunity to branch out in new directions.[5] While some people may be crushed by abrupt changes, highly resilient individuals are able to adapt and thrive. So how do we begin to develop this quality in ourselves and how can educators and trainers develop this in others? How can we make sure this is part of communication skills training, leadership training or any kind of soft skills training?

Our plastic brains

Neuroscience suggests that some people may be more adaptable than others and also suggests we can train our brains, whatever our age. The brain is plastic and flexible, and now new brain circuits can be developed through parenting, education and training that nurture adaptability. Such interventions are, however, thought to be more effective at crucial stages of our development, for example, adolescence. So at the very stage in life where some of us may be very self-conscious about moving beyond our comfort zone, being encouraged to do so can have a permanent impact on how our brain develops, making us adaptable for life! Interestingly, I suppose life events can also make us more adaptable. For example, I left home completely at the age of 16 and moved house and school several times before that. My family life was disrupted on a regular basis through circumstances and factors completely beyond my control as a child and adolescent. Although these events were stressful in their way and not things that I even wanted, the experience of them at a time when my brain was still developing has made me lifelong adaptable, which I have always valued. Many of our young people in the West, growing up in relatively conventional households, need, therefore, to be given far more opportunities to stretch their comfort zones, whether that is through adventurous travel, volunteering work, trying out new sports and interests or by training and courses that increase their self-awareness of their own communication styles, ability to work in a team and their presenting and performance skills.

Opportunities for being adaptable are all around you

It can be as simple as looking for opportunities to try out new things and being open to new ideas. In small ways, just like going to the gym, we can exercise our adaptability muscles by changing plans at short notice, dealing with unexpected demands gracefully and calmly and doing something new, like singing or learning a new language or another skill. Both singing and learning a new language offer other big fringe benefits and additional skills subsets. For singing: physical awareness, breathing control, presentation skills, listening skills, working in a team, performance skills and self-expression. For learning a foreign language: improving memory, protection against dementia, improving brain resilience, cultural awareness, differentiator at work and helping to understand communication styles.[6]

> every day there are opportunities for you to develop your adaptability skills

Experiential learning

Trainers and educators need to give people maximum opportunities to go out of their comfort zone through experiential learning, through 'real-play exercises' to encourage creativity and problem solving.[7] I think adaptability also needs to be better integrated into our education methods as an explicit skill. Many training exercises probably create stronger adaptability as an outcome, though this may not be explicit.

Comedy improvisation is a fantastic tool and we can all learn to embrace some of its principles. I have a very talented American friend and associate, Jon Wilkerson, who uses the principles of improvisational theatre to help people move beyond their own mental scripts and barriers. I want to share with you some of the principles he teaches because they are so valuable to changing behaviour. We also use these principles on our Advantage workshops through games and exercises to build awareness of all seven skills.

Improvisational theatre is a form of theatre popular in the USA. Instead of actors going on stage and performing memorised lines from a script, they must create a scene on the spot complete with fully developed characters, scintillating dialogue and a compelling environment. Life also has no script, which is why embracing these principles is so important.

To do this well, improvisational actors must be able to make bold choices, but they must also be quick to understand, accept and support the choices of others. They must be able take on different roles with speed and commitment. They must be able to lead as well as follow. They must have tremendous access to their creativity, but also must exercise judgement. They must be able to listen empathetically, but also to make quick reasoned decisions without second guessing themselves. They must be aware of their strengths and weaknesses and recover quickly from mistakes – even seeing them as opportunities. **These are the very same principles that allow a person to most effectively manage their own behaviour and accomplish their life goals.** These are also the skills of being truly adaptable.

Here are the principles; courtesy of Jon Wilkerson:[8]

- **Commitment** – means doing something with as much energy and enthusiasm as possible. When a comedy improvisational actor fails to commit on stage, the scene falls flat. When we fail to commit in life, our dreams grow dim. Whether we are applying for a job, leading a team on an important project, walking up to an influential person at a networking meeting or asking someone on a romantic date, we need to take the plunge, to gather ourselves and jump with both feet into the situation with the firm intention to be the best that we can be. Improvisational actors *practise* commitment. That's why they are good at it. And that is why we use improv exercises in our workshops – so that people can experience the power of commitment and experience themselves committing.

- **Listening** – the ability to shut off the voices in our head and really pay attention to the people and environment around us. This can be very difficult to do when we are nervous and busy thinking about what we should do and say. However, by really giving attention to what our client, team member or boss is saying, we can respond more appropriately than if we are constantly planning out our next sentence in our minds, or worrying whether we have a coffee stain on our sleeves! We also often block new ideas and opposing views, often without realising we are doing so, so being in the moment and truly listening with every ounce of our being is a key skill.

- **Grabbing opportunities** – opportunities are fleeting and, if we don't jump on them fast, they will leave us behind, kicking ourselves. You know that feeling! I know it too and we always know and sense when we have missed an opportunity. In improvisation, this is called 'accepting offers' and an 'offer' is defined as anything another actor says or does. That means *everything* is an opportunity! And if you are trained to do this, you will see opportunities that others won't even notice.

- **Support –** a general attitude of helpfulness that all successful improvisational actors carry with them every moment they are on stage. It is also a common characteristic of anyone who is especially effective at his or her job, whether as a waiter or a CEO. These extraordinarily successful people know that support isn't just praising co-workers or being able to do what someone else is already doing. People who are adept at support know that real help is looking around and noticing what's *not* being done, and then doing it! It means filling in what's missing. So to do this well, you need to be adept at listening, at grabbing opportunities and at committing.

- **Spontaneity –** the ability to act without over-thinking everything you do. It is having access to a sort of instantaneous judgement and being able to follow up on it immediately. It means not second-guessing all of your decisions. It requires good judgement that is built from experience, and it requires trust in your ability to recover quickly from bad decisions and learn from your errors. It is an essential companion to the other principles.

- **Fun –** what is fun? Fun is just fun! It means having a *positive attitude,* and leaning towards what you are doing and not away from it, or resisting it. When we head towards a challenge not only with a determination to succeed but with an expectation that tackling the challenge will be rewarding and fun, we run towards that challenge instead of stumbling towards it reluctantly.

Seven steps to adaptability

The following steps can help you improve your adaptability skills and raise your general awareness, which is where everything must begin. Remember, it really is like exercising a muscle, and requires work!

1 **Stick at things** Being adaptable doesn't mean flitting from one thing to the next. Adaptability is closely linked to

resilience, as well as perseverance. Resilient people stick at
things. They keep going, even when the going gets tough. This
is about your ability to concentrate, discipline and motivate
yourself to complete a task or project. Strong application is
underpinned by a sense of self-direction or free will, and these
in themselves create robustness. As a consequence you are
able to be more adaptable because you cope better with setbacks and rejection.

How easily do I tend to stick at things?

_____

_____

_____

**What are some triggers that make me want to
give up?**

_____

_____

_____

**What are some strategies I can put in place to help me
keep going when I feel like giving up?**

_____

_____

_____

2 **Be willing to learn** We never really stop learning. Be willing
to learn new methods, procedures and ways of doing things.
Take on new tasks. Try something different. Draw conclusions
from new information. And how about that foreign language
you've always wanted to learn or that choir you've always
wanted to join? It's easy to tell yourself you don't have time.
But this is your life and it's not a dress rehearsal. Respond
with energy to new challenges, the unfamiliar and the
unexpected.

What is a new skill that I have always wanted to learn?

_____

_____

_____

What opportunities are there for me to do this?

_____

_____

_____

How will I make time for this new skill? What am I willing to commit to?

_____

_____

_____

3 **Improvise** Don't over-think and second-guess everything that you do. Practise being spontaneous – accept that last-minute invitation, change your weekend plans, walk into the presentation smiling with confidence knowing that you will do well (as long as you've put the preparation in, of course!). Grab that opportunity, it might not come again.

What happens when I second-guess things and I'm not spontaneous?

_____

_____

_____

When can I next use improvisational skills? What's coming up in my life where I could be more spontaneous or just decide to attack something in a different way?

_____

_____

_____

4 **Flex those muscles** It's true that going to the gym will help you be more physically and mentally resilient, and we know that adaptability and resilience are linked, but I am talking about three types of flexibility: a) 'cognitive flexibility', using different thinking strategies and mental frameworks; b)

'emotional flexibility', varying your approach to dealing with your own emotions and those of others; and c) 'dispositional flexibility', remaining optimistic and at the same time realistic.[9] Look for as many opportunities as you can to exercise these types of flexibility. The opportunities are all around you in your day-to-day life.

When can I next try exploring different ways of thinking about an issue or problem?

_____

_____

_____

When can I next vary my emotional response to someone I don't tend to get on with?

_____

_____

_____

When can I next remain optimistic as well as realistic about a situation that is bothering me?

_____

_____

_____

5   **Adopt a 'can do' positive attitude to change** Even though it is natural to want to resist change, try and build up your ability to adapt and respond positively by literally changing your behaviour next time you are faced with a change. Again, start with small steps. You feel disappointed because of a change of plan? Respond enthusiastically even if you don't feel like doing so. Couldn't get tickets for a show you've been wanting to see? Smile and choose something completely different so you can embrace a new experience. Lost your job? Get upset, yes, but bounce back faster by taking positive action each and every day.

Over the next few weeks I am going to build up my ability to respond positively to changes. I am going to deliberately change my behaviour in three specific situations and note down the results here:

1 _____

2 _____

3 _____

6 **Get creative at problem solving** Research suggests that people who are able to come up with solutions to a problem are better able to cope with problems generally than those who can't. So, whenever you encounter a new challenge, make a quick list of some of the potential ways you could solve the problem. Experiment with different strategies and focus on developing a logical way to work through common problems. By practising these skills on a regular basis, you will be better prepared to cope when a serious challenge emerges.

What particular challenge am I currently facing?

_____

_____

_____

Here's my list of ways I might start to solve this problem:

_____

_____

_____

7 **Have a survivor attitude** Anything can be turned into a crisis or problem, if we want it to. Really, anything! Refuse to see yourself as a victim in any situation and always look for ways to resolve it. If you've always been quite a reactive person, this may be hard to do at first. Remember that you can never be in control of your circumstances and external events, you can only be in control of your own responses and behaviours. The trick is that if you focus on that, as opposed to the circumstances, chances are you'll influence the situation favourably anyway!

What's happening right now around me that could easily be turned into a crisis?

_____

_____

_____

Here's my list of survivor responses to this situation:

_____

_____

_____

_____

A day in the life of. . .

Let's take a magnifying glass to the skill of being adaptable through a day in the life of Fiona. We'll start with a brief introduction to Fiona, to give a quick snapshot of her life.

About Fiona

Fiona is a retired nurse and a widow. She has a small pension but is very concerned and worried about the future and how she will manage. Fiona lives in a small flat that she owns. She does a little part-time tutoring to supplement her pension but probably needs more money. She isn't able to afford holidays or travel, which she used to love. Her family all live overseas, including a daughter in Australia. She's lonely but doesn't like to admit this or show it. Fiona has a small network of friends she sees regularly and visits a local club where she exercises. She is also active online, mainly through Skype and keeping in touch with her family.

Fiona is generally positive about things, even though she worries. She doesn't feel there is much she can do about her situation. She doesn't like thinking about her finances and so avoids this. She's in her early sixties and has only ever been a nurse. She believes she is 'too old' to learn anything new and will confirm this to herself through anything she reads or watches on TV. The more she does *this, the more she finds information and articles and even research to support this view. She feels very sad that she can't travel more and see more of her family. Most of the time she actually feels fairly bored. A long time ago she used to enjoy singing but never took it any further and doesn't read music. Her husband died around five years ago and Fiona misses him and seems to have got herself into a bit of a rut.*

Let's have a closer look at a typical day in Fiona's life and how building the skill of being adaptable can help her.

Fiona's typical day

Fiona tends to get up very early and goes for a swim at her club before returning home for breakfast. She listens to a radio programme and does a bit of Sudoku and household chores before meeting a friend for lunch. This friend is busy starting a new flower-arranging business. Fiona is interested and compliments her friend on her talents. Fiona thinks to herself that she is 'not the sort of person to start a business' and that, anyway, even if she did have an idea for a new business, she doesn't have any money to get it going. Fiona tutors a nursing student at her flat mid-afternoon, which she quite enjoys as it keeps her active in the nursing profession. After that she does some gardening and then cooks dinner and watches a little TV. Today Fiona also runs into a couple of other friends. She bumps into one who has just started singing with a local community choir where no auditions or sight-reading is required. Her friend encourages Fiona to join but Fiona feels very timid and unsure about the whole idea of singing again and decides not to. Then she stops to chat with another friend. They chat about how terrible the weather has been and how soon the nights will be drawing in and there hasn't been much of a summer.

Fiona often surfs the Net of an evening or Skypes her family. She was supposed to be meeting up to go to the cinema with an old

work colleague this evening but at the last minute was let down.
The outing was planned some time ago and so Fiona felt very
disappointed by this and spent the evening at home alone.

What's going on here?

Fiona's life is ticking along but she doesn't sound terribly happy.
On the surface, her life seems to be active but actually it's almost
as if life is passing her by. She doesn't seem to be making the
most of her potential. She has adapted to her life as a widow, yes,
but she is not in herself adaptable enough to make more of her
life. Yet she is only in her early sixties and there are many many
good years ahead of her. She appears to have given up and be
resigned to her life as it is now. At the same time she is slightly
envious of her friends who seem to be involved in new things and
leading busy lives and have somehow reinvented themselves.
Fiona probably also feels a little isolated as her family lives
overseas and she is unable to afford the travel to see them. She is
worried about money and about her future, yet doesn't see herself
in a position to do anything about it as her 'working life' has
stopped. Her life could be so much happier if she exercised the
skill of adaptability. She might be able to earn some extra cash
and even save for a trip. Fiona is also quite bored – she has an
active mind but isn't really exploiting that and she seems to be
living the life of someone much older than she actually is. She
likes to plan ahead but she has lost touch with being spontaneous.

If Fiona puts some of the ideas about adaptability into practice, it
could all look quite different.

Let's revisit Fiona's 'typical day' six months later.

How Fiona's life has moved forward

Fiona was able to visit her daughter in Australia, as her family
kindly paid for this visit. The trip came as a welcome surprise and,
although it wasn't planned ahead as Fiona would have preferred,

the desire to see her family was strong enough to override this initial discomfort. While she was in Australia, Fiona had sufficient distance from her life to really think about some of the things she wanted to change. The trip away was refreshing and energising for her. She decided to spend a little time taking stock and putting together a plan for herself. Her part-time tutoring is rewarding and Fiona decided to try and do more of this. She offered her services at the local nursing training college, starting with taster sessions. This soon led to a regular group of student nurses wanting group tutoring, which is more cost-effective for them and means Fiona now has regular additional income.

Fiona's day is now spent more actively. In the mornings she is busy putting together revision materials for nursing students, which she plans to compile and offer through a new website she wants to develop. It's early days but she is hopeful that this may be another source of income. She continues to meet her friends but spends more time with friends who are active in various things and this gives her great support with what she is working on. Fiona has also taken more control over her finances by getting some sound financial advice. She has started to save a little money on a regular basis and is planning to take a short weekend trip soon with one of her friends. She also often meets friends at short notice – after all she is not on a fixed schedule and has no family ties.

Fiona generally feels more relaxed and happy about life, which means that now she really enjoys her time gardening, cooking or surfing the Net. Whereas, before, these activities felt a little functional, she now feels there is more purpose to them. She has started to try out new recipes and grow new types of vegetables. She finds that the more she focuses on the things she is able to do, the more productive and relaxed she feels, and the wider her comfort zone becomes. It's tremendously energising. She feels less lonely and has things to look forward to. She's even thinking *about taking a course for starting up small businesses, as well as learning more about using the Internet.*

She decided to give the choir a try too. She felt nervous initially, but found it helpful to think about all the new things she had been doing lately and then this no longer felt so daunting.

Adaptability is a skill we can all benefit from. It's not only something that can help you adjust to major life changes and upheaval, but it can also make your life happier and more interesting in the day-to-day. By becoming more adaptable day-to-day, you will be better equipped to deal with bigger changes that come your way. Because they will! And you may want them to.

Interested in learning more?

I've put together some extra resources here:

Books

Goldie, A. (2016) *The Improv Book: Improvisation for Theatre, Comedy, Education and Life.* Oberon.

Hollins, P (2017) *The Science of Breaking Out of Your Comfort Zone: How to Live Fearlessly.* CreateSpace.

Newmark, A. (2017) *Chicken Soup for the Soul: Step Outside Your Comfort Zone: 101 Stories about Trying New Things, Overcoming Fears, and Broadening Your World.*

Mckeown, M. (2012) *Adaptability: The Art of Winning in an Age of Uncertainty.* Kogan Page.

Poynton, R. (2013) *Do Improvise: Less Push. More Pause. Better Results. A New Approach to Work (and Life).* The Do Book Company.

Ryan, M.J. (2009) *AdaptAbility: How to Survive Change You Didn't Ask For.* Broadway Books.

Articles and websites

Buch, K. (2009) 'Adaptability – Leading Through Focused Conversations'. You can download this article from www.management concepts.com

https://www.kornferry.com/institute/adaptability-the-surprisingly-strong-predictor-of-career-success

How being adaptable can influence your career.

You can also find more tips, ideas, curated video clips and exercises to strengthen your optimism skills by visiting https://unimenta.com/adaptability/

Sign up too for daily tips – a daily quote, tip and video clip on one of the seven skills direct to your inbox. https://unimenta.com/seven-skills/

'Not everything that counts can be counted and not everything that can be counted counts.'

William Bruce Cameron

Chapter 2

CRITICAL THINKING

S ome of us may be familiar with critical thinking from our university days or further education. It's what you are meant to be doing, after all, alongside all the partying. While you could say that critical thinking is at the heart of academic study, it's more of a **process,** a way of thinking, understanding and expressing ourselves, than a single definable skill: being able to analyse, evaluate, apply reasoning, observation, experience and reflection to make decisions. Critical thinking also has links with being more empathetic, logical and fair-minded, reasonable and rational.

As a future skill, critical thinking is about complex problem solving, originality, fluency of your ideas and active learning. It's also about leveraging our brain's capacity to be creative, have ideas and truly flourish. Recent research and insights by neuroscientists are discovering that our brains can be rewired and trained each and every day and indeed throughout our lives.

What is critical thinking?

At a simple level, critical thinking means making an evaluation or judgement about what we see or hear about facts or a situation presented to us. For many people, this means making a quick mental decision in a fairly short space of time. Although this works most of the time, critical thinking is so much more than this. It's about questioning assumptions, evaluating a situation from different angles, solving problems creatively and using a reflective, considered approach. Its origin dates all the way back to Socrates who identified that our natural human tendency is to justify answers to questions based on emotion or impulse thinking rather than a logical or reasoned response. It would seem like not much has changed since then! Emotion and impulse thinking are subjective and we are all prone to it. A shocking amount of thinking that we do is actually quite biased and uninformed!

Critical thinking is smarter thinking. The ability to think critically is what makes us capable of tackling new challenges – and completing them well amidst a constant flow of ever-increasing digital information.

We have become used to using a 'light' approach. In a busy life, information comes to us in lots of different ways and our brain has to find ways to make sense of it all. The way we look at information online contributes to the 'speed' in making judgements and how we perceive data. Attention is a hot commodity and is a vital component of being able to think critically in a way that benefits us. I believe that our attention spans are getting shorter, not least through how we use our smartphones. According to neuroscientist Dr Jack Lewis, anything you do daily, intensively and over long periods of time changes your brain. That can sometimes be a good thing but unfortunately not so much when it comes to our habitual use of smartphones and the constant checking of messages and notifications. When we do this, we are training our brains to react to our phones multiple times a day. This not only creates a constant state of stress, putting us on high alert every time a message comes through, it also has a very big impact on our productivity levels and limits our brain's capacity for being creative and resourceful.

There is sufficient evidence to suggest that our graduates do not come out of university with strong critical thinking skills and, even more, that the current type of learning and teaching at university does not even really encourage critical thinking in depth.[1] For example, students who study courses entitled 'Critical Thinking' are more likely to learn how to label certain types of thinking than how to actually think critically for themselves and relate this to their own

Try this

Social media exercise

Observe yourself on social media. Deliberately and with intention look at a video or headline and then examine further to find what is underneath it. Don't take it at face value and be aware that you may subconsciously do just that. How do you USE social media – do you put into play your critical thinking skills, or not? Most of the time we don't and the more you use and check social media feeds, the worse this can become.

As fake news, advertisements and misleading websites grow, the implications of not leveraging our ability to think critically is magnifying.

work, life and goals. Most critical thinking and information literacy programmes in higher education are inconsistent. Critical thinking is an essential tool for the modern world, and it should be taught in a broad, coherent and effective way.

Education should emphasise the crucial importance of critical thinking skills more. We are living an an era of free access to all the information and knowledge we could possibly want. The actual skill we lack is the ability to truly understand, evaluate and analyse it all

On a deeper level, our ability to think critically and solve problems creatively is being constantly challenged by our changing world environment. A thinking skills explosion has not accompanied the information explosion.[2] If you want to succeed now and in the future, the ability to think critically is vital because growth and abundance of information increases on a daily basis due to our access to unprecedented technological innovation and information. Managing this amount of information is becoming much more challenging. We have a real problem of information overload, which has led to shorter attention spans and an inability to manage this information effectively.

Consider this

Every day we are exposed to literally billions of different types of information online originating from social media platforms, millions of hours of video content, multiple text messages and other online messaging applications and countless other platforms. Did you know that 90 per cent of data on the Internet has been created since 2016 according to an IBM study[3]. This information explosion is only set to increase, so sharpening those critical thinking skills is crucial.

Why critical thinking is a must-have skill

US executives say they need a highly skilled and agile workforce in order to compete in today's fast-paced, competitive global environment. Employees need to think critically, solve problems, innovate, collaborate and communicate more effectively – at every level within an organisation, according to a 2012 survey conducted by the American Management Association.

The 4 Cs

1 **Critical thinking and problem solving** – the ability to make decisions, solve problems and take appropriate action.

2 **Communication** – the ability to synthesise and transmit ideas, both verbally and in writing.

3 **Collaboration and team building** – working effectively with others, including people with opposing points of view and with diverse groups.

4 **Creativity and innovation** – being able to see what is missing and fix it.

The most important skill defined was critical thinking, and all of these skills are considered crucial in the next few years and beyond.

Critical thinking is 'raw material' for a number of key workplace skills, such as problem solving, decision making, organisational planning and risk management. These are the skills deemed to be essential for avoiding mistakes and miscalculations. Lack of critical thinking can lead to evaluating market and needs inaccurately through preconceived notions and assumptions. Quite often, too, people at the top of an organisation are automatically *assumed* to be bright and 'good' thinkers – the ability to think critically tends not to be assessed or measured the higher up an organisation you go. Critical thinking is even more important when sophisticated decision making and judgement are needed.

On a day-to-day basis, in your personal life critical thinking can help strengthen your relationships and help you to be more creative, resourceful and reflective when handling problems or difficulties:

- Thinking critically means you ask more questions, look for relevant information, think open-mindedly and communicate well to find effective solutions.

- Developing your capacity to think more critically will impact the quality of your decisions and judgements. They will be more informed and less biased or subjective.

The human mind is rarely objective so strengthening critical thinking skills keeps your mind objective, at least about those things based on facts. However, sometimes we will take opinions and subjectivity as a 'fact' too and it's all too easy to do this, especially if we are busy and distracted or spend too much time online.

It is so important to be clear about this as often we make decisions and judgements without all the facts or based merely on assumptions and subjective views.

Top tip

Human thought is amazing, but the speed and automation with which it happens can be a disadvantage when we're trying to think critically. Our brains naturally use mental shortcuts to explain what's happening around us.

A critical thinker is aware of their cognitive biases and personal prejudices and how they influence seemingly 'objective' decisions and solutions.

All of us have biases in our thinking. Becoming aware of them is what makes critical thinking possible.

Reflective thinking

By thinking critically, instead of reacting emotionally to a problem, we use strategies which:

- Help us learn from an experience
- Help prevent it from occurring again
- Result in a reasonable, effective solution
- Helps us make better decisions in the future

The quality of life we experience is in direct proportion to the quality of our thinking. Take a few moments to absorb that last sentence – quite powerful, don't you think?

'Thinking is skilled work. It is not true that we are naturally endowed with the ability to think clearly and logically – without learning how, or without practising. People with

untrained minds should no more expect to think clearly and logically than people who have never learned and never practiced can expect to find themselves good carpenters, golfers, bridge players, or pianists.' – A. E. Mander Logic for the Millions

Dr Linda Elder, an educational psychologist and an authority on critical thinking, defines the process as 'self-guided, self-disciplined thinking which attempts to reason at the highest level of quality in a fair-minded way. People who think critically consistently attempt to live rationally, reasonably, empathically.'[4]

Thus, critical thinking is also inextricably linked to cultivating self-awareness and crucial for developing all seven skills.

Critical thinking has been proven to have a positive impact on creativity. A 2012 study by Nusbaum and Silvia found that people high in fluid reasoning (closely connected to critical thinking) outperformed others in creative ideas.[5] Why is creativity important? Because creativity contributes to having fresh new ideas and being able to take the initiative amidst uncertainty. Creativity gives organisations and individuals the competitive advantage – original ideas and our ability to produce and articulate these makes each of us unique.

critical thinking and creativity are a match made in heaven!

The majority of cognitive ability tests include critical thinking. Such tests are used more now by companies, so you may be asked to take one at your next job interview. Increasingly, these tests are now being seen as the strongest and most consistent predictors of job performance, leadership effectiveness and creativity. The main reason these tests are so powerful is because they predict both what you can do right now and the extent to which you are likely to learn and develop in the future (Kuncel and Hezlett 2010).

An example of critical thinking at work

Ellen Kumata, a consultant to Fortune 200 companies has this to say: 'It can be easy to assume that an organisation's senior leaders should have all the answers but that is no longer the case. The closer you are to the actual on-the-ground work the more analytical and creative you need to be, You need to be able to test your own assumptions, not take things at face value and let go of any preconceived ideas.' This means that the need for far stronger critical thinking skills is relevant for every employee at every level of an organisation.

As the rate of complexity rises, the need for critical thinking is resurfacing. Richard Paul of the Center for Critical Thinking says: 'Consider this Critical thinking, if somehow it became generalised in the world, would produce a new and very different world, a world which increasingly is not only in our interest but is necessary to our survival.'

Try this

We are thinking critically and in a problem-solving mindset when we:

- Rely on reason rather than emotion
- Evaluate a broad range of viewpoints and *perspectives*
- Maintain an *open mind* to alternative interpretations
- Accept new evidence, explanations and findings
- Are willing to reassess information
- Can put aside personal prejudices and biases
- Consider all reasonable possibilities
- Avoid hasty judgements

Reflect on this for a moment. Try to raise your awareness of how often you might employ any of the above strategies and ways of thinking. Think back to a recent struggle, challenge or disagreement and work out to what extent you were able to get into the right mindset.

_____

_____

_____

_____

This also implies that in order to think critically and effectively we need to manage our emotions appropriately too – not always easy in the heat of the moment or during an argument.

How critical thinking helps us at work

You may well be one of the many people who feel overwhelmed by work overload, information overload and stress. Or you may feel overwhelmed sometimes or on a regular basis. Your strong critical thinking and problem-solving skills are the very ones that are going to be able to help you manage these problems and work and live smarter; skills such as rationality, self-awareness, honesty, open-mindedness, discipline and judgement, and the ability to be an active thinker, a sceptical thinker, to question, to analyse, in depth and faster than ever before.

We need to be able to question assumptions far more and seek out the _what_ and the _why_ of every situation. We need to be able to adopt different perspectives and have a much greater awareness of cultural differences. These are deductive skills. But good critical thinkers also need to be creative. They need to be able to see opportunities where others might only see obstacles. So they need to be looking for solutions rather than for problems and this is so much more than mere 'problem solving'.

Employers want employees who can think independently and autonomously, problem solve, use good judgement and make decisions. Decisions are often made at work without reflection or without all the key facts required to make a wise choice or judgement because a decision is needed quickly. And if you think about it, you are probably expected to make decisions a lot faster these days. That's OK isn't it? We make quick decisions all the time. Well, yes it probably is fine for much of the time, especially if you are able to apply a wider or deeper set of experiences to inform your decision, but it simply isn't a good idea where outcomes are critical. A good example of where critical thinking is very important is in project management. Without sufficient attention to detail, working out costs, resources, time management, team roles and priorities, a project in most industries will fail.

'The No. 1 thing we look for is general cognitive ability, and it's not IQ. It's learning ability. It's the ability to process on the fly' Need to make it clear to the reader that this is a statement made by Lazlo Bock. I suggest adding a spaced en rule after the quote and the run text on to 'Lazlo Bock, Senior...'

Lazlo Bock, Senior Vice President of People Operations at Google

David Garvin from Harvard Business School says that there is a general consensus that everyone needs to sharpen their critical thinking skills - whether that means question their assumptions or developing the willingness and understanding to look at problems from multiple points of view.[6]

It's especially important now: companies face huge challenges with global competition (including small businesses), emerging markets, technology changes and the political and economic landscape. Employees at every level, entrepreneurs, leaders and managers need to be able to think fast and act smart – often in situations that are complex, uncertain and where there might not already be an effective policy or existing procedure in place. All this means critical thinking is vital, and it also means that these critical thinking skills have an added layer of challenge to them.

Consider this

The ability to focus is a number one key skill today. The types of things that can distract us include irrelevant information, external distractions, interruptions, email, social media, all incoming information and mind wandering. All of these things happen lots of times each and every day. Training your brain to focus will boost your critical thinking skills as will managing your use and engagement on social media and online generally.

Because of neuroplasticity, our brains definitely have the capacity to develop effective critical thinking skills. It is a purely cognitive skill and there are exciting developments that inform how we can improve our critical thinking skills. There are three, in particular, that are important to note:

1 **Inhibitory control** – This is the ability to resist the strong inclination to do one thing in order to do something else that is more appropriate, or would better help you to reach a goal. This is important because it means that even if we feel like putting off an important project, we are able to resist this and choose behaviour that helps us get something done. This is well-documented research that proves we are able to control or regulate our behaviour, so there's no excuse! (Diamond *et al.* 2007). Inhibitory control will also help you manage how you use your smartphone and training your brain to reassess information and become more reflective rather than reactive is key.

2 **Working memory** – This is a mental 'jotting pad' feature of your brain that shares important information that you can use in the course of everyday life, helping you stay focused on a task, block out distractions and keep you aware (Gathercole and Packiam-Alloway 2008).

   What this means is that it is now proven that there is a feature in our brain that is critical to our ability to control our attention, concentrate despite distractions, successfully multitask, learn and understand what we read and generally improve our overall performance on measures of intelligence. Historically, it was believed that working memory was actually a fixed ability that could not be improved and, even worse, that it declined with age. This new research turns that around and that is good news!

3 **Cognitive flexibility –** Cognitive flexibility is our human ability to switch behavioural responses according to the context of a situation. The ability of a person to see different aspects of an idea or situation and switch their 'attentional set' can now be measured through neuropsychological tests and improved through training. '*The hardest part of learning something new is not embracing new ideas, but letting go of old ones.*' – Todd Rose

Try this

1. What is going on around you right now as you read this text? Where are you sitting and what distractions are there? Is your phone within easy reach? Are you near to other digital devices? What sort of information is coming at you? When was the last time you checked your phone for messages? What do you hear? What thoughts are going through your mind?

    _____

    _____

    _____

2. Simply beginning to be aware of these is the first step towards overcoming distractions more effectively.

    _____

    _____

    _____

3.   List some of the things you could do to minimise these distractions:

_____

_____

_____

Being a critical thinker is a lot more than learning a collection of techniques. It is a mindset, an attitude and a way of thinking that you adopt and apply on a consistent basis, every day. Becoming a better critical thinker is a bit like becoming a better athlete. We are all born with the ability to move, but to develop our

Critical thinking is much more than a collection of techniques – it is a mindset, lifestyle and more focused way of thinking

athletic skills we need to learn technique and practise. People who are athletic are usually good at multiple sports but excel at one or two. Critical thinkers also approach most problems effectively but excel in specific areas. The decision to build your athletic skills is a lifestyle decision. To be a competent athlete, you need to live a healthy and active lifestyle. Likewise, critical thinking is also a lifestyle issue. Critical thinkers approach every situation by trying to evaluate it accurately and make the best possible decision at the time.

Critical thinking case study

On our workshops, we often use critical thinking exercises with teams as a way to explore problem solving and raise awareness of our default behaviours. We worked with a fast-paced software company that has grown significantly within a short space of time. The problem-solving exercise was deliberately a simple one: forming a team circle and passing a hula hoop around the team. The team have to hold hands and the hula hoop is suspended from two team members' arms within the circle. Without exception, all teams rushed to complete the exercise without any kind of planning time, creativity or strategy. During the reflection process afterwards they acknowledged that this was their typical style because they are so results driven. This was despite being given planning time and being asked to complete the exercise a second time using more creativity.

The exercise gave the teams lots of food for thought in terms of integrating critical thinking skills into their problem-solving approaches!

becoming a better critical thinker is a bit like becoming a better athlete
Download this exercise for some quick ways to improve your critical thinking skills:
https://unimenta.com/critical-thinking/

The way we think about critical thinking is changing

Critical thinking has a long academic tradition and history, having its roots in philosophy and using deep reflection to help to understand our existence. The fundamentals of critical thinking in terms of gathering good evidence, separating facts from opinions and questioning and drawing sound conclusions by applying logical deduction are all well known. These skills can be analysed and discussed from a number of different perspectives and, indeed, this has been done widely and there are numerous studies and research articles to support this. Most of the traditional material on critical thinking is presented either from an academic angle or a psychological one (cognitive focus). More recently, neuroscience has contributed to a better understanding of critical thinking in terms of how our brains work and the patterns involved.

Try this

Replace any guesswork or gaps with facts and data, and challenge decisions that have materialised without any data or facts to support them. Always do your homework and check everything. And if you're not sure of something, say so, and find out.

The University of Phoenix's non-profit Institute for the Future 'Work Skills 2020' research underpins key drivers that are currently shaping our future as does the Pearson research into 2030 skills of the future. Both of these highlight the increased need for critical thinking to support creativity, problem solving and decision making, innovation, active learning and fluidity as well as quantity of ideas.

Let's take a closer look at six key principles that unpack why we need to rethink our critical thinking skills:

1. How we make sense of things

This is our ability to determine the deeper meaning or significance of what is being expressed or presented to us. In our fast-moving world, this requires a reflective, considered approach that does not come easily. For example, today, anyone can publish anything on the Internet and much of this information is actually flawed, biased or possibly even inaccurate. We need sharper critical thinking skills to discern the information we are constantly bombarded with and to remember that 'Googling' something is not the same as researching and understanding it properly. Reflection skills are also vital here to allow our brains space to process and put aside assumptions and prejudgement.

Consider this

How often do you question the first result that comes up when you Google something? You probably take it at face value because it came up in the first page of results. But that doesn't mean it's valuable, well written or even accurate!

The way we work is changing: as manufacturing and service jobs are automated, there is an increasing demand for the kinds of skills that machines are not good at – yet. These are higher-level thinking skills (critical reasoning skills – numerical, verbal and spatial) that as yet cannot be codified. So we need to be ready in ways we haven't been in the past. Just think for one minute about all the massive technological changes just in the last ten years. This isn't stopping any time soon and is, in fact, accelerating!

Not all jobs will necessarily become automated and there are key professions where critical thinking will be one of the most important assets because of its strong links with complex problem solving, originality, fluency of ideas and active learning.

2. Novel and adaptive thinking is needed more than ever

Critical thinking now includes adaptive thinking because most jobs demand and will continue to demand what is known as 'situational adaptability' – the ability to respond to unique, unexpected circumstances of the moment. In addition, given high rates of rising unemployment and changing work patterns and ways of working, everyone will need to up their ability to respond effectively to unexpected changing circumstances.

3. Computational thinking

This is the ability to translate vast amounts of data into abstract concepts and to understand data-based reasoning. Many more roles will require computational thinking skills in order to make sense of the vast amounts of information. This is already happening, and most people already feel huge amounts of pressure in their day-to-day work. It's only going to increase. Computational thinking will help and it probably means learning to use more of our brains more effectively. Some estimates say that we actively use only about 10 per cent of our brains – there is the capacity to do far more. From neuroscience we know that there are individual learning differences with the basis in the brain. We also know that it's possible to improve critical reasoning skills.

4. New media literacy

This is the ability to critically assess and develop content that uses new media forms and to leverage these media for persuasive communication. We have an explosion in user-generated media, including the videos, blogs and podcasts that now dominate our social lives, and this will be felt fully in workplaces over the next few years. Those who do not embrace these new media, or do not know how to use and manage them to the best effect, will simply be left behind. We are still learning how to use these new media and we need to learn this skill faster, in my view.

5. Managing our cognitive load

This is the ability to discriminate and filter information for importance and understand how to maximise cognitive functioning using a variety of tools and techniques. Given that the way we work is changing and the sheer amounts of information we are expected to understand, coupled with the constant distraction of social media and the Internet, this ability is crucial. We also have to learn how to unlearn our bad habits of what we think is multitasking but, in reality, is lessening our ability to retain key information. I know I keep talking about managing our technology, social media use and how we use our smartphones but that is because doing so is simply vital for developing the skills we need – not just critical thinking but all seven!

6. Becoming T-shaped

This is a literacy in and an ability to understand concepts across multiple disciplines and not just one. The ideal future worker is 'T-shaped' – they bring deep understanding of at least one field and often two or more, and they also have the capacity to converse in the language of a wider depth and breadth of fields. Lifelong learning will be of paramount importance in parallel with extended life spans. We may all be working for a lot longer than we thought and may want to too. So critical thinking and reasoning across different topics, subjects, specialist fields and disciplines will become more important, and those who rise to this challenge will have a competitive edge.

For me, these six principles point to significant gaps in our current ways of learning and absorbing information, as well as our education systems. The world of work is changing and our education system needs to be better prepared to equip our young people to flourish in it. Those of us no longer in the education system need to be prepared and get ready to expand and super-charge our thinking and life-long learning skills on a day-to-day basis.

What makes critical thinking challenging?

Perhaps the main barrier to developing effective critical thinking has been a lack of awareness of what it actually is and how important it is as a skill. In academic terms, there can sometimes still be a stigma to critical thinking training in that it is stuffy, too academic to be engaging and that it's an abstract concept. It certainly does not seem to be mainstream just yet, even though there is a growing awareness of its importance.

Creative problem solving sounds like more fun and is something that educators and trainers will happily include in sessions. Perhaps now, though, given the need for our critical thinking skills themselves to change, this brings yet more scope for a teacher or trainer to introduce a whole range of new types of exercises. To start with, we probably need to work on our own critical thinking skills each and every day. That begins with heightening our awareness of how readily we absorb and believe information and managing how we use our smartphones.

Try this great exercise for problem solving using a critical thinking mindset. You can download it here: https://unimenta.com/critical-thinking/

We are prone to making assumptions about any and every situation without necessarily having all the relevant information on hand and we do most of this automatically and very fast. We can easily make assumptions based on our own perception of a situation or issue without making sure we have all the background facts first. The media encourages this to a certain extent also with big headlines, leading photographs and possibly biased or insufficient information. So it can also be quite tricky to get right if we are expected to think critically with speed, and with even more information at our fingertips.

Here is a longer exercise you can try which will heighten your awareness about the sheer number of assumptions we can encounter in just one day!

Download it here: https://unimenta.com/critical-thinking/

Try this

Engage in healthy debate. Argue both sides of an argument and be aware of emotions and automatic assumptions that might come up and where these may come from.

We are also naturally prone to a number of tendencies – having awareness of these and using some kind of strategy every day to counteract them will give your critical thinking skills a huge boost. I highly recommend keeping a kind of learning journal where you can record some of this for an accelerated boost:

Tendency No. 1: Confirmation bias

This is when we take the evidence or information presented to us and deliberately look for components that support our point of view, instead of being objective. This is a completely natural tendency and quite hard to fight unless you do the exact opposite and actively try and seek out information that doesn't support your own beliefs. Try it! What is important here is to heighten our own awareness levels of how often and how quickly we might do this in every day situations and then deliberately do the opposite. Train your brain.

Tendency No. 2: Attribution bias

In psychology, an attribution bias or attributional bias is a cognitive bias that refers to the systematic errors made when people try to find reasons for their own and others' behaviours. What this actually means is finding excuses or justifying our own and others' behaviour.

This can cause us to pigeonhole actions of others. We are often too quick to attribute the behaviour of other people to something personal about them rather than to something about their situation.

This particular bias can be further divided into types:

Interpersonal Attribution: When telling a story to a group of friends or acquaintances, you are likely to tell the story in a way that places you in the best possible light. Ever done this?

Predictive Attribution: We like to attribute things in ways that allow us to make future predictions. If your car was vandalised, you might attribute the crime to the fact that you parked in a particular parking garage. As a result, you will avoid that parking garage in the future in order to avoid further vandalism. Ever done this?

Explanatory Attribution: We use explanatory attributions to help us make sense of the world around us. Some people have an optimistic explanatory style, while others tend to be more pessimistic. People with an optimistic style attribute positive events to stable, internal and global causes and negative events to unstable, external and specific causes. Those with a pessimistic style attribute negative events to internal, stable and global causes and positive events to external, stable and specific causes. (For more on explanatory style, please refer to the chapter on optimism.)

We may use any one of these biases almost subconsciously and every day so try to be aware of when this happens. Have fun with it.

Tendency No. 3: Trusting hearsay

This is all about believing information someone else tells us, even if there is no evidence to support it. We tend to take things at face value, especially gossip. And how willing are we to select a product or service based on others' recommendations or online reviews? Word of mouth is the strongest marketing tool, but it can also be a danger to our ability to think critically and independently if we take everything we hear from others at face value. Ask more questions, use social media platforms mindfully and work out yourself what you want from a product or service first. Always question first what someone else has told you – be aware that it is likely their spin on something and not fact!

Tendency No. 4: Memory lapses

No, this is nothing to do with having a 'senior moment' or any other type of memory lapse. This is more to do with the common human trait of 'filling in the gaps' with our own information or ideas, which may or may not be accurate. When we recall an experience or when we are explaining a problem, we'll often put our own spin on it and where any information is missing, or we don't remember it completely, we'll fill in the gaps quite naturally. Watch for when you do this next time you are recounting an event or issue to a third party.

Tendency No. 5: Accepting authority without question

In the sixties, famous experiments were conducted by the social psychologist Stanley Milgram where people were willing to administer ever more powerful shocks on the orders of an authority figure, even though they were not convinced it was right to do so.[7] This failure to think critically can continue to be seen in blind acceptance of people with 'expertise', or in positions of power and authority. Does this ever happen to you?

Tendency No. 6: Not admitting you don't know all the facts

None of us likes to look foolish in front of others. This trait can sometimes lead to quite wild fabrication and speculation! It's better to just admit you don't know something rather than 'fake' knowledge. It happens much more often than we think and can sometimes happen automatically through over-elaborating on facts, or by telling 'white lies' to appear more knowledgeable than we are. Watch for when this can happen easily at work too. You may notice yourself or someone else doing this at your next meeting.

Get more observant about these tendencies. Observe yourself when you use them – don't take yourself too seriously either – try a light-hearted approach – 'there I go again believing hearsay!' when you get embroiled in a (often online) discussion.

How to think more critically

The best way to do this is through building awareness and trying out different approaches. The skills you need to get ahead in critical thinking are based on a combination of natural ability through character traits and genetics and cognitive flexibility, meaning they are connected with how our brain functions. By understanding our character traits and developing our self-awareness, we can build these skills through changing our behaviour. By strengthening our brain and having a better understanding of how it works, we can also build any and all of the seven skills and never more so than critical thinking.

Critical thinking IS a purely cognitive function – deeply connected with our brain. It's really about a process: asking questions and then asking more, depending on the answers we get. It's about practising discipline and being more rigorous. Yet, as we can see from some of the natural biases we have, other character traits, emotional wellbeing and human tendencies can interfere significantly with our ability to think critically.

Flex your thinking

If empathy is also part of developing critical thinking, as Elder and Paul suggest in their book *30 Days to Better Thinking and Better Living with Critical Thinking,* then the more 'intuitive' process of considering another's point of view, including emotions, opinions, background, knowledge and intentions, is, to some extent, hardwired for many people. Taking a more reflective and considered approach to situations, conversations and external events will help you. Empathy will help you too – refer to the chapter on empathy for more. I did not realise until this second edition not only how much overlap there is between all seven skills but specifically between empathy and critical thinking which we might not at first consider.

Maria Garcia Winner, a leading specialist in social-cognitive defects, believes that how we think is inextricably linked to how we feel.[8] Social thinking is, basically, what we do when we interact with other people. Critical thinking, although an individual skill, is rarely conducted in isolation. Winner outlines these key elements of social thinking:

1 **Our thoughts and emotions are strongly connected.** How we think affects how we feel and how we feel affects how we think. We may not want that to be the case, but it is. Therefore, we need to know how to manage our emotions and thoughts effectively.

2 **We think about others, even if we have no intention of interacting with them.** We adjust our behaviour based on what we think others may be thinking about us. This is not based on anything factual! Only our own perception.

3 **We 'think with our eyes' in order to figure out other people's thoughts, intentions and emotions.** We read other people's faces and interpret what we think they are thinking from their expressions. Most of the time we'll also, often wrongly, go even further and attribute our perception of what they may be thinking or feeling to something we have said and done.

Winner says that when people learn how to think differently and flexibly, they can think anywhere and be happier as a result too.

By far, the best way to build critical thinking skills earlier is in how we educate young people. Building self-determination skills, such as goal setting, decision making, self-advocacy and problem solving, should all be included in career planning for young people. Critical thinking skills can also be taught from a very young age onwards.

Developing cognitive flexibility is seen as key to unlocking critical thinking in our brains. Cognitive flexibility is our human ability to switch how we behave according to the context of the situation. This is all about ensuring that the learning of any subject is within a flexible learning environment.[9] Knowledge should be presented in a variety of different ways and for different purposes. The more information added to a task, the more our competences are challenged. They need to be challenged for us to tap into our critical thinking skills.[10]

Consider this

Do you run or do you fight? Let's say you know you are physically fit and could box someone in a ring and win. But faced with an unknown opponent in the street, late at night, who is shorter than you, you may need to use some critical thinking skills. And supposing you have also had a drink? Doesn't make the process any easier does it? In one situation we may evaluate something a certain way but in another quite differently and we need to become more nimble and agile in this process.

Clinical psychologists Lauren Kenworthy and Benjamin Yerys say that cognitive flexibility is best taught to young children through a hierarchy of other skills, including physical flexibility (such as Yoga and spatial games), coping skills and recognising feelings, introducing 'heroes' and creating clear goals. Forward-thinking primary schools indeed often include such experiential learning. Unfortunately, this seldom continues once children reach adolescence.

Cognitive flexibility is so important to developing strong critical thinking skills because it gives us the ability to adjust nimbly to changing demands and priorities and it requires consistent consideration of new perspectives, new information and adjusting to change. If you're a flexible thinker, you are far more likely to find lots of different ways to problem solve, accept other ideas and try out new things. You won't be thrown by rapid changes, unexpected curve balls or even annoying people.

Improve your mental jot pad

Working memory is critical to your ability to control your attention, concentrate despite distractions, successfully multitask, learn and really understand what you read and generally improve your overall performance on measures of intelligence. It improves with age. There is now even software that can make you smarter. Dual-N Back training is software that gives you a mental workout by getting you to keep track of objects on a screen while, at the same time, keeping the sequence of auditory letter sounds.[11] As you train, you progressively improve your ability to hold more information in your working memory.

Top tip

Play strategy games, Sudoku and solve crossword puzzles to sharpen the working memory part of your brain.

Chess also improves working memory because you tend to play out sequences in your mind first and you maintain them on your mental jotting pad as you analyse the various options. In one study of older people, chess was found to be the single activity most predictive in reducing the risk of mental decline. The same goes for reading books and, the more complex the material you are reading, the higher the load on your working memory.

Dopamine has been shown to improve working memory and this can be sourced easily in eating the right kinds of foods such as carbohydrates (pasta, rice and potatoes), avocados, bananas, pumpkin seeds, leafy green vegetables, fish and poultry.

Other measures that help are getting sufficient sleep. When we are asleep, the brain does all its repairs and maintenance work. Ensuring we have adequate sleep is crucial for a strong brain.

It is also perfectly normal to feel drowsy in the mid-afternoon. Acting on the urge to have a 15- to 20-min nap is not just restorative, enabling you to continue your daily activities with greater efficiency but, perhaps even more importantly, it also vastly improves memory retention and creative problem solving.

Finally, don't use up your working memory through overuse of your smartphone. Regulate how often you use it. If you want to or need to work on a project or task that requires you to really use your brain, your knowledge, your expertise get out of the habit of multi-tasking and into the habit of unitasking. That means phone-free periods of time to work. I promise you fantastic productivity results!

Try this

What is your typical morning routine? Do you get up and go or do you take a more reflective approach? Reconsidering how you begin your day can have a big impact on your brain's ability to think critically, problem solve and be productive.

We only have a certain amount of energy and willpower when we wake up each morning, and it slowly gets drained away with decisions. This is especially true if you're making hundreds of small decisions in the morning that mean nothing yet will affect how you make decisions for the remainder of the day. **Try to have the first hour of your day vary as little as possible with a routine.**

Mine goes as follows:

Wake up 6.30 am and drink a very large glass of lemon water.

Write in gratitude journal and drink cup of tea.

Hot shower, time with family, breakfast and coffee.

Writing down intentions for the day (I do not plan my day in the morning, instead I do this the night before.)

Walking with the dog and the school run (without my phone.)

Only after this do I get down to work following my plan set out from the evening before.

I also tend to leave mornings for my most productive work and I don't respond or deal with email until the afternoon.

What is your current morning routine?

_____

_____

_____

What are some ways you could create a better morning routine for yourself?

_____

_____

_____

**you are what you eat,
quite literally, it seems!**

Take on the barriers to critical thinking

Next time you find yourself in a situation where you reflexively resort to filling in any gaps with your own assumptions, or automatically listen out for opinions and information that support your own viewpoint, or take what you hear at face value, stop a moment and take stock. The more you can spot your weaknesses, the more self-aware you will become. Remember that these are completely natural tendencies that we all do and, mostly, are wired to do. The more we can rise above these tendencies and fight, the more strategies we will develop for thinking critically.

Be honest and open

Communicate clearly, don't fabricate and don't fake knowledge. Prepare properly for meetings and presentations so you don't have to 'fill in the gaps' based on your poor preparation. Slow down a little and don't take on so much. Take the time to do things properly and well.

Seven steps to critical thinking

You can improve your critical thinking skills and raise your general awareness, which is where everything must begin. Remember, it really is like exercising a muscle and requires work! Using a journal to record your thoughts and experiences, even for a short amount of time, is very helpful.

1   **Question your assumptions**

Wherever the assumptions come from, question them. Critical thinkers are curious and look to find the what and the why behind everything. Become more forensic when presented with a situation and try to work out where assumptions are being made. We probably make them so automatically in so many situations without thinking. Now is the time to change that and to ask why. **Think about a recent conversation or challenging situation. Are you aware of any immediate assumptions you were making? Or think about a current difficult situation – what assumptions are you making and why?**

_____

_____

_____

_____

2   **Adopt different perspectives**

Get into other people's heads as much as you can! This is where empathy comes in. Involve others in decision making too. If you are fortunate enough to be working in a culturally diverse environment, find out how others might view a problem. You will uncover valuable insights. Look at a problem from as many viewpoints as possible while recognising weaknesses in reasoning. **Identify a current problem or issue that your team at work is struggling with.**

_____

_____

_____

Try to analyse the issue from as many view points as you can. Even better, run a creative problem-solving meeting and see what comes up! Think about turning the 'problem' into a statement and then let the conversation emerge.

_____

_____

_____

3 Get creative

See opportunities where others see obstacles and seek these out! A savvy smart thinker views setbacks and issues as opportunities for something new, or as a way to do things better or differently. Explore new ways of being creative and innovative. You don't have to be a 'creative person' – your brain naturally has the ability to think creatively.

Think of a recent setback you have experienced:

_____

_____

_____

What opportunities do they offer you for something new or another way of tackling something?

_____

_____

_____

4 Build in reflection time

It will always seem like there is not enough time for this, but make time for reflection anyway and make thinking and reflection a priority in any decision-making process. You can build in reflection time to your day – even five-minute pockets here and there can make a difference because a little more time allows for this careful thought process and better decision making to occur and become more of a default setting. You could even use your commute for reflection and mindfulness!

What are some other ways I could introduce some reflection time into my day?

_____

_____

_____

_____

5   Get past face value

Don't settle for surface impressions, or 'gut feeling'. Think about root factors and source issues and about what is really going on underneath. Don't believe everything you hear, not for a minute! We tend to do this so automatically, though. Oh, and whatever you do, don't gossip!

Have a quick peek at your favourite social media platform. What sorts of surface impressions come up for you immediately when you do this?

_____

_____

_____

Think back to when you experienced a 'gut feeling' or wanted to make a decision based on that. How accurate was your instinct in reality?

_____

_____

_____

6   Build your skills

Read, read, read and, better still, write, blog or try podcasting. Have more in-depth conversations on important complex topics. Explore current events more. Get involved in debates. Have a view and an opinion. Learn something new every day. Keep learning, keep curious. If you have children, encourage them to do the same.

_____

_____

_____

A day in the life of. . .

Let's take a magnifying glass to the skill of critical thinking through a day in the life of Lisa. We'll start with a brief introduction to Lisa, to give a quick snapshot of her life.

About Lisa

Lisa is in her twenties, a young entrepreneur with her own Internet fashion business, which is starting to become quite successful. She travels a lot for work and doesn't have a fixed office as such – everything is run from home and, as she is often on the move, she works mainly with her laptop, tablet device and smartphone. Lisa says she can work anywhere at any time and feels fortunate to have such a flexible business. Lisa spends a lot of her time interacting with virtual teams and with suppliers and buyers in the Middle East and Asia.

Lisa is energetic and extrovert and generally upbeat. She has a wide network of friends and she's very active on social media, both personally and through her business. She doesn't tend to read much and feels that she can get whatever she needs online. She started her business straight out of university. She'd always had a flair for fashion and her History degree, although interesting enough, did not really equip her for the world of work – so she's had to learn everything by doing it, and very fast. To her credit, she's built up a successful and thriving business.

Let's have a closer look at a typical day in Lisa's life and how building her critical thinking skills can help her.

Lisa's typical day

Lisa tends not to keep set hours. She gets up late and often works late into the night, because of time differences and also because being active on the fashion scene at evening shows and nightclub events requires this. Once up, she tends to get straight to her computer or iPad, checking email, several industry social media platforms and flitting from the business to the personal and back again. She is constantly distracted by her social media news feeds and articles and news she clicks onto. Once Lisa is up in the morning, it's often close to lunchtime so she tends to drink only coffee and then grab a salad for lunch. During lunch she hosts a conference call with suppliers and buyers. The afternoon is taken up with admin and setting up meetings. She books flights to Hong Kong and a hotel mid-afternoon. She then is presented with a bit of a crisis in that one of her suppliers can't meet a critical deadline. She immediately discusses this with her virtual team but they're unable to resolve this easily because of the overlap with other orders and deadlines. Lisa finds this very stressful and decides she will deal with this tomorrow, when she's had some time to think about it.

Lisa's social life tends to blend with her work. This evening, like most, she goes to a networking and media event that is combined with a business dinner. She gets into a conversation with one of her competitors, which doesn't go very well, and Lisa feels a bit discouraged but shrugs it off. Her business is doing great.

Lisa leaves the event and goes home in the early hours. Before bed she rechecks her email and social media feeds to make sure she hasn't missed anything before falling into a fitful sleep.

What's going on here?

Lisa is young and energetic and has, what sounds like, a thriving business. She's done really well to start it straight out of university and she obviously has entrepreneurial skills, which is great. At first glance it may not be easy to see how critical thinking skills might help her. Surely she got enough of that on her History degree? But what is happening, is that Lisa doesn't have the critical thinking skills that could make her and her business really flourish. She is in danger of burning out too because, as her business grows, so will the demands on her time and, at the moment, she doesn't have any structure to her day and is unable to manage the overload of information and data she is bombarded with day-to-day. Because of the constant online distractions, her brain is starting to become weaker at focusing and giving attention to any one task, making her really quite inefficient. Critical thinking would help her to work more effectively with social media. In her industry, too, innovation and creativity are high on the list of top competences that critical thinking can boost significantly. Critical thinking can also help Lisa problem solve more effectively and creatively, which doesn't always happen. The reason why that conversation with her competitor didn't go well? Lisa is not the greatest listener because her attention flits. In this instance, because she wasn't really focusing on the other person, her brain leapt into gear and gave her lots of assumptions and 'missing information' to plug those gaps where she wasn't focused.

Lisa decides to put some of the ideas on critical thinking into practice. Let's revisit Lisa's 'typical day' six months later.

How Lisa's life has moved forward

These days Lisa has a much better grip on social media. She's decided to use it more to the advantage of the business by becoming an expert in her field – she's doing this by blogging on a regular basis, which requires her to research quality content. She is starting to process some of the information and data coming at her online in a more orderly way. Writing her industry blog is enabling her to connect different ideas and see their relevance – in fact it reminds her of some of the coursework she did on her History degree, which she enjoyed a lot. Lisa also keeps her professional and personal social media activity separate. Although this has not been easy for her to do, she has recognised its importance. She now keeps

social media activity to set times of the day and has set up a
social media dashboard to make it easier to manage the
various feeds and posts. Because of the blog, her posts are
becoming more strategic anyway. Gradually, she is starting to
plan her activity and focus on specific areas at different times
of the day – i.e. blog and industry research, posting about
events, marketing activity, photography and image posts.

Lisa has decided to build in more creativity sessions with the
teams she works with. She has realised how crucial this is for her
business and in general, so now there are regular times when
Lisa facilitates freethinking innovation tasks and exercises. They
all enjoy this and it has led to some great new ideas. The supplier
problem that cropped up is something they've now resolved
through having more streamlined processes in place, which
weren't there before.

Lisa is getting better at listening. She understands that she can
quickly jump to conclusions sometimes so tries to slow down a
bit when talking to people, especially competitors. Part of this is
also because she has never felt hugely secure setting up her
business without a lot of knowledge of the industry, so,
consequently, when she meets competitors, she knows that
initially she might feel a bit threatened and she now uses this
awareness to ask more questions.

Lisa still keeps erratic hours, but these days she is more relaxed
and enjoys the evening events more. And when she gets home she
tries to wind down before sleeping, which means no iPad in bed!

Critical thinking skills can make a huge difference, as we can see
from Lisa's life. Many of us are living like Lisa, flitting from thing
to thing and stuffing as much as possible into our days. We can
be so much more efficient, creative and effective in our work and
in our personal lives if we practise and build critical thinking skills
into our day-to-day routines.

Interested in learning more?

I've put together some extra resources here:

Books

Berger, W. (2016) *A More Beautiful Question: The Power of Inquiry to Spark Breakthrough Ideas.* Bloomsbury.

Elder, L. and Paul, R. (2012) *30 Days to Better Thinking and Better Living with Critical Thinking: A Guide for Improving Every Aspect of Your Life.* Pearson Education.

Gathercole, S. and Packiam-Alloway, T. (2008) *Working Memory and Learning: A Practical Guide for Teachers.* Sage Publications.

Goldberg (2001) 'Building the brain's "Air Traffic Control" system: How early experiences shape the development of executive function', National Scientific Council on the Developing Child. Harvard University.

Harper, J. (2017) *Wait, What?: And Life's Other Essential Questions* Harper One.

Levitin, D. (2015) *The Organised Mind: Thinking Straight in the Age of Information Overload.* Dutton.

Lewis, J. (2014) *Sort Your Brain Out: Boost Your Performance, Manage Stress and Achieve More.* Capstone.

Winner, M.G. and Crooke, P. (2010) *You Are a Social Detective: Explaining Social Thinking to Kids.* North River Press.

Articles and websites

Diamond, A., Barnett, W.S., Thomas, J. and Munro, S. (2007) 'Preschool program improves cognitive control', *Science,* 381: 1387–88.

Kuncel, N. and Hezlett, S. (2010) 'Fact and fiction in cognitive ability testing for admissions and hiring decisions', *Current Directions in Psychological Science,* 19: 339–45.

www.criticalthinking.org

A website with lots of resources, articles and events to help sharpen your critical thinking skills

www.thinkwatson.com

Website with critical thinking assessments, research and articles

You can also find more tips, ideas, curated video clips and exercises to strengthen your optimism skills by visiting https://unimenta.com/critical-thinking/

Sign up too for daily tips – a daily quote, tip and video clip on one of the seven skills direct to your inbox. https://unimenta.com/seven-skills/

Chapter 3

EMPATHY

Developing skills that are uniquely 'human' such as active listening, caring and nurturing are key for the world of the future. Empathy – that is, the ability to understand and be aware of, co-experience the feelings and thoughts of other people – is probably one of the most important skills you can have. It is essential for enhancing our interpersonal relationships, overall life satisfaction and improving our ability to respond well to challenges. But what is empathy exactly? This word originally was coined from the German *einfuehlungsvermogen* drawing on the Greek 'em' for 'in' and 'pathos' for 'feeling'.

Literally translated, this means being able to feel what another person is feeling. Empathy is the ability to imagine yourself in someone else's position and to identify and understand another's situation, feelings and motives. Perhaps on first glance all this sounds a bit woolly.

What is empathy?

Empathy can be confused with sympathy. Sympathy reflects understanding of another person's situation, yes – but only viewed through your own lens or perspective. So it's based on **your** version of what the other person is dealing with. For example, a friend has just told you that someone close to them has died. You want to respond genuinely and you can sympathise because, perhaps, you also lost someone close to you a few years back and you dealt with it in a particular way. That may appear to be empathy but you're really only expressing it from your own perspective. In that sense, sympathy can actually be a form of judgement! Worse, you are probably not even listening actively if you are that ready to come in with your own story. In contrast, empathy is what you feel only when you can step outside of yourself and enter the internal world of the other person. There,

> **empathy rarely starts with the words 'at least'**

while still keeping your own perspective, you can experience the other's emotions, conflicts or aspirations from within the vantage point of that person's world. Really listening, therefore, is an important component of empathy as is paying attention. Focus on others is the foundation of empathy.

What others say about empathy

Brene Brown (Research Professor at University of Houston who has researched empathy, vulnerability and leadership over the past two decades) gives this very helpful summary of what empathy is:

- **Empathy is being able to see the world as others see it –** This requires putting your own 'stuff' aside and choosing to see the situation through the other person's eyes.

- **Empathy is being non-judgemental –** Judgement of another person's situation discounts their experience and is actually an attempt to protect ourselves from the pain of the situation.

- **Empathy is understanding another person's feelings –** We have to be in touch with our own feelings in order to understand someone else's.

- **Empathy is communicating your understanding of that person's feelings –** Rather than saying, 'At least you . . . ' or 'It could be worse . . . ' try, 'I've been there, and that really hurts', or (to quote an example from Brown) 'It sounds like you are in a hard place now. Tell me more about it' or simply 'I don't know what to say, but I am really glad you told me'.

Daniel Goleman, leading psychologist and expert on emotional intelligence says there are three kinds of empathy:

- **Cognitive** – this is being able to understand another's perspective. To do this requires genuine curiosity more than anything else, to get behind why someone thinks the way they do and why the do the things they do. Self-awareness is, again, key here. If we are able to be aware of our own feelings and where they come from and have effective ways of managing our behaviour then we can also apply this process with other people. This takes effort and of course a willingness to do so, but can be done!

- **Emotional** – the ability to feel what someone else feels is bound up with deep responses within our brain. We are able to subconsciously mirror someone else's body language quite easily and our brain's neurons light up when we do. However, the ability to do this on a deeper level is dependent on close attention to detail such as knowing that we are likely to have our own interpretation of someone else's feelings and awareness of emotional "cues" that come from body language, facial expressions and tone of voice.

- **Empathic concern** – the ability to sense what another person needs from you. For this to happen you, in essence, have to be able to manage your own emotions despite someone else's distress so that you can remain calm.

Empathy is a right-brain quality linked strongly to our interpersonal skills.[1] In our globalised competitive economy, the one thing that can't be outsourced or automated is an understanding of what makes others tick, creating trust and strong relationships and generally being caring of others. It is a skill that is becoming increasingly important in both our professional and private lives. Empathy is, if you like, your personal and professional competitive advantage. The skill of empathy can make you really stand out in a company, among individuals in a crowded and noisy marketplace and it can significantly enhance your personal and social relationships too.

Why empathy is a must-have skill

Why is empathy something we all need more of? First of all, without it you will never have strong listening skills or the ability to truly respect others and really value your relationships. Everything you do is visible to more people, mostly because of the amount we interact online, including how you communicate and relate to others.

We communicate so much online now that empathy is also often missing in everyday human interactions because we miss a lot of environmental cues and we don't pay attention. How many discussions, conversations and arguments now take place solely via messaging platforms? We live in a distracting world, where so much is happening that we forget to really focus on the person with whom we are communicating. We also miss vital signs and messages in facial expressions that appear on faces within the first few seconds. Our innate ability to empathise with others is weakening. We need to develop empathy because it is a natural skill that we have started to lose and strengthening it will make a huge difference to how we interact with others.

Empathy is also often referred to as 'social intelligence'. Socially intelligent people are able to assess quickly the emotions of those around them and adapt their words, tone and gestures accordingly. This has always been a key skill and now it is even more important for all of us, as we are called upon to collaborate with larger groups of people in different settings, virtual and non-virtual. Our social IQ will continue to be a vital asset. Social IQ is built into the human psyche to greater or lesser degrees and is something that can be developed. In a truly globally connected world, your skill set could potentially see you living and working in different locations and interacting with people from very different backgrounds.

You need to be able to operate and function well in whatever environment or cultural context you find yourself. This can demand not only specific abilities, such as language skills, but also an ability to adapt to, sense and respond to changing circumstances and new contexts.

The Internet has changed the way we communicate and makes the need for empathy even stronger. So many elements of communicating effectively as human beings simply get lost on social media interactions.

Empathy is probably the most important tool you have when it comes to interpersonal skills both online and off-line.

Consider this

Social media may very likely be a key part of your personal life. For most people it is. Social media, including online messaging platforms and direct messages can be great for connecting with others but is also highly prone to misunderstandings and hurt. Include empathy in your social media use too and watch your relationships thrive – post positive comments and limit use of social media too so that you are responding more thoughtfully. If you need to have a potentially difficult conversation with somebody, don't do it on messaging and social media platforms. Take the time to meet face-to-face. Communicating on social media is faster in the short term but can often lead to miscommunication and misunderstandings, which then take far longer to resolve and sometimes lead to real damage to a relationship.

How empathy helps us at work

In *Wired to Care: How Companies Prosper When They Create Widespread Empathy*, top business strategist Dev Patnaik states that organisations of all kinds can tap into a power each of us already naturally has: empathy, the ability to reach outside of ourselves and connect with other people. When people inside a company develop a shared sense of what's going on in the world, they're able to see new opportunities faster than their competitors because they have the courage to be more innovative and take risks. Where empathy plays a part is because the company is far more focused on sincerely understanding the market in-depth and with empathy, and they're doing this collectively.

An example of empathy at work

IBM was falling apart in the early 1990s[2] and seemed destined to become obsolete. The new CEO at that time, Leo Gerstner, instigated 'Operation Bear Hug', which was simply sending the top 50 managers out to really listen to customers' concerns and to think about how IBM could help address them. The same listening programme was cascaded down to other managers. 'Operation Bear Hug' revealed some major new opportunities for IBM to help companies leverage the power of the then emerging Internet, and this strategy literally turned the whole company around; a whole new product was created with a focus on service, rather than on product.

There are numerous studies that link empathy to business results. They include studies that correlate empathy with increased sales, with the performance of the best managers of product development teams and with enhanced performance in an increasingly diverse workforce.

Empathy is also crucial for strong leadership. Empathy in leadership is all about building trust. Leaders need to create an environment that is free of fear, anxiety and lack of trust as these all make people shut down because the brain's threat response engages and as a result creativity and productivity diminish.

Try this

Three essential practices – empathy, gratitude and generosity – that have been shown to sustain benevolent leadership, even in the most cut-throat working environments.

To practice empathy:

- Ask a great question or two in every interaction and paraphrase important points that others make.

- Listen with intent and willingness. Orient your body and eyes towards the person speaking and convey interest and engagement vocally.

- When someone comes to you with a problem, signal concern with phrases such as 'I'm sorry' and 'That's really tough'. Avoid rushing to judgement and advice.

- Before meetings, take a moment to think about the person you'll be with and what may be happening in his or her life.

To practise gratitude:

- Make thoughtful thank-yous a part of how you communicate with others. This works well at work as well as generally!

- Send colleagues specific and timely emails or notes of appreciation for jobs done well.

- Publicly acknowledge the value that each person contributes to your team, including support staff.

To practice generosity:

- Seek opportunities to spend a little one-on-one time with the people you lead.

- Delegate some important and high-profile responsibilities.

- Give praise generously.

- Share the limelight. Give credit to all who contribute to the success of your team and your organisation.

Empathy is part of emotional intelligence and self-awareness is the cornerstone of emotional intelligence. Emotional intelligence is not static and you can grow and develop it throughout life. Emotional intelligence grows through experience, openness and a willingness to learn and be more self-aware.

We live in an age of young, independent, highly marketable and mobile workers. In a popular *Harvard Business Review* article, 'What makes a leader', Goleman isolates three reasons why empathy plays such an important role, particularly now:

1 **The increasing use of teams, both virtual and face-to-face** – Even though the patterns of how we work are changing, we do not work in isolation and, in fact, are increasingly dependent on working in all kinds of different types of teams. The Pearson 2030 research into skills for the future stresses the huge importance of social and interpersonal skills as we navigate our way forward. The need for high-performing, multifunctional and strong working teams has never been greater.[3]

2 **The rapid pace of globalisation** – As organisations negotiate the cultural context in which globalisation and the spread of digital technology are taking place (Tett, 2017), this increase in cross-cultural communication can easily lead to misunderstandings. A survey by Ernst & Young points to surprisingly big gaps when it comes to cultural knowledge.[4]

3 **The growing need to retain talent** – Key skills are becoming scarcer as baby boomers near retirement age, and the war for talent is getting fiercer because it is harder to find employees with the right skill set. So this means looking after and nurturing the people you have who are good at what they do. Organisations can't protect jobs which are made redundant by technology – but they do have a responsibility to their people. This means nurturing agility, adaptability and reskilling.

'Leaders with empathy', states Goleman, 'use their knowledge to improve their companies in subtle but important ways.' This doesn't mean that they agree with everyone's view or try to please everybody. Rather, they 'thoughtfully consider employees' feelings – along with other factors – in the process of making intelligent decisions'.

Often, what employees feel is a result of what they are experiencing in the workplace. The quality of our lives is determined by whether the feelings we have on a day-to-day basis are primarily positive or negative. Positive feelings result in us feeling good, and when that's the case, we tend to perform better and contribute actively. It's common sense that feelings influence behaviour and results. So it's good business practice to consider employees' and colleagues' feelings and to seek to make them 'the best that they can be'. Consciously practising the skills of empathy has to be part of that.

Social media is becoming the biggest platform for many businesses and success relies not on selling, but sharing something interesting and relevant and by listening and understanding needs and different perspectives intimately. The ultimate aim is to create that strong relationship and credibility and then to sell. This takes time. And empathy! Empathy online is important because, unlike other communication channels, with the Internet all the power is placed in the hands of the audience and not the speaker![5] This is the case whether you are interacting in a professional or in a personal capacity. In social media, the target audience will gravitate towards exactly what they want, the way that they want it. They find the product or service rather than the other way round. Empathy with this target audience is key. That means listening to them and being able to put yourself in their shoes, rather than first putting your effort into selling your product or service.

More important now? You bet – because social media not only sharpens the breadth of information we receive, but gives all of us a far stronger and easier way to make quick choices. The use of social media in business is growing faster and faster as many come to recognise it as a powerful tool to build brand awareness and also, and this is the most important of all, create strong relationships.

Empathy case study

Billy Cripe, the founder of BloomThink, a social media and mobile strategy consultancy, is adamant that using social media to engage well with others relies on empathy. Social media is now used widely as a marketing tool. Successful use of social media correctly anticipates what a customer wants and provides content or product that is interesting and relevant, and precisely aligned to needs. That requires attention and focus – active listening. Honing empathy skills helps you to understand what market needs are and what is relevant content that fits the specific context. Empathy, in this case, makes your listening and your focus that much sharper. I never used Twitter until relatively recently. It has opened up a whole new world and propelled me into much more finely tuned social media empathy skills. It also forces me to respond and, where necessary, change a particular approach. Uncomfortable sometimes? Time-consuming? Yes, but completely necessary now.

What makes empathy challenging?

Generally, we do not think, see or perceive the world as other people do but we do spend a lot of our time operating within our own way of thinking, seeing or perceiving the world and expecting everyone else to be operating from the same paradigm. This is a waste of time, since they don't and they can't. However, practising empathy consistently across a variety of interpersonal situations in the course of our day requires work and a conscious degree of attention, as well as real effort. A key aspect of empathy is truly and actively listening, something we find very difficult to do.

> 'We think we listen, but very rarely do we listen with real understanding, true empathy. Yet listening, of this very special kind, is one of the most potent forces for change that I know.'
>
> Carl Rogers, American psychologist and founder
> of humanistic approach to psychology

How do you use empathy with someone who annoys you or frustrates you?

First of all it's worth looking at why this person annoys you in the first place – it may be their communication style or maybe they engage in behaviours you find rude or unpredictable. Or, for whatever reason you just don't like them! Using empathy can help you to maintain a more balanced approach to working and dealing with difficult people:

Reflect

Always remember that people generally are not necessarily irritating you or annoying you on purpose. Most of the time other people are just reacting to things that are going on in their own lives. How they do this will again depend on their own degree of self-awareness and ability to stand back and not project their issues onto you. Equally, you yourself can stand back and simply ask yourself 'what is causing ME to react this way' – it can well be that this person reminds you of someone else you don't like. So YOUR self-awareness is key here – an understanding of your own psychological makeup strengthens your capacity for empathy.

Stay calm

This is where you need to lean in to your emotional self-control and willpower – sooner or later this person will do something that annoys you and when this happens you will definitely feel a physiological reaction – so recognise the clues that you are getting triggered. Maybe your breath will quicken, your palms start to sweat and even your temperature may rise. Giving into these risks 'amygdala hijack' where you lose access to the rational, thinking part of your brain. So take a few deep breaths to help regulate your stress hormones and make it far less likely that you'll engage in behaviour you won't be proud of later. Being calm puts you in a better frame of mind to practise empathy for this other person – you're not caving, you're not shutting down – you are staying cool and collected and maintaining awareness of the situation.

Be curious

Your ability to understand someone else's perspective and feel what someone else feels tend to shut down when you're annoyed or frustrated. So cultivate curiosity.

Try and generate theories that may explain why a person says what he/she says, thinks what he/she thinks and acts the way he/she acts. Unearth curiosity – go so far as to ask yourself what motivates this person, what inspires and excites them? Maybe even reflect on his/her cultural background, education, family situation or day-to-day pressures. It's just about understanding perspective and acknowledging it – not necessarily agreeing with it or validating it. Maybe they are just having a bad day!

Focus on your similarities – easy to focus on the differences but TRY focusing on things you may have in common.

Be kind – when you're dealing with someone you dislike, it is easy to assume the worst and that mindset will show up in your behaviour too. So short-circuit that reaction and just do or say something that is surprising and nice. Compliment the person or offer to help with something. It has to be authentic though! Watch for passive-aggressive behaviours and be kind instead – empathy is a choice you can make in any scenario.

Have a (difficult) conversation – Coming from an empathy perspective, you can sometimes confront in a calm way – perhaps even say something like 'I'd like to explore how we can get on better' – this is maybe something you'll want to do if the relationship is high stake – someone you have to deal with at work or in a community situation. Also, never lose sight of the fact that it's likely too that this person may feel exactly the same way about you! If they drive you crazy, then chances are you drive them crazy too!

The things that are unsaid

We also need to be more aware of what is not being said or expressed, or concealed behind niceties. Empathy has to get right behind 'polite' behaviour and be able to bring sometimes uncomfortable issues out into the open. That means empathy works with information that is as accurate as it can be. That's done through careful listening, and the more willing you are to understand someone else's perspective, the more accurate the information they give you will be. How do you do that? By asking the right kinds of open questions and observing body language. If your goal is to lead or influence someone, the first consideration must be to your own personal behaviour. Most people absolutely do not listen with the intent to understand; most people are preparing to speak when their turn comes next. I know because I catch myself doing it numerous times a day. Empathy takes effort and conscientiousness.

Consider this

When you actively listen, you can literally transform the conversation you are having. And, because others don't often experience the gift of listening, when you take the time and attention to listen to them, they perceive this (and you) in a highly positive way. It's so simple really! But something that we find hard to do day-to-day and consistently.

Empathy is not only about really understanding someone's feelings and thoughts but also understanding real constraints and pressures that may not be revealed in an initial verbal exchange. An example of this is in a negotiation situation, where it's important to understand the objectives and constraints that underlie the discussion, both at a corporate level (if that is where you are negotiating) and at the personal level. This requires wider discussion and research around the immediate issue being negotiated.

Top tip

Be fully present when you are with people and tune in to non-verbal communication

You can start being fully present by putting away your phone, not checking your email and not accepting calls while you are interacting with someone.

The ego

Our strongly developed sense of individuality – or being a personal self, or ego – can make it difficult for us to experience this state of connection with others that using empathy suggests. The ego 'walls us off' from other people. We spend most of our day walking around focused on ourselves and looking at everything from our own perspective. This is completely natural and is probably heightened by our increasing propensity to react rather than respond to events around us. Therefore, empathy requires effort on our part, at least initially to kick it back into gear.

If you are discussing a friend's personal situation, you are very likely also to be looking at it from your own perspective – i.e., how YOU would feel if YOU lost your job – making true empathy harder still.

How to become more empathetic

The vast majority of a person's ability to recognise and respond appropriately to the needs and feelings of others seems to be based on social factors, such as upbringing and environment. A large 2018 study into the genetic basis of 'empathy', suggests that just 10 per cent of the variation between people's compassion and understanding is down to genes.[6]

It is true that some people are naturally good at empathy. Neuroscience suggests that empathy is connected with how our brains work.[7] So, although this means that some people may well be better at it than others, it also means that it can be learned. According to neuroscientist Dr Shanida Nataraja, Westerners use the left hemisphere of their brain too much, focusing on the logical, rational and analytical aspects of the mind. Why do we use this side so much? Well, partly because of the world we live in and its overload of information, and the brain processing required to handle it.

The right hemisphere of the brain is associated with seeing the whole picture, emotional expression, creativity, non-verbal awareness and visual and spatial perception, and it is the neural site of empathy. In fact, considerable research shows that the capacity to feel what another person feels is hardwired through what are called 'mirror neurons', which connect your brain like Wi-Fi with people you observe.[8] Functional magnetic resonance imagery shows that regions of the brain involving both emotions and physical sensations light up in someone who observes or becomes aware of another person's pain or distress.[9] Literally, you do feel another's pain or other emotions. Similar research[10] shows that generosity and altruistic behaviour light up pleasure centres of the brain usually associated with food or sex.[11]

When you walk down the street and someone comes your way, it's likely you will both move in the same direction, even though you are trying to get out of each other's way. This is because your mirror neurons sensed the person's intentions and you 'mirrored' their actions until your cognitive brain could engineer an opposing move that cleared the path.[12] These mirror neurons enable us to experience empathy and show that to a greater or lesser extent, we are each in fact hardwired to be empathetic.

This suggests empathy is a skill that needs to be mastered.

Start with yourself – if empathy is about understanding others and showing understanding and compassion, then this has to start with being able to do this to yourself. It's a bit like when they tell you on a plane to put your oxygen mask on BEFORE you help your child with theirs. Unless we are able to look after ourselves, we will not have the energy, resources or effort that is needed when it comes to others. Looking after yourself first also increases your own self-awareness – crucial for using empathy with people you may find annoying or difficult.

So why not start with self-care?

The first step of self-care is to pay attention to yourself and whether you are getting what you need physically, mentally, emotionally and spiritually – just on a day-to-day level. Quite simply you could start with a list – things that contribute to you feeling bad and things that help you to feel great and grounded. This is also important, not least because our levels of empathy aren't necessarily fixed for all situations and right across our lives. Your ability to empathise is compromised when you are under stress, tired or just not looking after yourself.

Here's an example, but yours may well look different:

Non-self-care list	Self-care list
Too many late nights in a row	Making sure I get to bed by 10.30 most nights
Thinking I should be somewhere other than where I am	Taking a relaxing bath or shower before bed
Not having a morning routine	Preparing ahead when it comes to food so that I eat healthy and tasty things

Non-self-care list	Self-care list
Comparing myself to other people	Being around friends and family
Not paying attention to my body	Dancing
Eating too much sugar	Going to Yoga class
Working too much, too long, too late	Practising mindfulness every day
Forgetting to do mindfulness practice because I've been Instagramming for too long	Writing in a gratitude journal morning and evening
Zoning out to box sets	Being honest to myself about myself
Too much TV in general	Paying attention to self-critical thoughts and changing the track to something more positive
Too much time on social media	Treating myself as kindly as I treat friends/family/work colleagues
Not taking a day off when I need to	Taking naps and rest when needed
Missing meals or not taking the time to sit down and eat them	Walking in nature
Not being around friends and family	Swimming by the sea
Being around too many people for too long	Having quiet time

Try creating your own self-care list!

You can download the exercise here: https://unimenta.com/empathy/

Writing a self-care list may seem like an odd thing to do – perhaps you've never really thought about this before but it is so vital when it comes to empathy and also plays a big role with building some of the other seven skills – for example, resilience.

We can also sharpen our empathy skills simply by being more aware of and paying more attention in our daily interactions with others.

Top tip

Try to empathise with people whose beliefs you don't share.

One good way to approach differing beliefs in conversation is to say, 'That's interesting, how did you develop that idea?' or 'Tell me more'.

Reading faces

According to Daniel Pink's book *A Whole New Mind*, if we are going to build our empathy skills, we need to get better at reading people's faces and body language, so that means paying far more attention to people we are interacting with than we normally do.[13] This is because facial expressions that demonstrate the real feelings underneath, which are not being voiced, are visible only for a few seconds,[14] but long enough to recognise easily if you are paying attention and are not distracted by your own thoughts. He says that what we need to begin to understand are the micro-expressions within these, which are there for an even briefer time.

How to read someone's face

Remember that a **micro-expression** is a subconscious flash of emotion across the face. It is difficult to fake a microexpression. A microexpression is a 100 per cent accurate reflection of what that person is feeling, which will then quickly be adjusted, once the conscious mind kicks in, to what they want you to see.

There are seven universal microexpressions: disgust, anger, fear, sadness, happiness, surprise and contempt. They often occur as fast as 1/15 to 1/25 of a second so you need to be quick!

The best way to practice reading micros is to watch recordings of interviews. Interviews with politicians and criminals are a good place to start!

Turn the sound off and watch the body language and expressions. Repeat it until you see the shifts and changes and you recognise them without thinking. Lastly, watch it with the sound on. What was said at the moment a micro-expression flashes on to their face? Was the actual expression congruent with the words themselves?

Top tip

Focus on the face. The next time you ask an important question in a meeting or negotiation, focus on the other person's face for at least four seconds, instead of just listening to the words coming out of his or her mouth. Develop a sensitivity for this and see if you can start recognising micro-expressions.

Active listening

Most people think they are great listeners. They think good listening comes down to simply not talking when others are speaking, letting the other person know you are listening through your facial expressions and verbal sounds and being able to repeat what others have said almost word-for-word. But that is not great listening. Most listening skills techniques say you should do those very things – remain quiet, nod and 'hmm hmmm' encouragingly and then repeat back to the talker something like: 'so let me see if I've understood you correctly. What you're saying is . . . .'

There's more to active listening than this though:

1 **Good listening is much more than being silent while the other person talks** It's all about asking questions! The best listeners periodically ask questions that promote discovery and insight because they challenge old assumptions in a constructive way far more than just sitting there nodding. A good question

shows that the listener not only heard what was being said but understood it well enough to want more information. The best conversations are active ones and a two-way dialogue.

2 **Good listening includes interaction that builds up self-esteem** This is about making it a positive experience for the other person, which does not happen if the listener is passive or critical. The listener helps the other person feel supported and creating a self environment to discuss things openly.

3 **Good listening is a cooperative conversation** Poor listeners listen only to find errors in reasoning or logic and use the silence to prepare their next response. Good listeners may challenge assumptions and disagree but the person being listened to does not feel like they are in an argument.

4 **Good listeners tend to make suggestions** This can only happen if the listener has built up trust and is able to provide feedback or suggestions in ways the other person will accept.

Good listeners are, in fact, like trampolines – you can bounce ideas off them and rather than just absorb them they are able to energise and help clarify your thinking.

Levels of effort in listening:

1 Creating an environment where issues can be discussed or where talking can take place comfortably.

2 Clearing away distractions like phones, etc. and focusing attention on the other person, making appropriate eye contact. This is really important too because it changes the way YOU feel as the listener also.

3 Really striving to understand the substance of what the other person is saying. Capturing ideas, restating issues to confirm correct understanding.

4 Observing non-verbal cues – so really being hyper aware of facial expressions, gestures, postures and lots of other subtle body

language signals. Over 80 per cent of what we communicate comes from these!

5 Understanding more and more the other person's emotions and feelings about the topic at hand and identifying them and acknowledging them. Validating the feelings in non-judgemental way.

6 Asking questions to clarify assumptions other person might have so as to help them see the situation in a new light – could also be about injecting some thoughts and ideas into the topic that might be helpful but not hijacking.

Each level builds on the next.

So you definitely cannot offer solutions unless you have built on the other levels first.

Most of us stop short of these final rungs on the ladder

Here are two key components of active listening:

Being interested in what the other person is saying, with a readiness and ability to listen. Now, we may not actually *be* interested initially but, curiously, by acting interested we start to become interested. How do you show interest? By everything from body language to reflecting back to the other person what is being said in what we say or write.

Being present. Most of the time, when others are speaking, we are focused on what we are going to say next or on our own thoughts and are less likely to be anchored in the present moment. We may have to force ourselves to be present, but when we are, it pays huge dividends.

So, the next time you communicate with anyone, set aside your own need to say the next thing and genuinely seek to understand. Don't push, be patient, be respectful, understand their emotions, clarify their statements and be discerning, sensitive and aware.

Top tip

Challenge yourself to have a deeper conversation with someone

Understanding a person's point of view or personal challenges requires conversation that moves past the weather. This doesn't mean you should necessarily ask about highly personal matters. Start by sharing a little more of your own experiences and perspectives and see if the other person opens up.

Try it this week! It's an excellent way to start developing empathy. While you speak to this person, think about using their name, smiling, encouraging them, listening, without interrupting. This singular conversation won't just be practice; it will lay the foundation for a much better relationship and connection and you might even enjoy yourself!

> **want to be liked? all you have to do is listen!**

> **empathy is the power of active listening**

Try it next time you are talking with your partner or friend. Then try it at work. You will see an immediate change, either in the direction your conversation takes or the outcome as a result of that conversation.

Download this active listening awareness-raising exercise to help you, if you like: https://unimenta.com/empathy/

Total immersion

Another way to develop empathy is to try to totally and completely immerse ourselves in what it might feel like to walk in another person's shoes. This is hard to do because it means consciously directing our awareness to something our mind does not naturally gravitate towards. That's because our sense of individuality and ego is so very strong and ingrained. However, it is possible. It's possible through consciously focusing on another person and stepping outside of ourselves; through really listening and making sure we understand. Most of the time we focus our attention only on ourselves. Every single experience, from standing in line at the bank to attending a meeting, is undertaken through our own personal lens. Try doing this a different way. It's hard work and it's exhausting but it does have an immediate impact. Try practising this focus in an everyday situation and notice the effect it has. An example: you go into your local bank to pay in some money. There's a long queue and you're in a hurry. Finally, you get to the window. Instead of conducting the transaction in a hurry and barely looking at the woman behind the counter, blaming the bank and by default the woman serving you, you smile and ask how she is and maybe even acknowledge the wait. The effect can be transformational. And you will certainly feel a lot happier immediately as a result. That is why customer-centric banks will train their staff to do just this, so it's you on the receiving end.

Why is empathy that powerful? Psychologically, empathy is crucial as it meets the critical human need of personal affirmation. After physical survival, the greatest need of a human being is psychological survival – to be understood, to be affirmed, to be validated and to be appreciated. So when you listen empathically, you are giving that person psychological affirmation of their value as a person. That is why it works every time.

Building self-awareness and focus

Apart from learning how to read faces, active listening and immersing ourselves, there are other key elements of empathy that we can develop. These are self-awareness, non-judgement and self-confidence. These are the subsets of skills that help build empathy.

Forum theatre

One fantastic technique that helps build awareness and non-judgement, which could be used more in mainstream education and training, is forum theatre.[15] This is a hugely successful tool to help understand others' perspectives through empathy – a low-risk, high-gain opportunity to walk around in others' shoes and explore language and behaviour. It works because the actors or audience members can stop a performance, usually a short, scripted scene depicting a conflict and ending on a 'cliff-hanger' where it appears there is no solution. You don't need trained actors for forum theatre, you can use two confident individuals. Once the cliff-hanger is reached, the audience can then 'get to know' the characters by asking them more about themselves and their backgrounds. The audience then suggests different actions for the actors to carry out on-stage in an attempt to change the outcome of what they are seeing. Forum theatre is a stressless investment for learners as they don't have to actually get up and role-play, but they still have a huge level of involvement; or it might allow them to challenge someone's behaviour on another's behalf. Scenes are based on real issues that have been given a dramatic context to bring out discussion.

Mindfulness

One way to activate right-brain thinking, the hardwire key to inter-personal skills and empathy, is by practising mindfulness meditation, defined as a heightened awareness of the present moment that comes about by observing thought patterns and emotion without judgement or getting overly involved.[16] This has been shown to create significant changes in the areas of the brain connected to attention and feelings. This kind of meditation results in an increased ability to focus, as well as to reflect and relax. But it also strengthens the right brain, which unlocks your hardwired empathy abilities.

> mindfulness meditation is on the increase and has many benefits ranging from productivity and efficiency to happiness, well-being and relief from depression.

Mindlessness – what we do most of the time

Mindlessness involves automatic, habitual thought. Your brain treats information as though it is context-free and true, regardless of circumstances. Mindlessness is most common when people are distracted, hurried, multitasking or overloaded.[17] Since people are hurrying, multitasking and feeling overloaded most of the time, we need to attack our default pattern of mindlessness. It is much more challenging to tap into empathy when you feel distracted or overwhelmed.

The power of mindfulness

Mindfulness helps you to be immediately more present and focused – both of these are key for great listening. It also encourages a more reflective way of interacting and responding with others. It increases empathy.[18] Mindfulness training is becoming increasingly popular in modern Western society, as reflected in the numerous initiatives to offer mindfulness at workplaces, schools and in magazines, as well as to incorporate mindfulness in traditional mental health interventions. One of the presumed benefits of mindfulness is fostering empathy. Cultivating compassion, which includes empathy, is one of the main aspects of the Buddhist traditions from which mindfulness arose.[19] This raises the possibility that being aware of the present moment enables humans to be aware of the experiences of others – that is, to empathise with others

Download some simple mindfulness exercises here: https://unimenta. com/empathy/

Practising presence

The way to be present with whatever you're doing is to learn to focus completely on doing that one thing. Choose one thing today you would like to be wholly and completely present for – it could be absolutely anything in your day, from drinking your morning cup of tea to being at a work meeting. Take the following steps:

1   As you begin the activity, pay attention to every aspect of it.

2   Take a moment to consciously collect all the information about your experience through your touch, your eyes, your ears, your smell and perhaps through your taste.

A How does the experience feel?

B What does it look like?

C How does it smell? Sound? Taste?

D What emotions come up for you as you do it?

E What is going on in your body as you undertake this experience?

F Now become aware of what thoughts enter your mind. As you become aware of your thoughts, you'll notice them jump to other things.

G Use your awareness to gently bring yourself back to your present task. Keep gently turning your awareness back to the present moment, time and again.

_____

_____

_____

Being mindful at work

It is possible to bring mindfulness to every aspect of your workday starting from the moment you wake up in the morning. Trying some of these should bring you a sense of calm and control and enable you to respond more effectively to daily events as well as boost your productivity levels!

1 How do you begin your day? Try starting the day more mindfully by slowing down, allowing time for breakfast, conversations and being present. If you can fit in a walk before work starts, then even better. Make a clear decision at the start of your workday to be present as best you can. Pause for a few moments before you start your work day to set this intention in your mind.

2 Use deep breathing at regular points throughout your day. You can even get apps or wearable devices that remind you to do

this. Most of the time we are simply unaware and forget to take those deep, nurturing, centring and reviving breaths.

3 Get into the habit of 'chunking' your work – focus on brain-intensive work first – writing reports, projects or preparing for a presentation and save energy-draining email for later.

4 When you do get to checking email, try to respond mindfully – take a few moments to gather your thoughts before composing your message. Keep it simple, brief and factual. Mindful email also means not overloading your recipient with too many ideas or a brain-dump.

5 You'll have lots of opportunities at work to practise active listening – engage in this with every workplace conversation you can possibly manage and if you've got a potentially difficult conversation? Schedule it in and prepare for it – mindfully!

6 Mindful exercises can be as short as you wish. Even one minute of consciously connecting with one of your senses can be classified as a mindful exercise. You don't need to close your eyes. You don't even need to be sitting down. Be creative about finding slots in the day to practice mindfulness exercises. At times of excessive pressure at work, practising a short mindfulness exercise can be a saviour. The process helps to rebalance your nervous system, toning down the fight-or-flight response and engaging the wise part of your brain, so that you make reasoned decisions rather than automatically react to situations.

7 Be grateful. If you feel like you're stuck in a job you don't enjoy, the first step is to practice gratitude. What's going well in your job? Maybe you're grateful for the money? Even though it may be less than you'd like, you probably prefer it to having no salary at all. You may not like your manager, but maybe you are friends with a couple of colleagues? You hate the office politics, but they give you insight into what you don't like in a job, so in the future you know what to look for.

After practising gratitude, you can then consider whether you want to continue in that role or need to find another job.

Seven steps to empathy

Here are seven simple steps to help you improve your empathy skills. Try these out as soon as you can in your next meeting or your next conversation. The exercises will have more impact if you record what happened.

1 **When were you last empathetic?**
   Think back to a situation when you showed empathy. Maybe it was when you were listening to a friend or colleague or when you gave a kind-hearted gesture.

   _____

   _____

   _____

   What was going on for you at that time – how were you feeling? *For example, maybe you were feeling optimistic and not distracted and maybe this had an impact on how able you were to show empathy.*

   Maybe you were focused on active listening, which changed the results of that situation for the better.

   _____

   _____

   _____

   What helps you demonstrate more empathy? *Tip: Think about the analogy with the oxygen mask and self-care. What sorts of things help?*

   _____

   _____

   _____

2 **Think about the last argument you had and what happened.** *Tip: Maybe the other person (or you) had underlying*

*concerns that were not fully expressed or addressed or did not feel
listened to.*

4. _____

_____

_____

What triggered the argument? Why did this happen? *Tip:
The more you are aware of typical triggers – for example, things
that escalate or worsen an argument, the more you can pre-empt
this happening in the future.*

_____

_____

_____

5. Sometimes empathy is the hardest to express with those
closest to us, such as our spouse, partner or child. That's
because we are so often caught up in our own priorities,
thoughts or feelings.

3 **Have a conversation where you actually listen.** *Tip: Be
present, put your phone away, ask open and interested questions.
Use some of the active listening described in this chapter. Try simple
things such as waiting until others fully express their points of view
before offering your own (hard to do at first!).*

**Identify the very next time you can have this kind of
conversation**

_____

_____

_____

What happened as a result? What did I notice? *Tip:
Recording what happened helps raise your awareness and heightens
the chance of you applying the same skills next time!*

_____

_____

_____

4 Slow down

Build in reflection time and mindfulness into your day as much as you can. If you are constantly rushing from one stimulus to the other, you are far less likely to be empathetic to others. Explore mindfulness. If nothing else, just try being still and silent for a short time and breathe deeply. This can be done while waiting for a train, instead of automatically pulling out your smartphone.

What were the effects of doing this? What did I notice about your day? What insights came up?

_____

_____

_____

5 Get better at reading faces and body language

This is something we probably don't ever consciously focus on. But try it. Really pay attention to facial expression and body language the next time you are in a meeting or discussion. **What was happening? What did I notice?**

_____

_____

_____

How sensitive was I to non-verbal cues? *Tip: Look at someone's face for that very first initial response, which is so hard to disguise!*

_____

_____

_____

6 Think about outcomes

So often we focus on outcomes but in the wrong way because we don't focus on the behaviour required to reach that outcome. For example, let's say my outcome is to have an enjoyable evening with my husband at the theatre. Well, that actually starts with how we interact with each other within minutes of meeting up after work. If my mood is negative or reactive, it will definitely result in defensive or irrational

behaviour of sorts on my part, which will impact the whole
evening. Another way is to actually change the desired outcome
to focus instead on the other person. My desired outcome, then,
is for my husband to have a wonderful and enjoyable evening.
Just by stating that and writing it down, I am more likely to
engage in behaviour that will lead to this positive outcome.

Think about an upcoming meeting – social or professional:

_____

_____

_____

What is your desired outcome for that meeting? *Tip: It
can be as simple as having a relaxing evening or something more
complex like wanting some kind of call to action.*

_____

_____

_____

What is your desired outcome for the other person? *Tip:
This is a bit trickier but really focus on them. It could equally be for
them to enjoy the evening or for them to feel like you can help them/
answer their need.*

_____

_____

_____

**Now think about how you can influence both desired
outcomes by your behaviour and through using
empathy.** *Tip: People are very good at sensing how we view them.
We translate this through a multitude of micro-gestures: frequently
checking email while they talk to us, picking up the phone when
they enter our office or looking away when they are talking.*

_____

_____

_____

7 **Start cultivating 'social generosity'**

Known as 'executive presence', this means that people walk away from you feeling energised and better about themselves and not the opposite, which is feeling drained! So help others to feel important, always see them as who they can become, the best of themselves. This connection can't happen without empathy. So pay attention, say positive things and listen when you talk to other people. Do this in small ways with family and friends and then at work for noticeable effect.

How and when could I start doing this?

_____

_____

_____

A day in the life of. . .

Let's take a magnifying glass to the skill of empathy through a day in the life of Jan. We'll start with a brief introduction to Jan, to give a quick snapshot of his life.

About Jan

Jan is a manager in his early forties. He's got an engineering background and is now responsible for health and safety compliance in an oil company. Jan is extremely hard-working and ambitious and wants to get on in his career. He knows this is the optimum time to get a prime senior position in the company. He works long hours and has a young family. His wife doesn't work and is at home with the children. Jan commutes to his work in the city from the suburbs. He is highly methodical and logical, working to clear structures and routines. He prides himself on his balanced lifestyle which includes exercise, a variety of interests and a strong social circle. He perceives himself as being well-liked and positively regarded both socially and professionally.

At the moment, Jan is pondering what to do about his recent 360-degree feedback exercise results. Overall, the feedback about his performance from colleagues, staff and his boss has been excellent. He expects total professionalism, dedication and hard work from his team. However, his scores on empathy have been fairly low in comparison and there have been qualitative comments such as 'he never fully listens to our point of view', 'he expects us to work excessive hours and we can't see the point', 'he's completely intolerant when we make mistakes', 'he doesn't cut any slack' and 'team performance is suffering'.

Actually, the feedback doesn't come as a total surprise to Jan, as he is aware that for some reason he doesn't empathise with others. His wife has made similar comments about his listening skills. He generally thinks that listening and considering employees' feelings is a bit out of touch with pushing ahead with work, and he doesn't have that much tolerance for anyone whom he perceives as not putting in as much effort as he does. He can see that his management style may be impacting on his team performance and also may be an impediment to his advancement within the company. Jan is doing really well and should get promoted fairly soon into a senior leadership position.

Let's have a closer look at a typical day in Jan's life and how building the skill of empathy can help him.

Jan's typical day

When Jan's in the office, he gets up at 7am and takes a bus or taxi to work. He has a healthy breakfast of porridge and fresh fruit and black coffee. Today he has meetings with his team almost all *day, with a short break for a working lunch. At least one week in every month he travels to overseas locations to meet the other teams engaged on offshore projects. He really enjoys his work. Most of the time he is home by 7 pm each evening and has dinner with his wife and most evenings he is also in time to help out his kids to bed. Jan is lean and fit and enjoys cycling and tennis in his free time. Today he gets home feeling a bit irritable and argues with his wife – mainly because she wants to talk to him about her day with the kids. This sort of argument is becoming more frequent, and neither Jan nor his wife is addressing the arguments at the moment. He's a bit preoccupied today, anyway, about his 360-degree feedback results. He is actually a bit upset by the comments and puzzled too, as he thinks everyone should be more driven these days and he thinks he communicates quite well, even if he is a bit abrupt at times.*

Jan genuinely enjoys his work and is driven to excellence and top performance.

What's going on here?

Jan is fairly typical of managers with a strong technical background who encounter issues with their management style in more senior roles. They are highly logical and use this logic to good effect in their decision making. They do, however, often lack empathy, or at least the ability to display empathy and this can heighten the more senior the role. In many technical occupations this may not be an issue, but certainly becomes more of an issue when interacting with other people. There are several elements to consider here. Although empathetic skills are developable to some extent, Jan will also need to desire to change, as such development requires hard work and commitment. Jan may also feel that if he goes 'soft' he may lose his cutting edge. In Jan's case, he can logically see the benefits of becoming more empathetic as it will improve team performance and his own promotion prospects. He is unlikely to be promoted if he is unable to lead his team effectively, and the perception he is giving is that he isn't. There is nothing wrong with demanding professionalism and dedication, as well as hard work, but if he were leading well, then his team would want to go that extra bit further and work longer hours, etc. It may well be that in his case he will never be able to BE empathetic in the sense that he can truly put himself in someone else's shoes. However, with support, he could use his highly developed logic to understand how his staff may react to his behaviour and modify his own behaviour accordingly.

One day, Jan watches a debate about why we need to develop our inner resources more strongly. He's intrigued because he agrees with the idea that people should be more self-reliant. He decides to start focusing more on his empathy skills.

Let's revisit Jan's 'typical day' six months later.

How Jan's life has moved forward

Jan's increasingly regular arguments with his wife, combined with his recent 360-degree feedback, propelled him to want to make some changes. His first step was to keep a daily log and note down situations at work where his style of interaction with colleagues might be leading to reduced performance in the team. For example, he asked a colleague when the quality standards on the Nigerian oilfield would be completed. His colleague said it was slightly behind schedule because of illness in one of the team members. Jan displayed his annoyance and irritation but caught himself just in time to try and tone it down a bit. He then used a coach to help him look at alternative strategies of dealing with this kind of situation. The coach helped Jan look at questions he could have asked, before reacting, that would have helped him understand the true nature of this issue – that is, is it really about resources and team members or more about the fact that the team did not feel comfortable telling him there was an illness in the first place? This helped Jan see that, in fact, it was his responsibility to ensure that deadlines are being met and that the team have the required resources to deliver.

Jan started to practise more active listening skills. He knew that the first ten minutes of coming home were probably the most important in terms of determining how the evening might go. Although he did not find it easy at first, his logic enabled him to recognise immediately his natural default way of 'listening', so he tried very small things such as asking his wife more questions about her day and not jumping in with his own immediate responses. Jan also recognised that by not demonstrating empathy skills at work, he was becoming someone that people were starting not to like, which was a shock in a way but also a wake-up call to raising his self-awareness. He's started to think first before responding and to try to deploy the same active listening skills at work, since it had such an immediate impact on his personal relationship.

Jan thinks about outcomes more and how to ensure those are reached through being more aware of his own behaviour. Snapping at work colleagues does not create an outcome of a positive, efficient team – when Jan looks at it logically from this perspective, it all makes a lot more sense. The team are, in fact, quite driven, like Jan is, but now they feel part of a real team. Jan now tends not to just tell people what to do but spends time explaining what and why, and talking through things in such a way as to get the team's views. They feel they are being listened to and Jan is able to get more out of them as a result. Jan gets their views but, being their boss, makes decisions that may or may not accommodate the team's views.

Jan will likely never be naturally empathetic, but by using his logic he is able to move beyond seeing empathy as something 'touchy-feely' and 'soft' to something that he requires to move ahead. He also notices that his own behaviour has a much greater impact on others than he realises, and that this can be either negative or positive depending on how he approaches a situation. He is also creating stronger relationships and it is these that will help him to move forward in his career. In fact, being promoted and achieving a more senior role is largely down to his empathy skills.

Empathy is not about being 'soft' or sympathetic. It can help us to develop successful and dynamic work and personal relationships. Those relationships are really our only true sources of competitive advantage or distinction and they also make us happier. Empathy, perhaps more than any other skill, is the most challenging to develop as our natural instinct to focus only on ourselves is very strong.

Interested in learning more?

I've put together some extra resources here:

Bazalgette, P. (2017) *The Empathy Instinct: How to Create a More Civilized Society.* John Murray.

Chaskalson, M. (2011) *The Mindful Workplace: Developing Resilient Individuals and Resonant Organizations with MBSR.* Wiley-Blackwell.

Ekman, P. (2004) *Emotions Revealed: Understanding Faces and Feelings.* Phoenix.

Goleman, D. (2004) *Emotional Intelligence and Working with Emotional Intelligence, Working with EQ.* Bloomsbury Publishing.

Goleman, D. (1998) 'What makes a leader?' *Harvard Business Review.*

Hardy, J. (2017) *The Self-Care Project: How to Let Go of Frazzle and Make Time Work for You.* Orion Spring.

Orloff, J. (2017) *The Empath's Survival Guide: Life Strategies for Sensitive People.* Sounds True Inc.

Patnaik, D. (2009) *Wired to Care: How Companies Prosper When They Create Widespread Empathy.* Prentice Hall.

Pink, D. (2008) *A Whole New Mind: Why Right-Brainers Will Rule the Future.* Marshall Cavendish.

Rifkin, J. (2010) *The Empathic Civilization.* Polity Press.

Wax, R. (2016) *A Mindfulness Guide for the Frazzled,* Penguin Life.

Whitelaw, G. (2012) *The Zen Leader: 10 Ways to go from Barely Managing to Leading Fearlessly.* Career Press.

Articles and websites

https://www.scientificamerican.com/article/what-me-care/

What, Me Care? Young Are Less Empathetic – A recent study finds a decline in empathy among young people in the USA.

Useful resources and tools on how to get started with mindfulness

https://www.mindful.org/meditation/mindfulness-getting-started/

https://www.headspace.com

You can also find more tips, ideas, curated video clips and exercises to strengthen your optimism skills by visiting https://unimenta.com/empathy/

Sign up too for daily tips – a daily quote, tip and video clip on one of the seven skills direct to your inbox. https://unimenta.com/seven-skills/

'If you have integrity, nothing else matters. If you don't have integrity, nothing else matters.'

Alan K. Simpson

Chapter 4

INTEGRITY

Integrity' is a word you hear almost every day, but it's not a word that people spend a lot of time thinking about. If you try to define it, what would you say?

The word *integrity* evolved from the Latin adjective *integer,* meaning *whole* or *complete.*[1] In this context, integrity is the inner sense of 'wholeness' stemming from qualities such as honesty and consistency of character. As such, one may judge that others 'have integrity' to the extent that they act according to the values, beliefs and principles they claim to hold. Doesn't that in turn depend on specifically *what* those values, beliefs and principles are?

Integrity was one of the most challenging chapters to write in my first edition of this book and we have noticed that on our experiential learning workshops it is also often the hardest one for participants to actually conceptualise and make sense of.

This is because integrity will vary from person to person, often significantly so. What you value and the principles you hold may not be the ones that I value and uphold. You can think of integrity like a moral compass, holding true to your values and beliefs and choosing to live by these in your day-to-day life. In many ways, integrity is about character. It is what you do when no one else is looking, and is of course heavily dependent on what we believe to be right, our values and how we choose to behave. For instance, is integrity about little things such as following through on a promise, or big things like not fiddling your expenses or speaking up to defend a moral issue? Or is fiddling your expenses a little thing and not following through on a promise a big thing? And surely, moral issues may vary from person to person too?

What is integrity?

Integrity can be defined as 'integrated', meaning congruent words, actions and thoughts and, therefore, congruence between what you say and what you do. In plain English, this is about walking the talk.

First of all, we need to make a distinction between principles and values as these are often interchanged. Principles and values can be thought of as the 'rules of life' that each of us chooses to live by. Principles are about the expected behaviour of a society, and these in turn have a collective influence on everyone. So principles might include concepts such as fairness, justice, diligence, honesty, compassion and even how we define integrity. Principles are different depending on the society or culture. I experienced this quite recently while working in Algeria. I was running training sessions on communication skills and personal development. I learned that apologising is a key principle in Algerian culture linked to honour. One of my trainees related a story to me about his sister criticising his behaviour and not apologising to him – seven years ago. He found it impossible to let this go even though I reasoned with him that forgiveness might heal the relationship and also free him too. In Algerian culture, honour can be lost in many ways, for example, Algerians believe that turning down a friend's request for a favour causes the other person to lose honour. Therefore, they will agree to do something rather than risk either party losing face. Other areas related to honour are criticising others, insulting them or putting them in a position that will be uncomfortable. By dishonouring someone you also spoil the relationship. I did not know this or understand this at the time. However, this core cultural value and principle was strongly upheld by my trainee. I'm not sure whether this demonstrates integrity or not but it does demonstrate the strength of principles and the potential power they hold.

Consider this

Integrity is behaviour-based, which means you can get better at it!

Values, on the other hand, are personal, subjective ideals, beliefs and individual traits that a person can feel affinity with and so they are not necessarily related to principles or standards. They may also change over time and through life. Values can include concepts such as freedom, security, power, creativity and adventure. How those values, in turn, are interpreted will also vary from individual to individual. After all, adventure could be defined as anything from a bungee jump to a love of travel or risky behaviour, which may have negative consequences.

> principles provide anchors and a sense of internal balance and values help us to develop our potential and our character

Values and principles are important because awareness of these helps you to understand who you are. If integrity is about being true to yourself, having your own 'moral' compass and a strong connection between what you say and your actions, then values and principles will, to a certain extent, define how you express your integrity.

Some common myths about integrity:

1   Integrity means just being honest and straightforward
2   A balanced and compartmentalised life means a life of integrity
3   Integrity is a natural quality. It's effortless, just 'part of who you are' and you either have it or you don't.

When we talk about integrity, we sometimes miss out on the importance of *consistency, honesty and truthfulness or accuracy* of one's actions.

Consistency is about being the same regardless of the situation. It's about not being unpredictable and not making decisions or communicating based purely on mood, emotion or feelings. Consistency in terms of your actions and behaviours has to be an active choice that you make – for example, if you just had an argument with someone before walking into your next meeting, consistency means that you will make a conscious choice to shift gears and let go of the negativity of that conversation and not bring that to the next meeting or even the next person you encounter that day.

Honesty or accuracy of one's actions requires intentionality and thought. How honest or accurate are your behaviours, actions and words with other people on a day-to-day basis? How kind are you – is there a link between integrity, kindness and honesty? Are there times when you are thoughtless and therefore behave out of line with your values?

To explore honesty and integrity more, download this exercise here:

https://unimenta.com/integrity/

When you are living your life with integrity, people should be able to visibly see it through your actions, words, decisions, methods and outcomes. When you are 'whole' and consistent, this shines through in your work, your family life and your social life.

Top tip

Do what you say you will do

Whether that is to your family, your employees, your team or even yourself, keep your promises. Follow through on what you have said that you will do – consistently, steadily and quietly.

It can be challenging to live with integrity all the time because we are human – we can mess up, emotions can come into play and impact actions. This is why building self-awareness is again as critical to integrity as it is to the other skills.

Self-awareness also helps us to strip away agendas that may even be hidden from ourselves, let alone others.

Stephen Carter, in his book *Integrity*, defines integrity as a virtue of character that requires three steps: 1) **discerning** what is right and what is wrong; 2) **acting on** what you have discovered, even at personal cost; and 3) **saying openly** that you are acting on your understanding of right from wrong.

The term 'discerning' refers to being able to make that moral choice between what is right and wrong. This alone is not enough; the second step requires you to act on that knowledge, such as keeping commitments, and the third is being open and taking initiative.

According to the FBI, integrity is 'total commitment to honesty in every aspect of a person's life. Integrity goes to the core of one's conduct, what people believe in their heart of hearts. It cannot be bought, claimed or bestowed. It does not come with office, title or appointment. It simply exists. The person who has integrity rarely claims it. The person who claims it rarely has it. Integrity is best manifested quietly in day-to-day living and in the workplace. It should be treasured above all things, for after integrity comes decency, honour, trust and principle.'[2]

Integrity can be seen as something that is present and known only to ourselves (what we do when no one else is looking) and something that is also recognised and perceived as highly positive by the external world.

Why is integrity a must-have skill?

Isn't integrity subjective and personal and, maybe at the end of the day, simply down to how we behave as individuals? Isn't there lots of room for integrity to be 'faked', or used as a way to justify (just about) any action? Maybe.

Integrity is a quality, and perhaps considered an old-fashioned quality that we have lost sight of. Dr Stephen Covey said in an interview, just before his death, that the economic and global crisis experienced some years back creates humility because pain humbles people and, because of this, makes them more open and teachable.[3] Dr Covey believed that principle-centred leadership was crucial in a changing and challenging world and that the key to this was understanding moral authority versus formal authority. Covey felt that moral authority came from being centred on strong principles which are universal and timeless and for leadership, in particular, it is principles such as fairness, truth, integrity, compassion and honesty were vital. These principles are the same whether leadership is a work, at home or in the community

Living with integrity means:

1 **You understand the** true definition of integrity and making sense of it for yourself. Hopefully, you'll be able to do this once you've absorbed this chapter!

2 **You intentionally reflect on** what to say, how to behave, how to make decisions in a way that is reflective of your own values and beliefs.

3 **You are the same authentic person regardless of the situation.** Whether people encounter you at work or with family and friends, there will be a consistency in your actions, words and behaviours.

4 **You recognise the impact that you have on others.** This means you are aware of your behaviour and the way your words impact those around you intentionally and oftentimes, unintentionally. It also means having the humility and authenticity to apologise if it is ever needed, communicate with empathy and have some perception of how others might be responding to you. Although this is not something you can specifically control, you can certainly influence it.

5 **You actively focus on the development of character and wholeness.** This means intentionally investing time in personal development and learning whether that might be by reading, getting coached, listening to the counsel of others, going to leadership development courses and reflecting on how to develop character.

6 **You encourage others.** You make a conscious choice to walk in integrity, and as others see that, they are drawn to this. Other people will have confidence that you will do what you say and believe.

When we live with integrity, we

● are authentic – conducting our lives in a way that is true to our values

● act consistently

● take responsibility and 'own' all of our feelings and behaviours

● do what we say we will do

● hold ourselves accountable

● communicate the truth respectfully and don't leave out important information

● actively listen and seek to understand others' points of view

● are emotionally open, receptive and willing to share our feelings

● don't have hidden agendas.

Try this

Tell the truth for a day

In the Jim Carrey movie *Liar Liar,* the lead character is constantly letting down his young son. On his birthday, his son makes a wish for his father to be unable to tell a lie for a whole day – this wish comes true.

The character Jim Carrey plays is unable to lie, mislead or even withhold a true answer. For a day, why not see how much you tell the truth – white lies don't count, or do they?!

We tend to associate integrity with leadership because it is about making the right decisions and it embraces ethics and 'doing the right thing'. We also come across it when referring to politicians' lack of it too. I think integrity is important simply because the world is changing so fast. It does not matter if you are a leader or politician or not. In the midst of change and stormy waters, integrity can become the very thing that differentiates you and makes you stand out. Of course, lack of integrity can do the same, but in this age of transparency and visibility, combined with heightened uncertainty and rapid change, demonstrating trust, honesty and doing the right thing is valued. Having integrity makes a huge impact when it comes to others being able to trust you. It means that you will be the person they come to, whether it's to confide in you, to support you or give you that much needed break or work opportunity.

Consider this

When we're stressed, we're more likely to get defensive and blame others. But if each of us could learn to give people the benefit of the doubt across the board – whether it's in an argument, about a job not completed or in response to feedback that suggests that someone's spoken badly about you – we would have less stress in our daily lives. One of the noblest behaviours you can engage in is to give someone the benefit of the doubt before rushing to judgement or negatively filling in the blanks yourself.

Thus, you will experience better relationships and far less stress!

Why have we lost sight of integrity? Gary Fenstermacher, Professor Emeritus at the University of Michigan, says that the kind of integrity as exemplified by the likes of Martin Luther King has become eroded in recent history. He says that leaders in multiple sectors of society have failed to exemplify discernment, right action and transparency; that integrity has lost out to pride, self-interest, ambition, greed and pursuit of power. I would also argue that self-interest, ambition and pursuit of power are very human traits. We are equally as capable of great integrity, as we are of greed and self-interest. Self-interest can lead us to act in ways that are not aligned to integrity and sometimes it is even the easier choice. A very simple example: if I've arranged to go out with a friend but something else comes up that seems more attractive or more urgent (an opportunity to do something else), I might tell the friend I'm not feeling well and cancel our arrangement. I'll probably not even have a conversation but instead use messaging or texting to cancel our outing. This serves my own interests but I know I am not telling the truth. It may be easier to do but inwardly I may feel uneasy or even upset with myself. Not acting in congruence with 'the right thing' will lead to a type of uneasiness within myself, even if I am able to justify my actions, and I won't sleep well at night.

Top tip

Consider the habits and skills you need to develop to enhance your integrity

You might need to stop certain actions (e.g., speaking impulsively or sugarcoating your responses). You might need to improve on others: building your personal courage (because fear holds you back from acting with integrity) issue apologies that are fast and simple, aimed at containing any damage, rather than justifying yourself.

While an action that displays a lack of integrity may seem like the best way to get ahead, it won't work in the longer term. It's more likely to be a one-off gain, which may undermine long-term success when it comes to needing someone's help, or his or her trust. It means that others won't necessarily trust you and, if you have setbacks, you will recover less easily. We can never know the true impact of our actions, although we will always seek to justify them.

An example of integrity at work

I agree to give a presentation at a conference because at the time it seemed like an interesting opportunity, and then nearer the time I cancel because I 'have too much on', or just can't be bothered to give the presentation I said I would do. Or some other attractive and paid work comes up, so I take that instead. It all seems quite legitimate and justifiable. But the resulting consequences in the longer term may mean anything from missing out on a potential networking opportunity to the conference organisers knowing one of my key clients and somehow they learn of my cancellation. Social media and heightened visibility now mean that such ripple effects are even more likely.

Can you be ruthless and have integrity?

Yes, when it comes to leadership. Shakespeare's play *Henry V* proposes that the qualities that define a good leader may not necessarily be the same as the ones that define a good person. Henry is a great leader – intelligent, focused, charismatic and inspiring to others. He also uses any and all resources to ensure he achieves his goals and is actually quite ruthless in doing so. Shakespeare's play focuses on events before and just after the Battle of Agincourt. Henry V acted extremely aggressively and harshly to prevent loss of life on the English side, but this ruthlessness is perfectly aligned with his values in terms of fighting for a belief in a God-given right to hold the French crown and acting in the best interest of the people fighting for him.

Can you be dishonest and have integrity?

Less likely, because integrity is rooted in morals and principles. Stephen Covey said that if there isn't deep integrity within a person, then the challenges of life will, ultimately, cause true motives to rise to the surface. Many people who do achieve strong leadership and strong success socially can actually lack what is needed for integrity. Dig behind the success and you are likely to find this reflected in any longer-term relationship they have, whether that's with a business associate, romantic relationship or a teenage son or daughter going through difficulty.

How integrity helps us at work

Many companies have integrity baked into their values or mission statements. It's typically worded through strong messages like, 'We act with absolute integrity' or 'We build value through integrity . . . '. Integrity is a powerful but often misunderstood concept. Many define integrity as simply honesty, and it is true that people with integrity are honest, but they are also much, much more than simply honest.

You can also think of integrity as a kind of 'energy' a person brings with them to everything they do.

Many companies operate with a degree of integrity. We also know many that don't. According to Ernest Huge and Doug Park in 'The Best Companies Have the Most Integrity', great integrity in companies comes down to two things[4]:

By simply following through on what you say you're going to do, you visibly build trust and credibility.

1   **Being emotionally honest and open** – for example, not withholding information, such as why someone has been fired or promoted, the company's economic position or delaying bad news.

2   **Being principled** – behaving in a way that is consistent with stated values and beliefs and being uncompromising about those principles.

Here are some examples of integrity in the workplace:

- Being sincere and not just telling people what you think they want to hear.
- Being real and genuine, not shallow and artificial.
- Being a 'promise keeper', 'walking your talk' and promising only what you will deliver.
- Being consistent and predictable.
- Being committed and reliable: saying 'I'll have the report done next Thursday' and keeping to that.
- Being candid and forthright, not political or manipulative or getting people to do things without them knowing your real intent.

How often do YOU choose these behaviours in your day-to-day work?

_____

_____

_____

_____

It may be easier to count up the organisations that we know or have worked for that **don't** display integrity. It's important, when we think about integrity, to remember that it can only come from the

Consider this

In big ways and small ways, in visible or invisible situations, employees have the opportunity to demonstrate their integrity – or lack of it – every single day: John was a software developer who was working on a code to optimise a specific process. His approach was not working out as he had envisaged and he was encountering several problems and issues. Rather than patching together a solution that was not optimum, but that would allow him to save his work, he went to his team. He explained the dead ends he had run into and that he thought that they could create problems for the continual development of advanced features for the software product in the future.

The team discussed and worked through the problem. John scrapped all of his code and started from scratch with the team's input. His new solution gave the team the ability to expand the product's capabilities easily in the future.

individuals who make up the organisation. That is why, even if you are surrounded by a lack of integrity, if you want it, you need to start with yourself.

Integrity requires effort and conscientiousness

Look at the list above and think about how often you yourself display these behaviours at work on a daily basis. There is a great saying from Alcoholics Anonymous about 'keeping your side of the street clean'. It means that even if someone is annoying you or behaving with a lack of integrity, all you need to worry about is yourself and your own responses. That means being responsible for yourself, your actions and being honest about the way you yourself behave – even if people around you are demonstrating a (perceived) lack of integrity themselves.

The way you behave (remember that integrity is behaviour-based!) and the alignment between your words and your actions impacts trust and results.

Integrity at work case study

One study found that 'an improvement in only one-eighth of a point in the behavioural integrity score of a hotel's managers led to a boost in hotel profits of as much as 2.4 per cent of revenues'. When it came down to it, this small movement was, in fact, down to the 'little things', as in keeping a promise, sticking to an arrangement made or following through on something.

According to Tony Simon, assistant professor at Cornell University who was involved in this study, integrity really isn't about having some kind of higher moral code and much more about simply having actions and words that reflect each other. If this is so, then isn't being late for something sending the wrong message completely? Isn't our inability to really focus, really listen to each other, actually saying that we really don't care? It gives the perception of a complete lack of respect for the other person, suggesting that they are less important to you. Perhaps they are but if that is not the case, you need to amp up your integrity behaviour.

Consider this

Integrity is valued by employers as a much sought-after trait in employees. But employers also need to exemplify integrity at work. From high-level decision making to how people are treated, integrity will be reflected in a company's corporate culture. In a more interconnected and virtual world, it is likely to become an even more important quality as we collaborate across different cultures.

Some employers are now using integrity tests in recruitment.

An integrity test is a specific type of personality test designed to assess an applicant's tendency to be honest, trustworthy and dependable. A lack of integrity is associated with such counterproductive behaviours as theft, violence, sabotage, disciplinary problems and absenteeism.

Integrity is really about three essential things: being authentic with yourself, with others and doing the things you have said that you would do. Maintaining authenticity is about self-awareness – knowing what you want out of life, who you are, what your positive characteristics are and your negative qualities and behaving consistently in line with your values. Self-awareness means you actually have to start thinking about these things in the first place. It's not something most of us naturally do.

Keeping commitments builds trust, and in a perfect world we would not break them. But it's become too easy to do just that, as we hide behind technology, our 'busyness' and our lifestyles.

Workplace integrity starts with honesty, decency and trust. It makes a difference to your professional development and in your immediate environment as it has an impact on others. You are not likely to be promoted if you are perceived as not being trustworthy or honest. Your day-to-day work is going to be pretty unbearable if your colleagues/employees/clients don't trust you or you don't treat other people well. And the higher your role in the organisation, the more important this becomes.

Integrity in the workplace can perhaps also be likened to that buzzword 'accountability'. Accountability means putting our word and reputation on the line. Someone is counting on us and we should care that someone is counting on us. But the realities of twenty-first-century business can make accountability seem daunting. Following through on a commitment used to be fairly clear and linear and followed a recognised framework or process. Today's workplace commitments and projects can often be ambiguous, and we may need to create our own frameworks with many ways and approaches to reach a goal. In this context, being accountable can also mean being proactive and responsible; responsible for outcomes, project results and, if you are in a leading role, also responsible for engaging employees and treating them well, as well as leading by example.

Try this

Manage your time well

Use a different approach: get rid of your to-do list (track projects and deadlines on a calendar instead); resist over-scheduling (you can't cram 12 hours of work into 8 hours, so stop trying); and estimate times realistically (let's face it, most tasks take longer than we think they will). Slow down a bit too. Plan your week, plan your day. Get up earlier.

What makes developing integrity challenging?

if you want integrity in the workplace, always start with yourself

Some argue that integrity is closely connected with upbringing and early education and, of course, these do have a huge influence. Integrity, though, is an **internal** system of principles that *guide* our behaviour. Integrity is, therefore, a choice and, even though integrity is certainly influenced by upbringing and exposure, it can't be forced by outside circumstances. Of course, there are factors that can encourage or discourage integrity. A person lacking in self-esteem, friendship and financial stability, for example, may be more likely to act without integrity. Someone else with higher self-esteem, a strong support system and a balanced life is more likely to act with integrity. Integrity comes from the daily practice of doing the right things.

What makes integrity challenging is likely to be linked to the human traits I mentioned earlier – greed, self-interest and pursuit of power – as these will influence what you do. For example, do I pay cash to my plumber so that he will give me a lower bill, knowing he is likely to pay less income tax on it or even declare it at all? Or do I justify it because I am not involved in some big tax scam and, anyway, everyone else is doing it? If I really want something, to what extremes am I prepared to go to get it? If I want to display integrity, how difficult is that if everyone around me seems to be doing anything but?

A life with integrity is an examined one. There will be times when we behave with what seems to be a lack of integrity or acting in our own self-interest. Sometimes that may be down to reacting to circumstances or lashing out because of pressure we might be under. Our ability to act with integrity may well be better demonstrated by our subsequent actions, such as learning what triggers stress responses and developing the self-awareness to look after ourselves, or by our ability to be honest, apologise swiftly and put something right. If we are stressed, it might be difficult to act with integrity because our actions and behaviour are likely to be heavily influenced by stress factors. Under those circumstances, it may feel we have no choice.

If acting without integrity, such as deliberately stealing, lying or hurting others, is a choice, then what underlies that choice is how we justify the action. Today's choice for honesty seems to be 'it's OK as long as you don't get caught' or 'it's not that bad, everyone is doing it'.

Try this

Keep a journal where you can record your daily actions. Then try for just one day to record your actual actions with others. Be aware of how you might justify certain actions and write these down too. The purpose of such an exercise is to simply heighten awareness of how we justify our actions, that is all.

_____

_____

_____

Our speed of life and the urge to act in our own self-interest can definitely form barriers to building integrity. Things that become 'the norm', such as cancelling that meeting at the last minute, dictate the action. This can then escalate to bigger things as we find it easier to justify an action. We also seem to be so much busier than before, with numerous demands on our time, commitments to juggle and deadlines to keep. The more we juggle, the harder it becomes to keep promises.

'Whoever can be trusted with very little can also be trusted with very much' – this is a verse from the Bible. The message is that how you handle the small things will dictate how you handle the large things. We are certainly quick to judge others based on this. How many parents have, like me, told their daughters going on a first date that the way their date behaves at dinner, from addressing the waiter to simple table manners, will tell her everything she needs to know?

Barriers to integrity can also be created if one is easily influenced by current trends and norms and by what is going on around you. If you are working somewhere where it is 'normal' to fiddle expenses or where this practice is readily accepted by others, then maybe you will do it too if you're easily influenced, can justify your actions and make the active choice to do so. You are less likely to if you believe this is wrong and you choose to act by what you believe in. Perhaps we need more role models who can exemplify integrity.

Try this exercise for some ways to bring integrity into your day-to-day life – you can download it here: https://unimenta.com/integrity/

How to live with more integrity

I think integrity begins with small things. The small things tell you a lot about a person. On a very basic level, integrity is about knowing the difference between right and wrong – it's our conscience, if you like. Any action can be justified and what may be wrong to one person may well be right to another. Each person will have their own moral compass. Perhaps to strip this back, integrity is simply about doing what you say you will do, being honest and forthright. Walking your talk. Doing the right thing even when no one is looking, caring or acknowledging this.

do sweat the small stuff

Integrity can be lived in the small things. Being late for appointments, failing to return calls and emails, changing plans at the last minute and not completing projects on time are an everyday occurrence. These may seem like small things, but they are not! If I'm honest, I even have to remind myself that actually it is not OK to be late, cancel at short notice or request extensions to deadlines for something I've miscalculated. It's become so easy to do, though, and we are all guilty of it and we all do it. So one way to live with more integrity is to put a stop to these kinds of behaviours.

'People may doubt what you say but they will always believe what you do.' Anonymous

Consider this

How you drive says a lot about you – how you treat people you don't know; how you handle anger; and the extent to which you suffer from entitlement. Perhaps you'd like to believe that someone who drives slowly or non-aggressively is simply less busy than you, but driving in a cooperative manner that is mindful of your fellow commuters is actually a sign of integrity. Let's all try to practise it more when we're behind the wheel.

These days we think nothing of changing something at the last minute, without undue concern about the person we have let down. In fact, you are probably finding that more and more appointments or meetings come with a last-minute call or a text or an email announcing a late arrival or a change of plan. If it's not you sending those texts, you're probably on the receiving end of them. Part of this is, of course, because we can. Our lifestyles and our reliance on technology encourage this. So does our love of what we think is multitasking as we hurtle through our lives. Social media and smartphones are creating a strong tidal pull towards what's known as 'polychronic behaviours'.[5] At least two generations have already been taught to process information in this way rather than chronologically and in sequence. Our mobile devices are always on, interrupting us with notifications about what others are doing and saying. This forces us to embrace more switching between tasks, more fluidity in our daily activities.

Try this

1. When was the last time you cancelled a meeting or appointment or signed up to take part in something and then cancelled/changed your mind?

    _____

    _____

    _____

2. When you communicated the change of plan, how did you do this? Did you use text messaging or some other online messaging? Email? Or did you make a phone call? (Most cancellations are via email and messaging.)

    _____

    _____

    _____

3. Do you have parameters in place for how you use your smartphone? Is it ever switched off? Do you put it away when you are relaxing watching a movie at home?

    _____

    _____

    _____

Stop multitasking

Multitasking is really only possible when two conditions are being met:

> texting, emailing and watching a film while posting on social media is not multitasking!

1 one of the tasks is so well-learned it is almost automatic and does not require thought or concentration, for example, eating or walking; and even reading for leisure.

2 the tasks involve different kinds of brain processing. A good example of real multitasking is reading a book while listening to classical music, because reading comprehension and listening to music engage different parts of our brain.

When you are using the same part of your brain to process information through your laptop, tablet or smartphone, your ability to retain that information is actually declining significantly. Your ability to focus your attention is also reduced, which in turn leads to constant distractions that have an impact on the way you behave and on the way you treat others.

Top tip

Before you make a commitment . . . stop and soberly reflect on whether you are 100 per cent sure you can deliver.

What has all this got to do with integrity? Because it has become so acceptable now to cancel something at short notice or change arrangements or just do several things at once, if you actually are consistent, keep your word and can be trusted to be on time, you stand out. Everything we do now is so much more transparent and visible. Integrity really is our inner guiding compass and has an impact on how we behave and treat others. We are going through a period of intense change in probably every aspect of our lives – consistency, trust, values and honesty are like a harbour in the storm.

Integrity inspires trust and creates trust. Lack of integrity creates mistrust and lowers respect and openness. It really is that simple.

Try this

Listen more and multitask less

Consciously, actively and empathetically **listen**. Get rid of distractions. Lessen your technologically driven multitasking and give other people focus and attention. You will be a far better communicator and you're less likely to cancel arrangements and fail to deliver. Be more thoughtful and respectful of others. Think twice before you pick up your smartphone to send a cancellation text.

---

be the harbour in the storm

Integrity is one constant in our extremely fluid world and it goes where you go. And a bonus: if you are acting in line with what you believe in and know to be right, you will, quite simply, feel happier and less stressed.

Try this

The taxi driver gives you a blank receipt as he drops you off. You are on an expense account and can claim back expenses retrospectively. Do you write in the exact correct amount?

_____

_____

_____

You're backing into a tight parking space in the work car park and you accidentally dent someone's car. Nobody has seen you. Do you leave a note taking responsibility?

_____

_____

_____

You are paying for some shopping. The cashier makes a mistake with the change and you get more money back than you were meant to. Do you say something?

_____

_____

_____

Can integrity be developed? Of course it can, as it's your own personal choice and it is behaviour based. You can develop and strengthen integrity in lots of ways, from deciding to be accountable and responsible to following through on your promises and commitments. You are the person you are today because of the choices you made yesterday. In other words, integrity is developed each and every day in the smallest of actions, as well as the bigger ones.

'Characterize people by their actions and you will never be fooled by their words.' Anonymous

Integrity is about character. Can character be developed? Certainly it can! Being consistent, honest and doing what you say you will do, and practising this, is a great start. Have an opinion and stand up for something, don't sit on the fence. Think about what you value and the principles you hold dear and where these have come from. Some of these may be a product of your upbringing or conditioning and may not be traits or characteristics you want to keep. So knowing yourself is important. How can you be true to yourself and keep your side of the street clean if you don't know yourself, your strengths and weaknesses, what makes you tick and what you are accountable for? If you observe negative behaviour in others, you do not have to emulate it. That is always a choice.

It is a really good idea to spend some time identifying your own values and on our workshops this is one of people's very favourite exercises to do. Find a quiet space and try it – you can download the exercise here: https://unimenta.com/integrity/

In terms of your professional life, what sort of work do you do? Is this in line with your values and beliefs? If not, it's probably not the right environment for you. And in your personal life, what sort of relationship are you in and does it enhance your life and bring out the best in you, and vice versa? These, too, are connected with integrity because it will be easier to live a life of integrity if how you live and work is aligned to your inner compass.

Seven steps to integrity

Here are some easy ways to start developing your own integrity. It's always helpful to keep a record of what you are doing, or to at least record the processes you are going through and the results you experience.

1 **Start with working out what your values are**

    It can be helpful to start with your own values. These will be unique things that you value, that are important to you.

    The first step is simply to write them down. The list could include anything, from 'being results-focused' to 'creativity' to 'patience' to 'respect'. Don't know where to start? Reflect and think about what makes you happy, what makes you angry, sad, gives you energy, tires you? And then think about the value behind that.

Examples: Someone you work with is unfocused and distracted, often surfing the Internet or taking personal calls. This makes you angry because you are a team player and very results-orientated. Or your partner comes home from work early and surprises you by announcing he/she is taking you out for dinner. This annoys you because you value predictability, or it makes you happy because you love spontaneity.

Another way to discover your values is to identify your role models and write down why you like them – you will soon find common denominators in your descriptions that can indicate what you value. Or think about moments in life when you were on top of your game and felt unbeatable. What was going on at that moment – if you can identify those feelings, you will find the values that match. You can do the same with times when you felt angry or frustrated.

Once you have a list, try to clarify these values – how do these values manifest (or not) in your life. Do you see them showing up in the work you do, the things you do day-to-day? If not, you can start to put this right. You can start making decisions that enable these values to be present in your everyday life. If competition is a value, for example, this can be fulfilled by the nature of your work and/or by playing a team sport. If love and caring are values, how is this visible in your relationships with your partner or family?

Every Sunday I sit down and plan my week. Not just what I am doing and when, but how each of my activities and actions are aligned to my values. For example, because having a strong work–life balance is extremely important to me, I plan my life around that value rather than allowing work and deadlines to eat into family time. At the same time, I still need to be accountable to work deadlines, but I also don't neglect to bake a chocolate cake! Both are important to me (and the chocolate cake to my family). Download our values exercise here – https://unimenta.com/integrity/

2 **Be responsible**

It's easy to claim responsibility when things go well, but it's much harder when they don't. A truly responsible person, however, accepts responsibility either way. So next time you take on a project, be 100 per cent responsible for the outcome. Not a little. Not somewhat. Not pretty much. Own it 100 per cent – good or bad.

Start being more accountable. Keep promises and do things that you said you would do. Make commitments and stick to them. The more you do this, the easier it will become, and it will also be enjoyable because all your relationships, both personal and professional, will benefit. Start with the little things and go from there. Ownership and accountability – demonstrate these.

We alone have the power to manage our lives and careers. The sooner we accept this fact, the better. Start being more proactive (see the chapter on being proactive).
Identify something that you can commit to and stick to in the coming weeks:

_____

_____

_____

3 **If you have to let someone down, do it with integrity**

If you absolutely do have to change an existing commitment, be open about it, state the problem, listen, get involvement and solve the issue by agreeing a new commitment or an alternative solution. Can you do that with your smartphone? Probably not; unless you speak to the person or see them face to face, it will be very difficult to demonstrate integrity and get the right message across.
The next time you need to cancel something or change something, commit now to doing it in person or on the phone.

_____

_____

_____

4   **Be personally accountable**

This, like responsibility, is a willingness to answer for the outcomes of your choices, actions and behaviours. When you're personally accountable, you stop assigning blame, 'should-ing' on other people and making excuses. Instead, you take the fall when your choices cause problems. Are you accountable for your actions even if nobody holds you accountable – or nobody catches you? You bet you are. So be your own 'accountability cop' and police yourself. On the long and winding road of life, choose accountability every time. **Think about different projects or tasks you have taken on – either professionally or personally. In what ways can you ensure you are accountable for your part in these?**

_____

_____

_____

5   **Start with yourself**

If there is a problem or difficulty at home or at work, look first to yourself. Ask four specific questions:

What is the problem?

_____

_____

What am I doing, or not doing, to contribute to the problem?

_____

_____

What will I do differently to help solve the problem?

_____

_____

How will I be accountable for the result?

_____

_____

_____

6 **Be boring**

Being consistent and predictable may sound boring, but in our world of uncertainty, rapid change and roller-coaster lifestyles, being consistent, reliable and predictable are positive attributes and they demonstrate integrity. Use them every chance you get.

When can I next be as predictable and as reliable as I can?

_____

_____

_____

7 **Manage expectations**

Of yourself and of others. The most direct route to self-empowerment is to be clear about expectations – not only what you expect, but also what's expected of you. To do that, you need to ask questions, make agreements and clarify. Otherwise, you risk suffering the source of much upset: missed expectations. Communicate clearly.

Think about a project or task you have coming up or that you are organising. What is expected of you?
What questions can you ask to ensure that there is clarity?

_____

_____

_____

A day in the life of. . .

Let's take a magnifying glass to the skill of integrity through a day in the life of Sharon. We'll start with a brief introduction to Sharon, to give a quick snapshot of her life.

About Sharon

Sharon is in her mid-forties, has two children at primary school and works part-time. Her partner works full-time. Sharon has a portfolio career, with several key clients for whom she delivers marketing and PR services. Sharon is quite stressed. Her life seems to be full of rushing around from one meeting or commitment to another; there is always something going on. Sharon is very good at her job but sometimes doesn't follow through on deadlines because of pressure piling up. Because she is good at what she does and has a positive disposition, she is often able to extend deadlines but she is aware of overpromising and under-delivering. She also often misses social arrangements with friends because of work pressures. Sharon juggles being a mum with all of this, but feels like she isn't doing that particularly well either. Recently, she has started subcontracting some of her work out to associates to help alleviate some of the pressure.

Let's have a closer look at a typical day in Sharon's life and how developing integrity can help her.

Sharon's typical day

Sharon gets up early and gets the children ready and takes them to school. She has a chat with the other mums at the school gate and then rushes off to the train station where she parks in the wrong place and gets a ticket. As a result, Sharon is late for her meeting so she checks her emails on her mobile while at the station. Sharon arrives at the meeting flustered, saying that the train was late. The meeting is about a new project and this time Sharon is leading a team of associates. They agree roles and responsibilities, though none of this is documented, and Sharon is confident that the project will go well. She ducks out of the meeting early, leaving the team to continue with their planning. On her way to pick up the children, she decides to cancel meeting with friends that evening as she doesn't feel up to it – she pleads a headache, which is sort of true. Sharon rushes home with the children and cooks. She eats their leftovers, as she forgot to have lunch, and heats up a take-away for her partner to have when he comes home. Sharon puts both kids in front of children's TV. She opens a bottle of wine at 6pm and drinks half of it. It's been a tough day and she deserves it. Sharon thinks her partner really could be doing more to help with the household but it's never been discussed. She is too tired to talk to her partner when he comes home and, after putting the children to bed, Sharon stays up late watching TV and trying to wind down. She goes to bed quite late but does not sleep well.

What's going on here?

Sharon's day is typical for many working mums in terms of what they have to juggle and be mindful of, but she is not handling any of it particularly well, even though some things such as cancelling her arrangements with friends and being late for her meeting could be easily justified. After all, who isn't rushing around these days?

However, as an ongoing lifestyle, quite a few relationships in her life are thinly stretched. Her work relationships are stretched because she is starting to become unreliable; the new associate relationships and project may unravel because expectations are not clear and because Sharon is not holding herself accountable. Her relationships with her friends (which could form a valuable support network) are suffering because she keeps cancelling at short notice. She isn't spending any quality time with her children. Her partner is last on the list so her primary relationship is suffering. And finally, Sharon is neglecting herself. So how can integrity help? It can help through raising self-awareness and creating more accountability. Sharon needs to clarify her own values first and what is important to her and look at her life through these. This will help her to be more in control and to make some changes. Integrity will also help with being more accountable and responsible and managing herself and her time in a different way.

What happens if Sharon starts putting some of the principles of integrity into practice?

Let's revisit Sharon's 'typical day' six months later.

How Sharon's life has moved forward

These days Sharon is much more at peace with herself and is starting to feel happier. She spent some time working out what was most important to her: her relationships with her family and having interesting, rewarding and fulfilling work as well as passion, security and fun. She could clearly see that none of her life currently was aligned to these values, and started thinking more about how she might be contributing to some of the pressures because of this misalignment.

Sharon decided to have a frank and clear discussion with her partner about their relationship and about how to share some of the childcare. Her partner was only too happy to give more support and, consequently, Sharon has two days a week when she does not have the responsibility of getting the children ready for school nor getting back in time to cook the evening meal. Sharon uses this time to plan her schedule and to catch up with emails. And sometimes she uses the time to go for a swim or to have a beauty treatment.

Sharon also calls a meeting with her associate team to look at how they can put systems and processes in place for team roles and responsibilities. She accepts that project accountability must rest with her and that, now she has a team in place, her own role is going to be much more about managing and leading that team. She actually finds she enjoys this type of role far more.

Sharon is also more aware of how cancelling or changing things, whether meetings with friends or extending project deadlines, is not really conducive to effective work nor strong relationships.

She really does value her network of friends and sees them as vital to her support and well-being. She knows that, these days, it's more acceptable to cancel things but she's making a more focused effort to only say yes to commitments when she honestly feels she can follow through.

And these days, of an evening, she more often than not finds time and energy to enjoy her children and spend evenings with her partner that enable her to relax and feel energised for the following day.

Sharon's example shows how integrity makes a difference day-to-day and that this then has a positive ripple effect on fundamental relationships, decisions and life direction. Integrity is satisfying and rewarding because it means we can be our authentic selves and ultimately do and achieve more.

Interested in learning more?

I've put together some extra resources here:

Carter, S.L. (1996) *Integrity.* HarperCollins.

Cloud, H. (2007) *Integrity: The Courage to Meet the Demands of Reality.* Collins Business.

Covey, Dr S. (2004) *The Seven Habits of Highly Effective People.* Simon & Schuster Ltd.

Demartini, J. (2013) *Values Factor: The Secret to Creating an Inspired and Fulfilling Life,.* Berkley Books.

Fenstermacher, G.D. (2009) 'How did we get here? The loss of integrity in American life.' Speech at Pennsylvania State University.

Killinger, B. (2010) *Integrity: Doing the Right Thing for the Right Reason.* McGill-Queens University Press.

Scott, K. (2018) *Radical Candor: How to Get What You Want by Saying What You Mean,* Pan.

Articles and websites

You can also find more tips, ideas, curated video clips and exercises to strengthen your optimism skills by visiting https://unimenta.com/integrity/

Sign up too for daily tips – a daily quote, tip and video clip on one of the seven skills direct to your inbox. https://unimenta.com/seven-skills/

'The pessimist sees the difficulty in
every opportunity; an optimist sees the
opportunity in every difficulty.'

Winston Churchill

Chapter 5

OPTIMISM

How optimistic are you really? How do you view difficult events in your life? Research demonstrates that optimistic people are more successful, healthier and live longer. For many people there is an 'optimism bias' hardwired into the brain, and even if you feel that you are more pessimistically orientated, optimism can be learned.

Optimism and pessimism are explanatory styles of thinking about life events which predict a positive versus negative mood and expansive versus inhibited behaviour. People with optimistic explanations of life generally feel happier and more energised to cope with obstacles, seeing them as challenges rather than failure experiences. Optimists are more likely to analyse whether setbacks are situational, rather than personal, and are then able to develop plans to remove obstacles to their goals. Pessimists are more likely to view life problems as personal failures, blame themselves, feel unhappy and give up trying to change.

Irrespective of whether you think of yourself as a glass 'half-full' or 'half-empty' kind of person or even somewhere in between, optimism really can be learned.

The world is not divided into pessimists and optimists after all. We each have the capacity to be optimistic and passionate about life.

Easier said than done – sure, of course it is! And in a world where we are experiencing constant change and challenges and where most of us feel overloaded or stressed so much of the time being able to tap into that optimism is more important than ever.

What is optimism?

Optimism is often confused with 'positive thinking', as in viewing everything with rose-tinted glasses as a bit of a 'Pollyanna', no matter what the situation is. *Pollyanna* is a traditional story about a young girl, newly arrived in a small town. Her persistent view is that every situation and every person has something good and that this should be constantly emphasised to make life happier and easier. The Pollyanna attitude is sometimes used to describe someone who simply refuses to acknowledge any negativity whatsoever, and generally is used to refer to someone who is somewhat idealistic and outside reality in their thinking. Positive thinking isn't real optimism though. Optimism is often misinterpreted as being joyous, cheerful and content all the time, always smiling – like Pollyanna. But really it is much more about leading a rich life, taking the good with the bad and getting better at learning how to reframe the bad.

People generally like to view themselves as being positive – glass half full; but not everyone. For instance, doctors in our workshops describe themselves as overwhelmingly negative and glass 'half-empty' – this is because they see life or death situations every day; where do you find the positive in a death situation or serious illness? For them it was important to still look for the positive experiences of each day rather than the 'always look on the bright side of life' approach. Looking for positive experiences that have taken place over the course of a day is also the case for people working in extremely traumatic situations such as war zones and crisis areas.

Our natural optimism bias can lead to irrational optimism, or what I call irritating optimism. For example, almost all of us believe we are in the top 20 per cent of the population when it comes to driving, having a successful relationship or being effective at work. We all think we are good at these things. Almost all of us are also irrationally optimistic about our health and lifespan – all of us like to think that we will live long and healthy lives. We also hugely underestimate the likelihood of losing our job or getting an illness such as cancer. In business, optimism can lead to unrealistic forecasts. Those in sales know that over-optimism tends to produce over-commitment. Collective optimism can also lead to large-scale disasters. Over-optimism by a very large number of people about their repayment capacity on mortgages led to the housing bubble and recession in the USA some years ago.

> overly optimistic assumptions can lead to disastrous consequences, but an optimistic bias can also inspire, motivate and protect us

Tali Sharot, in *The Optimism Bias,* says that we need to be able to imagine alternative realities and need to believe that we can achieve them.[1] That is, in essence, where this bias or tendency comes from. Such faith helps motivate us to pursue our goals. Optimists generally work longer hours and tend to earn more. Economists at Duke University in the USA found that optimists even save more. And although they are not less likely to divorce, they are more likely to remarry.

Forget positive thinking

Positive thinking has a lot to answer for. There is a huge industry built on the back of positive thinking. Barbara Ehrenreich, in her book *Smile or Die*: *How Positive Thinking Fooled America and the World,* explains how positive thinking has become something like a cult in the USA and that people are actually addicted to it. Putting on a happy face is the only way forward, no matter what the circumstances are. Any negative thoughts must be banished as they will, in turn, lead to negative results. Books such as *The Secret* by Rhonda Byrne, a huge bestseller worldwide, have not helped this trend and simply feed into an already vulnerable mindset that accepts that everything that happens to you is dictated by the 'law of attraction'.[2] This then leads to false optimism where mindset is all that matters. This can actually be very dangerous. *The Secret* sells itself by promising that 'Everything is possible. Nothing is impossible'. This sounds great, but the truth is we cannot change outcomes by thoughts and affirmations alone. In fact, this statement is simply not true. We can achieve far more than what we believe may be possible by a combination of hard work, self-belief and healthy optimism. In that context anything, certainly, may be possible.

> Positive thoughts and affirmations are largely a waste of time when it comes to learning optimism

Psychology journalist Oliver Burkeman even goes so far as wanting us all to start thinking more negatively. He believes society's obsession with positivity is actually making most of us unhappier. In his book, *The Antidote*, Burkeman draws on personal experiences and scientific research to introduce a new, refreshing way of thinking called 'the negative path'.[3] The negative path is all about embracing those feelings we're taught to avoid – failure, pessimism, insecurity, uncertainty and anxiety. It's not about feeling gloomy, but instead seeing the bigger picture by being more realistic about happiness. Healthy positivity doesn't mean covering up how you are feeling – happiness is not the absence of suffering but the ability to rebound from it.

Healthy optimism

The 'positive thinking movement', with its linear, over-simplistic solutions, ignores the balance that is needed between negative and positive thinking and the different responses to adversity: action by approach (extrovert) or avoidance (introvert) personality types. An avoidant optimist's glass is neither half full nor half empty. It is simply at the level that he/she chooses to fill it to. Martin Seligman, a leading authority on optimism and positive psychology, says in his book *Flourish* that we've been living in a bit of a 'therapy century' and that the therapist's job traditionally has been to minimise negative emotion by psychological interventions that make people less anxious, angry or depressed.[4] Along the way, parents and teachers have joined in with minimising negative emotions. What is more essential, however, is to learn to function well even when you might also be feeling sad, anxious or angry. Even if you had all the therapy in the world, there will be days when you wake up feeling blue, worried or uncertain. This is the case for all of us. What's far more important is to not only fight those feelings but to actually live your life heroically, which means functioning well even when you are sad. Abraham Lincoln and Winston Churchill were two severe depressives but also highly competent and well-functioning human beings who dealt with their 'black dog'. The British actor Stephen Fry has openly admitted to manic depression, which he somehow manages to rise above most of the time, and refers to himself as being an optimist. So perhaps he is one of the 'avoidant optimists'?

Genuine optimists stay grounded in the real world. They size up situations accurately and, if there is a problem, they face it and seek solutions. They play the hero in their own lives, which leads to personal growth and offers a real chance for improving any situation.

glass half empty or half full? It depends!

The Hallmarks of Healthy Optimism Include:

1 **Accurately assessing a situation,** including asking questions, questioning assumptions, weighing up the facts, differentiating between facts and feelings and having a **perspective.**

2 **Seeing problems as temporary and not pervasive.** Being able to acknowledge your own role within a situation, feelings and actions. Less blame laid on self or external factors.

3 **Having faith in your own ability to implement solutions,** adjust and move forward constructively. Knowing that there is something you can do. You may not be able to change an external situation, but you can be more in control of yourself within it.

Why is optimism a must-have skill?

Each of us really does have untapped potential and strengths that we generally do not use to the full. The world we live in and the world of the future invite us to step up to the plate and examine that potential, perhaps more so than we may ever have done before. It is an exciting era of opportunity and change. Real optimism requires you to have your eyes wide open and not shut. Real optimism invites you to assess accurately the situation, face problems and take responsibility for your actions and seek solutions. Real optimism invites you to live a happier and more fulfilled life of your own choosing.

There are five elements essential to lasting contentment. These are positive emotions and the extent to which you experience them; levels of engagement with your work and the world; relationships; meaning/purpose; and sense of accomplishment and we need each of them to feel contented and happy.[5] Ask yourself to what extent these are in your life and how you could go about encouraging more of each. It's like taking a little health check of your optimism levels. Go to https://unimenta.com/optimism/ to health check your own!

Optimism is more important than ever, because it invites us to experience hopefulness and it also helps us to be more robust during difficult times. It enables us to be more accountable and proactive (see the chapter on being proactive).

While we can't say for certain why some people respond more positively to life's events, it is increasingly clear that your mental outlook can have a big effect on your physical health. Optimism motivates individuals to take control of their lives, while depression has the opposite effect and is linked to a sense of hopelessness because if you are depressed you can't engage in actions or events that will help to make your life better or solve a problem. The exact nature of the relationship between optimism and good health is still unclear. Martin Seligman says that it might be that optimists, as opposed to pessimists, are more likely to take care of their health because they believe in the potential positive outcomes. Or, it could be that optimistic people are more likeable and build better and more effective social networks, which have been associated with longevity. Another possibility is that optimistic people may have had less trauma or difficulty in their lives (a high number of negative events in a lifetime can correlate with bad health). 'All of these are plausible', says Seligman.

Try this

Good and sufficient sleep is associated with positive personality characteristics. Are you getting enough sleep every night?[6]. Here are some simple things you can try to make sure that you are:

- Try to go to sleep and get up at the same time every day.
- Limit naps to no more than 15-minute power naps if you need them.
- Spend more time in natural daylight.
- Avoid bright screens within 1–2 hours of bed time.
- Be smarter about what you eat and drink – that means less alcohol right before bed and no heavy meals – eat earlier and lighter.
- Cut back on lots of sugar in the evening too and instead have snacks like banana or milk to promote sleep.

Positive people are also more likely to see the opportunities within a situation, even when things are tough. This is probably more important than ever now. Optimism is a key part of being resilient – to thrive despite failure, setbacks and hardship (see also the chapter on resilience). Optimism points towards being future-orientated and going back to that hardwired belief that

the best is yet to come
Optimism also relates to how we think about the past and, in particular, how we might think about the causes of anything negative. Optimists tend to believe that the *cause* of a negative event can be changed and that problems in one area of life won't necessarily lead to problems in all areas.

Happiness is an inside job!

each of us does have, albeit to a greater or lesser extent, that things can indeed get better. Low optimism results in fear and uncertainty about the future, which in turn can result in passivity and a decision to not take action to make anything better.

How optimism helps us at work

Optimism in the workplace invites possibility, innovation and collaboration because optimism feeds into being more open to more opportunities. Generally, if you are perceived as being optimistic, you are more likely to get on well with your colleagues, be seen as a solutions-person and someone others want to be around.

Oprah Winfrey, when once asked what she wished she'd learned earlier in life, said 'I wish I'd known how to distinguish radiators from drains'. She explained that 'radiators' are people who give out warmth, honesty, positivity, energy and enthusiasm, which other people respond to. 'Drains' are people who are negative, downbeat, suck the energy out of others and don't like themselves. We can probably all think of people at work who we would consider 'drains'. At work and in life too, you want to be a radiator. That may not always be easy, especially if you are coping with pressures, setbacks, demands and challenges. But it's absolutely essential now. It's like cultivating your own immune system so you are better able to handle the pressures.

are you a radiator or a drain?

An example of optimism at work

A study by mathematician Marcial Losada[7] looked at the effect of negative emotions in the work setting. Losada and his team observed behaviour in company meetings behind a two-way mirror. He measured positive versus negative statements, self-focused or other-focused, or people who favoured inquiry or advocacy.

He found that high-performance teams have a 6 to 1 ratio of positive to negative statements, while low-performing teams were under 1 to 1. That gap makes a huge difference. The best performers scored high on profitability, customer satisfaction ratings and evaluations by others.

High-performance teams were more flexible, resilient and not stuck in self-absorbed defensive behaviour. High-performance teams asked questions as much as they defended views and had attention outward as much as inward. Low-performance teams had lower connectivity, asked no questions and had almost no outward focus.

Negative teams got stuck in negative, self-absorbed advocacy. Negativity causes teams to lose good cheer, flexibility and the ability to ask questions. Each person defended their views and became critical of all else.

Buddhist monk Matthieu Ricard says that happiness comes from a deeper sense of flourishing that stems from an exceptionally healthy mind. So it is all to do with how we interpret events and think about them rather than an emotion, pleasurable feeling or a mood. You can

Top tip: try this for one day!

Be a radiator

If you can radiate energy around you, everyone will pick up on it. And if you're a drain, they'll pick up on that even more. Be aware of the high negative impact of being perceived as a drain. If you are having a bad day, try, before you enter the office meeting, presentation or boardroom, to centre yourself, ground yourself and take control. It takes effort but you don't have to let a temporary bad mood project on to everyone else around you. In fact, if you allow yourself to do that you'll only feel worse.

always change the way you look at the world. Happiness and optimism are choices. But we also often turn away from happiness, surprisingly and this is because we are looking for it outside ourselves when it needs to come from within. So we will always be disappointed if we seek happiness from our circumstances. What needs to change is how we think about them and what actions we take. If we can learn to cultivate this habit day-to-day, it is possible to experience immediate calm and control. Sometimes that can mean simply stopping, taking stock and reflecting before responding. I'm a huge advocate of taking time to slow down and reflect more – for me this has an impact across all seven skills but especially optimism. This also means nurturing a sense of awareness about how something may make us feel and why. It can be very easy to be affected by other people's actions and moods and get sucked into their drama. The trick here is to avoid over-personalising things – it's possible to acknowledge how they might be feeling and how it in turn impacts your own feelings. Whether you choose to react to it or not then becomes your choice, over which you always have control!

Look for opportunities

Become a seeker of solutions. There are always opportunities. Try finding them in any situation you have coming up; for example, you were going to go on holiday this year but you've decided you now can't afford it and that you cannot take the time off from work either.

Opportunities for you include still taking a little time off and having a 'staycation' and getting to know your own hometown, spending time with family doing things at home or eating outside in your garden and acting as if you were on holiday.

Another example is if you have suffered some kind of a setback at work or a promotion or deal you were hoping for did not work out. This is an opportunity for taking stock, reappraising your role at work and forging stronger communications with your team as you pull together.

Healthy optimists are going to be good at evaluating a situation from different perspectives, weighing up different options and coming up with solutions. Optimists are always going to want to focus on being part of the solution rather than part of the problem. They'll be better at working within a team too because they'll be effective at creating strong connections and working to strengths.

Workplace engagement is a hot topic. Disengaged workers affect (or 'infect'!) others with their attitude – their emotions and mindsets impact others' moods and performances tremendously. How we feel at work DOES matter. There are clear neurological links between feelings, thoughts and actions. When you are in the grip of a strong negative emotion, you focus mostly and sometimes only on the source of the pain. We don't process information as well, think creatively or make good decisions. Frustration, anger and stress cause that part of us to shut down.

An interesting survey of managerial roles at Hanover Insurance Group by psychologists Greenberg and Arakawa found that a manager's optimism didn't necessarily directly influence the engagement level of employees they managed but did have significant impact on their own engagement on the job, which in turn affected the performance of the team.

Case study: an easy way to inject some optimism into the workplace through Pecha Kucha

Pecha Kucha is a format of presentation where you are limited to a maximum of 20 slides with only images. At Intel they got employees to share things about their lives outside work through using Pecha Kucha presentations at meetings. It made an immediate and significant impact and fostered a much stronger sense of collaboration.

We get very rigid when we're in a negative or pessimistic state. Negativity constricts thinking, puts us in a defensive crouch and prevents us from seeing the bigger picture.

Positive emotions broaden and build. Negative emotions hold you back. Positive emotions make you more curious. You explore more, take more initiative. You're looking outward, open to connection and trying new things and interacting with others. Negativity constrains your experience. A negative frame of mind puts you in 'leave me alone' mode, bunker mode. You're on alert.

Try this

Identify the emotion in a negative statement – whether it's something we are saying to ourselves or hearing from others around us. For example: 'I FEEL hopeless about xyz' is different from saying something like 'I'm just hopeless' or 'the xyz situation is hopeless'. Defining emotions helps to shrink them down to size rather than magnifying them through the language we use.

Saying things like 'We'll never be able to xxxx' is also an emotional statement – the best approach here is to bring facts and circumstances to the situation to identify practical action steps. So saying 'we'll never be able to buy a house' is emotional and gets you feeling stuck rather than starting to look at the facts, different options and 'what if . . .' scenarios.

What makes optimism challenging?

There are some natural barriers to developing optimism which are important to understand and build awareness of. Some of these link to our own perceptions of what optimism is and to what degree we believe we are naturally optimistic or negative. We also all have a natural human tendency towards irrational optimism.

The positive illusion

This is where someone generally views themselves in a positive way – something that mentally healthy people do very well – perhaps too well sometimes.[8] The danger is when this personal view leads to biased behaviours.[9] It's easy to have an inflated sense of our own strengths but be less aware of our weaknesses, or even of how we are perceived by others. Most of us also justify our responses and reactions quite easily and in our favour. Most studies find that people tend to have inflated views of themselves anyway. The research indicates that the relationship between people's self-evaluations and objective assessments is relatively weak. One explanation for this is that most of us do have mild positive illusions (Taylor & Armor 1996[10]). These illusions can influence decision making and taking an objective view. This could be why 'positive thinking' in the simplistic way it is put forward can actually be dangerous, as it feeds directly into and nurtures this 'positive illusion', which we all possess to a greater or lesser extent.

Optimistic people are more likely to focus on the opportunities, but we also know that too high a level of optimism can cause potential problems to be ignored, leading to possible negative events or an over-optimistic estimation of a situation. It's like being overly confident. Lower levels of optimism are more likely to cause people to focus on the obstacles lying in their path, but if they are too pessimistic then they may never seize the opportunities in the first place.

If most of us show a natural optimistic bias (which can, as we now know, be irrational), how do we remain hopeful of keeping the benefits of optimism while at the same time still being aware of its possible downside? The answer is to be more aware of our own tendency towards optimism bias and have a better understanding of what being optimistic actually means. There is vast misinterpretation of optimism and being 'positive', and we need to cultivate a much clearer understanding of what I am going to call 'healthy optimism'. That means being self-aware, being in control of our responses, being accountable and being solution-orientated.

Expectations and optimism

Some people believe that if we have low expectations, then we won't be disappointed when things don't work out and will be pleasantly surprised if they do. As Homer Simpson says: 'Trying is the first step towards failure'. Actually, in practice there is sufficient research to show that having high expectations increases your happiness, regardless of whether you succeed or fail. What matters is how we *interpret* the events we encounter. This is repeated over and over again in different research studies on optimism and happiness. Psychologists Marshall and Brown found that students with low expectations of their exam results were, yes, not surprised when they failed but they didn't **feel** better.[11] And if they did well, they put this down to 'luck'. Students who expected a high result and failed didn't feel worse because of failing. In fact, they felt inspired to do better the next time.

Try this

Optimism day-to-day – it is the *frequency* of your positive experiences that are a much better predictor of your happiness than the *intensity* of them.[12]

This is about making sure that mildly nice things are happening each day – simple stuff like getting outside, wearing clothes you love, walking with the dog, hugging your family, a cup of tea in the sunshine – it's the small stuff here that actually matters! Happiness is the sum of hundreds of small things. The main thing is to commit to some simple behaviours – meditating, exercising, getting enough sleep and to practise altruism. One of the most selfish things you can do is to help others. Nurture social connections. Write down what you're grateful for.

_____

_____

_____

Affirmation and visualisation

One of the biggest issues I have with books like *The Secret* and the many other self-help books and articles on visualisation techniques and affirming that all is well is that they give the wrong impression that having a positive attitude and outlook on life is simple – all you have to do is chant some affirmations and visualise yourself into a better place and so it will be. Hundreds of self-improvement techniques suggest that if you want a better job or relationship, you simply visualise yourself into the perfect dream job or describe your romantic partner and that by doing this you will start to attract the right kinds of decisions and influences into your life. People respond well to these sorts of messages because it all seems so easy. While a small element of visualisation and affirmation may be true (if you are positively expecting better outcomes, you are more likely to put yourself into situations where these may occur), research and, I would argue, common sense put this on its head. In one experiment at New York University by Gabrielle Oettingen, individuals were asked to visualise their dream job.[13] Those who reported that they frequently fantasised about such success also reported receiving fewer job offers and actually often ended up with lower salaries. In another study, at the University of California, students were asked to spend a few minutes each day visualising themselves getting a higher examination result.[14] Even though they were only doing this for a short amount of time each day, it actually caused them to study less as a consequence and so get a worse result.

I believe that overuse of visualisations and affirmations makes you less equipped to managing potential setbacks as well as putting in the hard work and effort needed to reach your goals.

Matthew Killingsworth Future of Happiness Research[15] has recruited more than 15,000 people in 83 countries to report their emotional states in real time. This is about how moment-by-moment details of a person's day affects their happiness – the first ever large-scale study of happiness in daily life. A major finding is that people's minds wander half the time which seems to lower their mood. No matter what people are doing, they are much less happy when their minds are wandering than when they are focused. So this would suggest that to increase our optimism and well-being levels, we should pay more attention to what our minds are doing. Yet the focus of our thoughts is not usually part of our daily planning – it's usually about what we will be doing – how about the question 'What am I going to do with my mind today?'

Go to https://unimenta.com/optimism/ to download a great exercise to redefine your morning routine.

The moody blues

It is true that optimism produces a positive 'mood', and this in turn is a big motivator for us. Our mood influences the way we view life and how we process information, and events will change depending on our mood, which in turn has an impact on our thoughts. Yet some people are very moody and 'up and down', with no consistency or predictability. How they respond to negative events (and even positive ones) is completely dependent on how they might be feeling at that particular point in time. We are all probably prone to 'moodiness' from time to time. Moodiness is related to lots of different elements, from genetics to hormonal influences, to natural disposition. However, those who can accept that they have the power to control their lives and circumstances and their responses, rather than being swayed by every change they experience around them, are far less prone to moodiness.

If your self-esteem is low, it may also influence how optimistic you are. Lower self-esteem can often mean that you automatically take responsibility personally every time you experience an event. For example, let's say you arrive at work (or school or a concert) and run into a colleague (or friend). This person doesn't acknowledge your greeting and actually looks away. One way of responding to this is to assume that you've done something to cause this: that you've upset this person, they're angry with you because of something you think you might have said the last time you met them.

This assumption can happen very, very fast and if you have low self-esteem you will be more prone to this. Social media feeds into these kinds of assumptions too. Healthy optimism says there may be a number of causal factors that have nothing to do with you: perhaps your friend/colleague has received bad news, wasn't wearing their glasses, was distracted or upset, in a rush, etc. Healthy optimists are less likely to automatically personalise events around them. However, even they are prone to assuming something worse if, on that particular day, they are experiencing stress or some upset.

How can we shift our moods so that we can limit the negative sway over our thoughts and emotions? We can do it by:

1   **reducing the negativity in our lives**

2   **changing the way we react to events**

3   **having more positive experiences**

4   **choosing intrinsic goals that bring the most satisfaction**

Try this exercise to work out how to shift yours.

You can download it here: https://unimenta.com/optimism/

We need to think about how to build healthy optimism into our day-to-day lives, rather than a vague nod at 'being positive' or being in a 'good mood'.

Consider this

Work out your explanatory style

How do you tend to respond to events in your everyday life? What is your default response if something does not go according to plan or you get some bad news? Take some time to understand yourself. After all, you're the only one who can!

How to become more optimistic

A growing body of scientific evidence points to the conclusion that optimism is hardwired by evolution into the human brain. It shows that our brains are not just stamped by the past but are constantly being shaped by the future. A recent study scanned people's brains as they processed both positive and negative information about the future. The results showed that we are, indeed, hardwired to be optimistic. Brain neurons will faithfully encode desirable information that enhances optimism but fails at incorporating unexpectedly undesirable information. So when we hear a success story, like somebody winning the lottery or succeeding at work, our brains immediately take note of the possibility that we too may become immensely rich or hit on an award-winning idea. It's what keeps people playing the lottery too. But hearing something far more realistic, such as 50 per cent of all marriages fail, we immediately do not count ourselves within the half that might fail. Nor in the 75 per cent of second marriages that fail. Why? It comes back to our tendency to be optimistically biased.

So we need to keep mindful of this bias, but at the same time, acknowledge the fact that us, a sailor who circumnavigated the world by himself having the bias means that healthy optimism can definitely be learned.

your brain is constantly being shaped by the future

For example, why do some people write proposal after proposal to get their book published by a mainstream publisher? They must know, on some level, that there is far greater probability of writing a book that few people will actually buy rather than a bestseller? They either have other reasons for writing the book or genuinely believe that theirs could be the bestseller. People who self-publish are also at risk of the bias that they will produce a best-seller. Or what about an actor who goes to audition after audition, despite the fact that a shockingly tiny percentage of actors actually earn a living from this career and an even tinier percentage become famous. They are likely to be passionate about what they do and see others achieve it, even if that is only a minority, and so believe that success is a definite possibility for them too.

Healthy optimism means we still pursue our dreams but we may approach them differently or work harder and more proactively, setting clear goals and being in control. I probably submit around 30 or more major consultancy proposals a year, of which perhaps 2 are successful and result in an actual paid contract. Each time

Try this

Study after study points to the huge benefits of cultivating an attitude of gratitude

Writing down what you are grateful for

Keeping track of all the things you appreciate in your life can improve your mood, health and sense of perspective too. Practising gratitude boosts your immunity, helps you sleep better, reduces depression symptoms. Even if you are feeling yucky, reflecting on a few positive things can shift your mindset instantly. The best way to do this is to write a journal – either by writing down at the end of the day the good things that happened or finding some positives to be grateful for – that is, your health, hot shower, coffee, good food, a home, etc. Just writing down three good things is sufficient.

_____

_____

_____

I submit a proposal I am convinced it will win and I know this is the right attitude to have. I also get better each time I write one. But I know that the end decision won't actually be about how good the proposal is. It will be decided as part of a short-list of equally competent consultants, using criteria based on a combination of cost, location and experience. Knowing this, I accept that I have to put in the work of writing 30 a year to get the 2, and I don't really worry about it too much or personalise the rejection when it comes.

Optimism and managing stress

There are two ways we typically approach a problem or stressful situation, whether that is a major life crisis or a day-to-day hassle such as being late because of a train being delayed. The first is emotion-focused coping, which is about trying to make yourself feel better by calming your feelings through meditation or relaxation or looking at the positives. The second is problem-solving coping, which means you are actively trying to turn the tide, decide what is needed and create a solution. It's probably better to use emotion-focused coping when it is too late to change the situation or when the stressor is outside of your control. It doesn't help, though, where you yourself need to take action to change an outcome. Wishing a huge project at work would get smaller or looking at the positives of producing it won't change anything, whereas tackling it and taking action will.

'Optimism seems to reduce stress-induced inflammation and levels of stress hormones such as cortisol. It may also reduce susceptibility to disease by dampening sympathetic nervous system activity and stimulating the parasympathetic nervous system. It is the system that governs what is called the "rest and digest" response – the opposite of flight or fight.'
Jo Marchant PhD, science journalist and author.

Faking it

Generally, we believe that how we feel influences how we behave. If we are feeling happy, we'll smile and if sad, we'll show a corresponding frown or grimace. However, even as far back as the nineteenth century, William James at Harvard University hypothesised that behaviour and feelings were a two-way street.[16] So, if you want to feel happy, start smiling. However, nothing came of this and for decades we have had self-help books telling us to change the way we are thinking and the behaviour will follow.[17]

The psychologist James Laird decided to test James' theory in the 1970s.[18] He got volunteers to create an angry expression by clenching their teeth and frowning and to create a happy one by smiling. The results showed that the volunteers felt much happier when smiling and much angrier when showing an angry expression. Subsequent research shows that this same effect applies to just about anything in our everyday lives. Simply by acting, or 'faking it', you take significant steps towards feeling the way you want to feel. Behaviour first then feelings, rather than changing our thinking first. Much simpler!

Take confidence: most self-help encourages you to think about times when you've done well or were particularly proud of an achievement, or even to visualise yourself giving a confident presentation. But, if instead, next time you give a presentation you walk in with a confident stride, open body language and a smile on your face, you will automatically feel more confident. I've experienced this so many times that whenever I now give a presentation I prepare for it like an actor going on stage!

Top tip

Try acting as if . . .

This can be very powerful. Try adopting a 'power pose' for confidence – standing straight, shoulders back, chest forward, both feet grounded. If you're a habitual procrastinator, spend ten minutes acting as if you couldn't be more interested in what you're trying to do and start the task – you'll find that within a very short space of time you will have a strong desire to complete it. Or break things down into smaller steps first – the key is taking action, not waiting until you 'feel better'.

The ABCDE model and explanatory styles

Psychologist and author Martin Seligman says that the key to optimism and pessimism lies in our 'explanatory styles', how we explain life events (good or bad) to ourselves. The following model summarises this and, to some extent, we are all capable of responding in either way. Seligman believes that optimism can be **learned** and that anyone can learn it through asking themselves more questions before automatically defaulting into a negative response. Try it for yourself, and try to raise your awareness of how you would respond by default. Then keep asking questions to move towards healthy optimism. We use this exercise on our workshops and everyone – from lawyers to software engineers, from sixth formers to the unemployed just love it. You can download it to try it for yourself here: https://unimenta.com/optimism/

Ways of experiencing an event	Healthy optimism	Negative response
Experience/negative event/ problem/situation or incident	More likely to look at event or experience positively. Will not see a negative outcome as 'negative'	Will scan for negative experiences and tend to find (or think they find) what they are looking for
Attribution and personalisation – the difference between personalising something and externalising it	Externalise – so you give yourself the benefit of the doubt. Don't automatically take responsibility for the situation or outcomes with no clear cause	Over-personalise – a tendency to solely blame yourself, even if there are very likely to be numerous other causal factors and reasons
Attribution pervasiveness – specific and temporary or global and permanent?	Tend not to blame yourself for an incident, i.e. getting upset and shouting doesn't mean I'm aggressive, forgetting my briefcase on the train doesn't mean I'm an idiot	Tendency to catastrophise by extending a specific situation to how you are all the time
Attribution permanence – temporary or permanent?	After deciding whether you have a role or responsibility in the negative outcome or situation, realising you have a weakness or problem to sort out and basically working on that problem. Or cut losses and benefit from self-perceived strengths	Continue to catastrophise and be resigned to the problem or issue being unsolvable

Ways of experiencing an event	Healthy optimism	Negative response
Dispute	Weigh all the possible explanations you can find. If you're at fault, you accept you did something wrong and put it right. Or you may decide the issue was not that important and either work on the things that are workable or preventable in future	Don't dispute anything. Instead, think of the first thing you can do to blame yourself and continue to focus on your shortcomings
Consequence/resolution	An optimist will accept that something unfortunate may have happened. You take ownership of your level of responsibility in it, resolve and plan to do things differently and move on	You're more likely to feel terrible about the consequences of the situation, give up and tell yourself there is nothing you can do

Seligman's ABCDE model[19] is based on this. The model begins with the Ellis ABC model of Adversity, Belief and Consequence:

- **Adversity** (the event): My husband comes home and snaps at me.
- **Belief** (how I interpret that event): 'What a complete jerk. I can't believe he's being so disrespectful, aggressive and rude.'
- **Consequence** (feelings and reactions that result from that interpretation): I shout back, throw dinner away and leave the house angry.

In the journey to learning optimism, you have to first understand your own natural reaction to an event and your own interpretation and belief of that. Seligman usually asks his students to keep a journal for a few days to record various instances.

Seligman then adds 'D' and 'E' to the model. These are **D**isputation and **E**nergisation:

- **Disputation:** (provide counter-evidence to dispute either my interpretation of things or the cause of the event): 'I am overreacting. I don't like this shouting but maybe he's had bad news. It's not like him to be aggressive. He must have had a terrible day. Something has really upset him. I'm sure I snap too when I'm upset or angry.'

  This is certainly not an easy first thing to do in a situation. The natural tendency will be to react. Successful disputation, over time, leads to more positive feelings and a more realistic interpretation of events. It also means that we stop allowing an adverse event to dictate our response and that we have a better and healthier way of evaluating life experiences.

- **Energisation** is the successful dispute of negative beliefs and a happier outcome.

Seven steps to optimism

Try out some of these approaches to raise your awareness and strengthen your healthy optimism. Try to record your experiences if you can. Even better, keep a diary, journal or blog for a few weeks.

1 **Embrace negativity**
   This doesn't mean being pessimistic but instead, as Oliver Burkeman says in his book *The Antidote,* **accepting** that negative experiences are just as important for our lives as positive ones. If you can accept that, then you'll be better equipped to develop a positive 'indifference' to negative thoughts or setbacks and have a better way of dealing with them. Life has its ups and downs and we need to embrace each and every one of them and grow from them.

Choose to do this right now with something that is not going so well for you at the moment:

_____

_____

_____

2   **Rethink happiness**

Happiness can be yours right now – in fact, it is yours right now, not something that is forever in the future. Let go a little and relax. Go with the flow more. Take some time to define what happiness and well-being really mean to you – they should be about balance, rewarding work, a loving relationship, a network of friends and family, good health; many of these things are inside your control. So practise letting go of the things that aren't and accept them. That way lies real happiness and contentment.

What are some things I could let go of?

_____

_____

_____

What are some easy ways I can bring more happiness into my everyday life?

_____

_____

_____

3   **It's as easy as ABC . . . DE**

Try the ABCDE approach of dealing with a problem or any event. Record how you interpret something and what impact that has. What's important here is to realise that it's not the external problem or event that makes you feel a certain way, it is your own interpretation of it! Remember that Seligman's students practise ABCDE for a period of time and note down the results – and so change starts to happen.

Download the exercise for ABCDE here:
https://unimenta.com/optimism/

4 **Ditch the self-help books**

For years I read self-help books. I was quite proud of my
collection! For some reason, they made me feel better, but I
rarely carried out any of the exercises in them. Did you know that
publishers of self-help books refer to the '18-month rule'?[20] They
say that the person most likely to purchase any self-help book is
someone who, within the past 18 months, bought a self-help
book that evidently didn't solve their problems! They're making a
lot of money and they certainly made a fair amount off me! So
just get rid of books, affirmations podcasts, and downloads that
are too strongly about self-help; they will **not** make you happy or
more optimistic. You have to do that yourself, and you CAN!

Do I have any self-help books? What are they?

_____

_____

_____

Am I willing to get rid of them?

_____

_____

_____

5 **Stop trying to think positively**

Apart from anything else it's exhausting and, if you become a
Pollyanna by being continually overly positive, you may just
find that you really start annoying other people. The way to
healthy positivity is through getting to know yourself, taking
responsibility and understanding how you tend to respond to
things. After that, it's about taking action.

_____

_____

_____

6 Find ways to relieve anxiety and worry

We are all prone to worry and stress. It is up to us to manage ourselves to handle that. So look after yourself. If you're working hard to a deadline, make time for an early morning swim or treat yourself to a massage. Make sure you relax and switch off properly in the evenings so you can sleep well. The fact is that the more you can achieve healthy optimism, the less prone you will be to worry because you will simply feel far more in control of your life and are more likely to accept that events that cause worry and stress are a normal part of our lives.

What are three practical things I can do that will help me to worry less?

_____

_____

_____

7 Make time for gratitude

Note three things you are proud of today and three things you are grateful for. Make this a daily habit!

_____

_____

_____

A day in the life of. . .

Let's take a magnifying glass to the skill of optimism through a day in the life of Paul. We'll start with a brief introduction to Paul, to give a quick snapshot of his life.

About Paul

Paul is in his mid-thirties. He is single and lives in a house share in a large city. He is well qualified and has a Masters degree in Geography. After graduating, he spent more than eight years teaching English as a foreign language in Japan, but returned to the UK when the language school he was working for went bust. For the last two years he has been working in administration for the City Corporation but was recently made redundant. He was kind of expecting it as there have been a lot of cutbacks lately and he wasn't getting on that well with his boss. He is quite heavily influenced by what he reads online and hears on the news and feels generally pessimistic about the future. It seems like three are 'no jobs' and, although he has updated his CV several times and applied for various jobs that fit his experience and background, he has not been able to find anything. He has a collection of self-help books and podcasts and, for a long time, was a great believer in using affirmations and positive thinking to help himself overcome his negative thinking tendency as he knows this is not healthy. Lately, though, these books are not really doing anything to help him so they are gathering dust and he rarely listens to the affirmation podcasts any more.

He has a few friends, most of whom are in a similar situation. He feels depressed, although he has always felt slightly depressed throughout most of his life. Generally, he doesn't see much of a future for himself and dreams about going off travelling again and leaving the UK, as things just 'seem to be getting worse'.

Let's have a closer look at a typical day in Paul's life and how building the skill of optimism can help him.

Paul's typical day

Paul usually gets up at about 10 am and goes for a swim in the local pool or for a run. He has breakfast either at the sports club or at a café in town as he doesn't like eating alone in his flat. He goes to the local library and reads a paper and borrows a few books as he enjoys crime thrillers. He browses through some of the psychology section too. He goes back home and reads for a bit, surfs the Internet and looks at a few job recruitment sites. In the afternoon he has an appointment at his local unemployment office, where he has to legally attend on a regular basis. He gives them a bit of an update on his job search but doesn't get any real encouragement or support. He tells himself, 'I really am a loser, not even the job centre can help me'. He buys a take-away and watches TV. Later that evening he meets with one of his friends, drinking a few cans of lager. They reminisce about the 'good old days'. The weekends are similar and Paul doesn't really do a lot of socialising, although he sometimes visits his sister for Sunday lunch. Generally, though, Paul is stuck and not doing much to improve or change his situation.

What's happening here?

People with a pessimistic interpretation of events may naturally have a tendency towards doing so, as does Paul. Paul's main issue is how he is 'explaining' events in his life. At the moment he is doing this through the 'three Ps':

Personal – Paul believes that he is the cause of his redundancy. 'I was outspoken to my boss' or 'The boss didn't like me.' However, optimists would see the situation as not caused by themselves but by outside factors – 'My company was looking to cut costs and unfortunately my role was deemed superfluous.'

Permanent – Paul sees the setback as permanent: 'I'll never get another job.'

The optimist would see the situation as temporary – 'This setback is just temporary. Lots of people are being made redundant in the public sector but I can always go back to teaching English as a foreign language, either here or abroad, and maybe enhance my qualifications. I'll sign on first and get some unemployment benefit and then consider my options.'

Pervasive – Paul sees this event as pervading his whole life. 'I'm a loser', 'I'm hopeless' or 'I'm a loner.' He generalises one adverse event to all other areas of his life. An optimistic just sees one event, which may not even be adverse. 'This is actually great news! I hated the job anyway and this redundancy gives me impetus to look for a more fulfilling job. I've been relatively successful in getting work and I've had a very interesting life, having lived in Japan for eight years, and also I managed to save a lot of money there.'

However, Paul doesn't fall into this category as he is not naturally optimistic. He can start to try actively looking at the events in his life from different perspectives, though, and once he does this it will definitely help him. The difficulty is that the longer he allows himself to be in his current mindset, the worse it may get. The circumstances themselves could become worse because of his current way of thinking about them. What this also means is that anything he reads in the news and online or any attempts to find work will feed into this mindset, so he will be able to confirm that there are indeed 'no jobs' out there and that the situation is bleak – a self-fulfilling prophecy. His friends, in similar situations, will confirm these views or, rather, Paul will attribute the comments he hears around him to supporting the whole negative outlook.

What would happen if Paul were to try and put some of the principles of healthy optimism into practice? Let's revisit Paul's 'typical day' six months later.

How Paul's life has moved forward

Paul is feeling better because he understands better his explanatory style and how he tends to interpret things around him. He recognises that he has got himself into a rather negative spiral and that what he chooses to read or listen to online, his lifestyle and the friends he has are only feeding into that. He is more discerning now about what he chooses to read online and does not react to every post or headline he sees. He has started to realise that he can take some control over his own responses to things and experiments with looking at his situation from different angles. He actually has a lot of strings to his bow and is well qualified with international experience, so he spends a bit more time making sure this is explicit in his CV. He still goes for a swim in the mornings but has ditched going to the library and poring through newspapers. He catches up quickly with the news on his phone rather than spending time watching 24-hour news channels and he has also switched off news and other notifications on his phone so that instead he is choosing when to view news and social media. Paul has also been taking a few cookery classes and has made some new friends, and this has really had a great effect on him. He's looking after himself more and certainly saving money by cooking at home.

Instead of applying for jobs, he has started to think more about what he has to offer and has been taking the initiative by visiting language schools and suggesting some opportunities for new types of classes that could be offered. He is actually quite confident, as he has been teaching and presenting for some years but lost touch with this skill after returning from Japan. He hasn't found a permanent job yet but he spends some time each day using a different approach to look for work, and he has started teaching a couple of evening classes on cross-cultural communication, using his experiences in Japan as examples. He's also started doing some volunteer work with disadvantaged young people in his local community. The volunteer work is adding some useful skills and experience but, more importantly, it makes a powerful difference in that Paul is starting to feel better about himself through helping others. He can see that he does have much to contribute and make a difference. He has also started to note down what he is thankful for in his life. Although gratitude journals are often a feature of self-help, they can actually be very valuable if used alongside positive optimism. For someone like Paul, who is prone to negativity, this is a useful and easy tool to gain perspective.

Optimism can be learned, it can be developed. It isn't something static that some people just 'have' and others don't, and positive thinking, by itself, will not help you to be more optimistic. We all need to start learning to develop healthy optimism. This requires becoming more self-aware and, to a certain degree, working on ourselves consistently. There are opportunities all around you to do this each and every day.

Interested in learning more?

I've put together some extra resources here:

Burkeman, O. (2013) *The Antidote: Happiness for People Who Can't Stand Positive Thinking.* Canongate Books Ltd.

Ehrenreich, B. (2010) *Smile or Die: How Positive Thinking Fooled America and the World.* Granta Books.

Huffington, A. (2015) *Thrive: The Third Metric to Redefining Success and Creating a Happier Life.* WH Allen.

Marchant, J. (2016) *Cure a Journey into the Science of Mind over Body.* Canongate.

Murphy, S. (2015) *The Optimistic Workplace: Creating an Environment That Energises Everyone.* Amacom.

Ricard, M (2003) *Happiness – A Guide to Developing Life's Most Important Skill.* Atlantic.

Seligman, M. (2011) *Flourish: A New Understanding of Happiness and Well-Being and How to Achieve Them.* Nicholas Brealey Publishing.

Seligman, M. (2006) *Learned Optimism: How to Change Your Mind and Your Life.* Vintage Books USA.

Sharot, T. (2012) *The Optimism Bias: Why We're Wired to Look on the Bright Side.* Robinson.

Articles and websites

https://www.nbcnews.com/better/health/how-train-your-brain-be-more-optimistic-ncna795231

An article on how to train your brain to be more optimistic underpinned by lots of research on optimism and some practical tips

www.pursuit-of-happiness.org

Lots of articles and resources on optimism

www.actionforhappiness.org

A great website with constantly updated tips, ideas, facts, events and courses to promote happiness and optimism

https://positivepsychologyprogram.com – lots of resources, articles and tools that strengthen positive psychology approaches

You can also find more tips, ideas, curated video clips and exercises to strengthen your optimism skills by visiting https://unimenta.com/optimism/

Sign up too for daily tips – a daily quote, tip and video clip on one of the seven skills direct to your inbox. https://unimenta.com/seven-skills/

PERMA – *If you are interested in taking a quiz and finding out your PERMA score, you can do so here:* www.authentichappiness.org for free

'If opportunity doesn't knock, build a door.'

Milton Berle

Chapter 6

BEING PROACTIVE

Most people, if you were to ask them, think of themselves as being pretty proactive. We have so much choice, information and freedom now, coupled with a strong sense of individuality, and we operate within that cozy bubble the majority of the time. We focus on results, making decisions, dealing with change and managing our complex lives. This sounds proactive but is likely to be far more reactive. Why? The fast pace of our lifestyles, the sheer overload of information and the increasing use of technology in every sphere means that we are living in more of a reactive way, perhaps even unintentionally. Living reactively, we feel we are getting more done as we multitask our way through multiple demands on our time and focus. The reality is that we are less effective, there is little time to reflect and we often don't realise that we often get in the way of our innate ability to be responsive. Being responsive means not immediately using our default reaction to every single comment and situation that comes our way. Being proactive means responding rather than reacting to stimulus. Whether we are responding or reacting, we can still come across to others as being energetic, highly motivated and active, which is why it's easy to think we are being proactive when we are not.

What is being proactive?

We each have the capacity to be proactive or reactive and there can be an underlying genetic bias in favour of either. Being proactive takes more brain energy as it requires us to make a choice and to actively think. Being reactive can be, and probably is, easier as it takes little thought to be so and can even become a default behaviour without us realising it. Unfortunately, we also feed into this kind of behaviour every time we pick up our phones as the immediate nature of messaging and texting platforms only reinforces reactive behaviour.

Stephen Covey famously said in his book *The 7 Habits of Highly Effective People* that there is this small space between stimulus and response where we can choose how we want to respond to something.[1] So we literally have the power to control how we respond. But isn't that small space rapidly shrinking? Even if we are being proactive in some areas of our life, this may not be consistent or enough for it to make a real difference.

Consider this

How many times, in the course of your day, do you make time for reflection and pausing?

When you're proactive, you are creating situations based on a strategy you have actively created for yourself.[2] It's about taking purposeful action against a clear, specific goal. It's also about being more aware in the present and actively creating that small space so that you are responding to what is coming in around you rather than reacting to it. Part of that has to be about managing time on social media and instant messaging platforms as well as how we read and respond to email and work messages. If you are 'always on', you are more likely to be quite reactive to others' messages and demands. Proactive behaviour can be about changing yourself (personal development) or changing your environment through making suggestions to others, taking forward new initiatives and looking for opportunities to contribute in some way.

know the difference between reacting and responding

Reactions are triggered by circumstance; responses are tailored to it. It is, by far, easier to be reactive and our lives now positively encourage it because we are constantly rushing from one thing to another or replying to multiple messages sent to us via multiple platforms. So, how can we get back in touch with being truly proactive in our lives and tailoring our responses so that we are more effective, calmer and happier too?

'I believe that everyone chooses how to approach life. If you're proactive, you focus on preparing. If you're reactive, you end up focusing on repairing.'

John C. Maxwell, leadership and management expert

First of all, being proactive is a skill and a mindset that we are all capable of. Anyone who consistently creates something of value is being proactive. In fact, often, our productivity in life is directly proportional to our level of proactivity. People who are proactive aren't just a little more productive than reactive people. Covey stated that people who take the initiative typically achieve, on average, **5000 per cent** or more quantifiable results in their lifetime. That's a massive difference when you think about it.

There are two aspects to being proactive:

- **Long-term and strategic** – This means being open for new opportunities, anticipating and preventing problems, persevering despite obstacles, achieving positive results and taking control of your own life. It also means being more self-aware and building in more of a work–life balance for yourself. You are using your own principles and values to make decisions, set goals and work towards your objectives.

- **Short-term** – This means small things you can do in the moment, how you use that space between stimulus and response and, more importantly, making sure that space gets bigger, whether that is reflecting before you respond to that email, focusing and listening attentively, making time for yourself or taking a deep breath before you respond to an aggressive colleague or boss.

Being proactive boils down to these four things:

1 **Self-awareness:** This is the key to being proactive because if you're not aware of your negative reactions, it's impossible to take the initiative to change them into positive actions. You also need to know your strengths and weaknesses and why you are likely to respond a certain way. Remember too that reactions are not always negative – what we are addressing here is reactive behaviour. Because of the huge increase in messages coming at us and the urge to want to respond to them all immediately, we are likely to not be that discerning about what we are responding to.

2 **Willpower:** Being self-aware does not, by itself, lead to proactive behaviour. In their book *Willpower: Rediscovering Our Greatest Strength,* Roy Baumeister and John Tierney say that, together with intelligence, self-control turns out to be the best predictor of a successful life. However, we are not necessarily that good at exercising our willpower, so we need to practise that. *Willpower* is filled with advice about what to do with your willpower and how to use it for best effect. Build up its strength, the authors suggest, with small but regular exercises, such as tidiness and good posture as well as automating some of your regular daily routines.

3 **Responsibility:** Being proactive means having a sense of responsibility for your own life. That is 'response-ability', as in the ability to respond. Proactive people's behaviour is a product of their own conscious choice, based on values and things that are important to them, rather than a product of their conditions, based on feeling and emotion.

4 **Self-mastery:** Being proactive means having complete mastery over your thoughts, emotions and beliefs. It also means having control over your actions and never blaming

someone else for your mistakes or negative circumstances. Being proactive starts with self-awareness and grows with willpower and taking responsibility for your actions. It is the key to creating personal happiness and the kind of life you desire.

When I think about my own life I can see these four elements clearly. I believe I have a high degree of self-awareness in terms of knowing and understanding my own strengths and weaknesses and why I am likely to tend to respond a certain way. Knowing this means I can always choose a different response, either in the moment or when it comes to planning ahead and taking specific action towards something. I may not always get it right, and exercising willpower certainly helps. Sometimes that can mean something very simple, such as being disciplined about my time or refraining from making a default negative comment, however much I may feel like doing so at the time! It most certainly means managing myself online. It is very, very easy to spend huge swathes of one's life online posting comments, videos, captions or responding to others. Not only that but multiple platforms, instant messaging and group chats create that urge to keep posting messages. We all need to become more thoughtful about how we are using these channels because the way we use them does not free up any reflection space or just brain space to think clearly or respond effectively which means many of us are going about our day in a constant state of high alert.

I've mentioned earlier that I plan my week based on my values and what is important to me. This means I can be, and am, extremely productive both in my work and my leisure time. Perhaps, most importantly, I believe completely that I am in control of my actions (what I say and what I do) and in the choices I make about my life. I also take risks and make a lot of mistakes. If someone asks me to do something I have never done before, I am very likely to say 'yes'! If I am not happy with the way something is going, I am very likely to take steps to change it.

Try this

1. How much of my day do I spend on social media and instant messaging platforms?

_____

_____

2. Do I have certain times of the day when I am 'phone free', i.e. after a certain point in the evening?

_____

_____

_____

_____

3. What's my typical morning routine? How can I encourage more reflection time into my morning?

_____

_____

_____

Why is being proactive a must-have skill?

When we face uncertainty and circumstances that are outside our control, we are less in control over our lives. As a result, many people struggle with anxiety, lack of sleep, worry and even depression connected with circumstances such as job loss or insecurity, financial problems, fear of the future and other stresses including the famous FOMO – fear of missing out activated through our social media use. Being proactive is a way of feeling more in control of our lives and of our futures. In a world that can seem out of control, proactivity is essential because proactive people don't allow the environment or their circumstances to dictate how they think and behave. They recognise and accept situations over which they have no control and do not waste energy worrying about them. It's a choice, but it's a hard one for some people to accept. How many times do you hear people complaining or voicing their views on external factors, from small things like the trains running late to current affairs and exploding news stories? How many times do you find yourself reacting to stress or feeling affected by the weather (especially when everyone around you is also complaining about it!)? How many times do you allow yourself to engage in idle gossip, which is another form of moaning? Remember that much of this now happens online. Beyond that, how many times do you take the initiative, whether it's to change something in your personal or professional life or to try something new and actively seek ways to persevere even if you fail at first?

Try this

Don't talk about the weather

In the UK we have this compulsion to talk, moan, rave and go on and on about the weather! It's easy to engage in this banter and it's even easier to react to it when someone throws weather comments your way. See if you can stop talking about the weather just for one day. It may seem like a silly thing to do, but when you think about how strongly weather seems to affect our daily actions, you can see that it is one more thing we are giving energy and focus to that is outside our control. Be proactive, enjoy whatever weather the day brings and choose your response when someone else moans about it.

Being proactive is important because only you can create the kind of life you really want, only you can be responsible for your reactions and responses to events around you and your circumstances, and only you can really be in control of your own happiness. You are far more likely to do that if you see yourself as the one at the centre of your life and the one in control of it and steering it forward. By focusing on what you can control – for example, your behaviour and how you respond and other factors that you can actually do something about – you directly start to expand your ability to influence others and influence your circumstances. But if you only zero-in on what you can't control and allow yourself to be reactive or to blame others, this ability to influence massively decreases and you just get stuck in a negative spiral.

Try this exercise for how to make your own luck!

You can download it here https://unimenta.com/being-proactive/

Try this

On way to become more proactive in your life is to pay close attention to the language you use when speaking with other people and to yourself. The following are several examples of how to be proactive through the way you speak to yourself and others.

REACTIVE LANGUAGE	PROACTIVE LANGUAGE
'I can't' or 'Why can't I. . . ?'	'How can I. . . ?'
'I should' or 'I have to. . . '	'I want to', 'I choose to', 'I'd like to. . . .'
'Why can't I stop doing that?'	'What would I rather be doing? What's one small step I can take towards making the change I want?'
'That's just how it is.'	'What can I do to change this?' Or, if you cannot change the circumstances, ask yourself, 'What can I do to change my personal experience of what is happening?'
'If only I had more time. . . ' Or, 'I'm just too busy to do what I really want.'	'How can I make time? What is most important right now? What can I let go of to make time for what's most important to me?'
'If only they would change. . . '	'They are who they are. What can I do to meet my own needs or to change this relationship?'
'I can't do this all on my own.'	Proactive: 'How can I receive the support I need?'

Being proactive makes you feel happier, too. By focusing on positive change, and by feeling more in control as a result, you are creating a situation much clearer from worry and anxiety. If you are stuck in anxiety and in focusing energy on preventing something bad from happening, you are likely to feel less happy and even less in control of anything.

if you want to move ahead in your career or reach a personal goal or achievement, be proactive, resourceful and responsive

An example of being proactive at work

A review on proactivity at work (Grant & Ashford 2008)[3] emphasised that today's workplace is one of flat hierarchies and dynamic conditions. This has only become more so since this review came out and demands a different kind of employee. What is needed now is an employee who is future-orientated and a self-starter not needing constant supervision and instruction. Grant and Ashford also argue that, 'Employees do not just let life happen to them. Rather, they try to affect, shape, curtail, expand, and temper what happens in their lives.' That is a strong definition of being proactive and is as relevant for work as it is for our daily lives.

How being proactive helps us at work

For a start, people's working patterns have changed and will continue to do so – we are far more likely to be moving jobs more often now, which means we have to be much more proactive and manage our own careers. If you engage in proactive behaviour, you are more likely to be effective in your work and career and you are more likely to be working in the field that best engages your skills and talents.

When you are proactive in your own life, you are more likely to have healthy and positive communication patterns and when faced with a challenging situation you'll be better able to handle it resource-fully, creatively and with a positive attitude.

If you are not able to be proactive in the workplace, you might even start to be perceived as a liability. Why? Because you may be more dependent on others or on external events and, therefore, require more 'maintenance'. In today's workplace, you need to be a self-starter and focused on how you can make a difference. Work has grown far more complex, so proactive behaviour can often be perceived as the differentiator for keeping your job. Be non-proactive at your peril. Organisations themselves need to be more proactive and stay ahead of competitors. Smaller organisations tend to be better at this as they are able to respond faster. The flatter hierarchy can become in larger organisations, the more autonomy managers can have to make key decisions, this will start to change.

Are you 'high maintenance' or 'low maintenance'?

Proactive behaviour at work can be displayed by doing something that is self-initiated, change-orientated and future-orientated. Here are some examples:

- An intern asks for feedback on her performance (self-initiated) so she can work out what skills to develop (change-orientated) and can add a testimonial to her CV or LinkedIn profile (future-orientated).

- Someone in a junior position does something unexpected but incredibly useful and valuable, without being asked: a personal assistant provides her company director with a folder of useful conferences and events that are worth attending for networking purposes (self-initiated) in the coming year (change- and future-orientated).

- A project manager approaches his appraisal by conducting a self-evaluation of recent projects (self-initiated), coming up with examples of how he can stretch his skills (change-orientated) for new projects (future-orientated).

Try this

What are some proactive choices and actions you can take that are self-initiated and change-and future-oriented?

Self-initiated:

_____

_____

_____

Change-initiated:

_____

_____

_____

Future-oriented:

_____

_____

_____

Being proactive at work can also be viewed as having foresight and acting ahead of anticipated events. So, the more efficient you can be in managing day-to-day tasks effectively, the more nimble and open you are going to be, which encourages proactivity. If you're proactive, you are far more likely to plan, set yourself goals and manage your time well – all of these are important for both life and work. If you are proactive, you cause things to happen rather than waiting to respond after they have happened. You are active rather than passive.

Learning how to be proactive is all about paying attention, noticing the brief moment between the external event and your internal response. As you pause, reflect and consciously choose your response more and more often, you will surprise yourself by realising that you do indeed know how to be proactive and create the life you want to live!

How proactive you are at work will be, to some extent, influenced by personal and situational factors. If you feel, as an employee, that you have a lot of autonomy and freedom to make work decisions, then you are more likely to be proactive because you feel more confident to be so. You are likely to feel confident about taking the initiative and making suggestions knowing that this is actively encouraged.

According to a 2010 review by Bindl and Parker, there is ample evidence that this proactive behaviour at work is strongly influenced by the atmosphere in an organisation, its corporate culture and its management.[4] So someone who may naturally be proactive in their day-to-day lives may be less so at work if the environment is not conducive. If you're a company wanting proactive employees, then create the kind of atmosphere to allow that to flourish. Equally though, even if your workplace does not seem to encourage proactivity, you can still look for opportunities to take initiative and make suggestions. Being proactive is always about operating within your circle of control and you always have a choice about how to behave or what action to take. Be sensitive to what is around you, take notice and listen – then take action.

The benefits of managers who encourage proactivity are huge. Proactive employees tend to show increased work performance, more entrepreneurial success, higher commitment to the organisation and higher job satisfaction. The organisation flourishes through, in itself, being proactive and competitive. So if you are in a leadership or managerial role, look for ways to actively encourage and support this in the people you lead and manage.

Try this

When you need something, you can either wait for people to figure it out on their own – which might take a very, very long time – or you can simply speak up. Reactive people usually stay silent, hoping that others will pick up on their signals or magically put the pieces together correctly. Even worse, reactive behaviour sometimes can include complaining, magnifying and gossiping to others about whatever is lacking. Be proactive instead. State your needs clearly, communicate with clarity and kindness. Being proactive in your daily work (and life) is actually a very effective form of stress management.

Another study (Gerhardt, Aschenbaum, Newman 2009) showed that when employees are allowed to set their own goals and manage their own time and environment, they perform more productively.[5] The study also recognised that proactive skills can be taught to those who may not naturally have them and recommended that employees who demonstrated these skills already should be actively encouraged to use them to the fullest benefit of the whole organisation. To encourage and 'train' proactive behaviour, let employees know you are interested in their thoughts and ideas about the business, welcome new suggestions and provide opportunities for suggestions and ideas to be shared openly. Make sure you enable employees to be truly accountable for their work too and trust them to own whatever project they are working on. This creates confidence and confidence creates boldness and a willingness to try different approaches.

Consider this

Be solutions focused

One of the greatest traits of effective people is good problem-solving skills. We are all going to run into problems. It's how you handle them that makes you effective. The most effective way to handle a problem is to focus on finding a solution. Focusing on things that are out of your control is a waste of time, so focus on what you can control with the final outcome.

Networking is definitely seen as a proactive behaviour. Networking should not be the transactional 'working a room' approach, but far more about building genuine relationships, both face to face and online through professional social media channels. LinkedIn is one of the number one recruitment sites because companies recruiting can search easily for specific skill sets.[6] A good LinkedIn profile is now seen as being more reliable than a CV – this is because it is quite difficult to lie on your LinkedIn profile; if you've been to a particular university, for example, you are likely to have connections and endorsements that reflect this. LinkedIn makes it easier to show off your projects and work and recommendations from others who know your work. Best of all, LinkedIn allows you to connect with as many people as you wish and create many different professional connections. As with any other social media, it needs to be used thoughtfully. There can be a fine line between networking and self-promoting. We love to run networking events in connection with our workshops – the emphasis is very much on bringing people from different industries together and 'seeing what happens'. It's about creating an environment where people can have meaningful conversations, feel that the time spent was worthwhile and leave feeling enriched with new ideas and connections. People are free to decide if they want to take any of the conversations forward. When it comes to networking and even though many great professional working relationships may begin on online, they are best nurtured through regular face-to-face meetings.

> relationships are the key to successful networking face-to-face and on sites such as LinkedIn

Whether networking online or offline, it will always be about nurturing relationships, visibility and transparency. Just as you can't expect to walk into a crowded room and make meaningful connections without looking to help or collaborate with others, sticking a profile up on LinkedIn and not actively following the professional network etiquette is not being proactive. What is the etiquette online? It isn't always clear. Aside from the obvious things regarding how your profile is written and a clear headshot (the equivalent of being appropriately dressed for a business function), you need to be interacting with your network by posting interesting articles, inviting others to connect with you using more than the generic LinkedIn invite message, seeking out and offering opportunities and support. All of this is self-initiated, change-orientated and future-orientated.

What makes being proactive challenging?

Woody Allen once famously said that '90 per cent of life is just showing up'. To some extent this is true, I suppose, but proactivity has to be more than merely 'showing up'. If we are proactive by nature, we are also more likely to be resilient and positive (see the chapters on resilience and optimism), and we need to be because we are likely to take a lot of knocks. If you're being proactive, you also have to be prepared for rejection and 'no' answers. If we are not proactive by nature and take a few knocks and then are not resilient enough to bounce back, that might prevent us from being proactive in the future – that is, 'I did show up but nothing happened!'. Proactive people persevere in their efforts. They won't be happy with saying things like, 'Well, at least I tried' or 'I did my best'. So often you hear these sentiments as a kind of rationale for why something did not work out as expected instead of actually acknowledging that just maybe one's best was not good enough and to work out how to get better or try out different approaches.

Proactive personality traits have been proven to be related to other personality dimensions, such as extraversion and openness to experience.[7] If a person is naturally introverted, this may prevent them from being as proactive as they need to be but not always. The available research also clearly shows that proactive behaviour comes from more than just personality. It's also strongly driven by situational cues, such as an autonomous environment or a supportive coach, for example. So someone who is introverted can be influenced to be proactive positively by a coach and can be coached towards changing their behaviour and reaching desired goals, thus becoming the driving force in their own life. Because being proactive is also strongly linked to optimism and resilience, an introvert who consistently takes positive action and is resilient is far more likely to be proactive and their possible reluctance at times to 'reach out' as an extrovert will not impede this at all.

being an extrovert doesn't necessarily mean you'll be proactive, and being an introvert doesn't necessarily mean you won't be

Being proactive can make demands on your time and mental and physical resources because it often means doing things over and beyond what might be expected or required. Some people are naturally lazy or don't want to be bothered with making an effort to be proactive. Again, this is a personal choice. 'Effort is one of the things that gives meaning to life. Effort means you care about something, that something is important to you and you are willing to work for it.'[8] (Carol Dweck, *Self-Theories: Their Role in Motivation, Personality, and Development.*) It could well be that people who 'don't want to be bothered' really do mean it, and if there is something that they care enough about, they are actually able to find it in themselves to be very proactive.

Another barrier to being proactive is a tendency to blame circumstances for a negative situation. This will then result in reactive behaviour. So, if someone treats you badly and you respond by reacting aggressively or negatively, you are more likely to feel bad as a result. If you are proactively pursuing a goal, suffer a setback and then blame your circumstances, you are defaulting to being reactive. One of the reasons being proactive is strongly connected with optimism (see the chapter on optimism) is because optimistic people will tend to think differently about setbacks or a negative situation.

'Look at the word responsibility – "response-ability" – the ability to choose your response. Highly proactive people recognize that responsibility. They do not blame

> *circumstances, conditions, or conditioning for their behavior.*
> *Their behavior is a product of their own conscious choice,*
> *based on values, rather than a product of their conditions,*
> *based on feeling.'*
>
> Stephen Covey, American educator and author

Our fast-moving lifestyles also mean that, in the short term, that space between stimulus and response is very small. We are busy and focused and flit quickly from one deadline and task to another with energy and flair. We consider ourselves to be proactive when actually it's just more of the reactive. Our very perception of what being proactive means can be, in itself, a barrier.

Try this

Slow down

If you're constantly rushing from task to task, deadline to deadline and day-to-day, it's easy to feel out of control rather than in control. Take time to reflect. Take time to plan your week, take time to plan your day. And that doesn't mean a checklist of things you have to get done. It means conscientiously thinking about how you want to approach different situations and events and what goals you want to pursue.

_____

_____

_____

Procrastination can be a huge issue when it comes to being proactive. This is mainly because of our inability to handle distractions. We are probably all familiar with logging on to our computer to do something specific whether that is paying a bill or working on a project and then getting side-tracked by an email or a thought to search a term or look something up on a web page. Suddenly a significant amount of time has passed.

that space between stimulus and response is getting smaller and smaller

Procrastination can also manifest itself in other ways like staying up too late and binge-watching box sets or avoiding having a potentially challenging or confrontational discussion.

According to Dr Piers Steel, author of *The Procrastination Equation*, 95 per cent of us are procrastinators![9] And some of this must surely be driven by our frenzied lifestyles and shorter attention spans. We surf the Internet instead of tackling that project, or we put off making an important phone call or a crucial task because something else today has eaten into our time. We all do this to a certain extent so that means we are all prone to procrastination and this can threaten our ability to be proactive. Planning and self-discipline have to be key components of being proactive.

'the most important thing is what is right in front of you. Focus on things one step at a time, one action at a time.'

Oprah Winfrey, American media executive, talkshow host and philanthropist

Try this

Eat the elephant one bite at a time

If you find yourself procrastinating, putting something off or just not giving something your full focus and attention, break things down into manageable steps and celebrate incremental progress. What's important is to take that first step. Writing a report? Can you get the headings and the structure done? Set some manageable goals for yourself, achieve them and track your progress.

Put simply, being proactive means doing the things you need to do before you need to do them – like regularly changing the oil in your car instead of waiting for it to start sputtering and making strange noises. When you are proactive, you keep your car running smoothly and prevent costly repairs further down the line. The investment in getting your oil changed regularly is minimal compared to the consequences in the longer term of not doing so.

Top tip

Being proactive *takes time,* since you have to consider your options, weigh alternatives and *make your own decisions* in order to achieve your goals. A reactive behaviour is influenced by the environment and outside forces.

Possibly one of the biggest deterrents to being proactive is fear. This is usually fear of the outcome, that is, rejection, failure or just something changing. That is why doing things in small steps that help remove that fear is important. Find ways to remove that fear and you will take more risks, be more innovative, feel more confident and be more proactive. That is a virtuous cycle, as the more proactive you are, the more risks you are likely to take because you feel more confident and in control.

Try this

Can you identify a specific time in the recent past when you failed to be proactive and regretted it? What happened and what were the results? Looking back, what would you have done differently?

_____

_____

_____

How to become more proactive

I revisit Stephen Covey here because proactivity is such a central focus of his book *The 7 Habits of Highly Effective People* and the very first habit is being proactive and responsible for our own lives. Viktor Frankl (Holocaust survivor)[10] says there are three central values in life: the experiential (that which happens to us), the creative (that which we bring into existence) and the attitudinal (our response to difficult circumstances). What matters most is *how* we respond to what we experience in life. Proactivity is grounded in facing reality but also understanding we have the power to choose a positive response to our circumstances. It's also about understanding what factors we can influence and what we can't. There is no point in devoting energy to things outside of our control, but by focusing on elements we can ourselves change, our chance of influencing those very things we can't control seems to magically change!

Try this exercise for some immediate ways to become more proactive in the midst of a difficult situation. You can download it here – https://unimenta.com/being-proactive/

If being proactive is a habit, then habits can be learned. It is said that it takes 21 days to form a new habit. However, we know from things such as resolutions made at the beginning of a new year, that many of us cannot even last a few days, let alone 21 days. It's as if we've forgotten how to stick at things and persevere. Think about the Olympics. Olympian athletes spend years perfecting and honing something very specific in order to compete. They believe in their abilities, their resilience in the face of adversity and in the opportunity to triumph. And

think like an Olympian

they keep at it. Their mindsets, their attitude, their determination, rigour and their psychological processes are applicable to anyone seeking to be proactive. The clearer your goals and the more excited you are about them, the more motivated you will be to achieve them. Habits are developed when we believe they are worth developing.

If you want to be proactive, then the goals you set for yourself need to be things you really want to do and you need to make time for planning and setting them. Not many people sit down and plan their lives, their years, their months, their days. Sure, some of us make to-do lists, keep diaries and so on, but it's not the same. There is a long-term aspect to being proactive, as we know, and that is where the goal-setting and life management comes in.

How we respond in the moment and day-to-day is the short-term aspect of being proactive.

Remember:

- **Long-term and strategic** – This means being open for new opportunities, anticipating and preventing problems, persevering despite obstacles, achieving positive results and taking control of your own life. It also means being more self-aware and building in more of a work–life balance. You are using your own principles and values to make decisions.

- **Short-term** – This means small things you can do in the moment, in that space between stimulus and response. These things may include reflecting before you respond to that email, focusing and listening attentively, making time for yourself or taking a deep breath before you respond to an aggressive colleague or boss.

> to be proactive in the short term means being more thoughtful and reflective, as well as more self-aware

In order to be proactive in the long term, it's important to develop foresight. This means learning to anticipate problems, understanding how things work and looking for patterns while at the same time not expecting how things went in the past to be a predictor for how they might go in the future. Proactive people are able to pre-empt possible obstacles by working out ways to manage them in advance.

Try this for developing foresight:

1. **PREDICT** – Learn to anticipate problems and events. That means taking the time to understand how things work, read documentation fully, question your own assumptions and look for patterns. Use your imagination when predicting future outcomes so that you are not expecting the past to be an accurate predictor for the future. Proactive people are always on their toes. Come up with a few scenarios for how things might unfold.

2. **PREVENT** – Proactive people foresee potential obstacles (without leaning to negativity) and exert power to find ways to overcome them before those obstacles turn into cement roadblocks. Thus, they will prevent problems that others would simply say in hindsight were unavoidable. Don't get swept up in feelings of powerlessness. When challenges approach, confront them head-on before they grow into real problems.

3. **PLAN** – Plan for the future. Avoid one-step 'here and now' thinking and instead anticipate long-term consequences. Bring the future into the present – just ask what can you to today to ensure success tomorrow? Every decision is a link in a chain of events.

4. **PARTICIPATE** – If you're proactive, you are an active participant and you are involved. It's all about taking initiative and being part of the solution. You are always going to be one piece of the whole and you influence – and are influenced by – the actions of others. Don't simply react to them. Engage with them. Make a contribution.

5. **PERFORM** – You must be decisive and willing to do the work now. You need to override any natural tendency to procrastinate and instead take ownership of your actions and decisions and hold yourself accountable. Stand behind your decisions. If you've been proactive, then you have taken careful, thoughtful steps to choose the right path rather than reacting emotionally and impulsively to your environment.

The role of education

Education and training can definitely help develop proactivity, and research supports this.[11] Parents can help children and teenagers to be proactive, and indeed must if they are to develop strong proactive habits later in life. When a child meets with failure or problems, it's important to help him/her understand how to interpret that and what actions can be taken to improve the situation. It's important for a child to learn that he/she can impact his immediate environment for the better by actions taken, and that even if those initiatives don't work out, he/she can try something else.

Consider this

It is a great aim to help a young person set goals and then work to achieve those goals. However, if we don't do this ourselves, it might be hard to teach this to our kids! Anything that enables incremental progress, such as learning a sport or a musical instrument, encourages proactivity.

Young people need to be taught to be proactive because of their strong natural tendency to react to situations based on their feelings and emotions at the time. Obstacles can quickly become overwhelming to anyone when too much time is spent devoting energy to them. This saps energy and creates hopelessness. Teenagers need to learn how to focus on specific personal goals, create a plan of action, outline necessary steps and set a deadline. Parents and carers need to demonstrate a problem-solving way of thinking. If young people have a role model, whether that's a parent, teacher or other respected adult, and they see this person solving problems without complaining or worrying, they will want to imitate this productive and proactive mindset. Help your kids take responsibility for their lives but do the same yourself! That means not being a victim of circumstances, not being reactive yourself, nor blaming others.

I mentioned the role of coaching in developing proactivity and this can be very beneficial in goal-setting and being accountable to someone else for carrying out the action needed to achieve those goals. Quite often people are simply not proactive because they just have low levels of accountability, both to themselves as well as to others.

Teaching or helping others be more proactive is made up of two main components:

1. taking responsibility for action instead of expecting someone else to think for me, and
2. systemic view – an ability to understand how making a change or shift now will impact something in the future.

Both of these can be taught, but they also need to be practised often and in a positive way. Taking responsibility for action (being accountable) has to do with several emotional skills, so this can be harder to teach. For example, a fear of failure that leads to avoidance has to be treated differently than resistance to change.

Seven steps to being proactive

Try some of these to help you develop your proactivity skills, both in the short and long term. The results you experience may surprise you! Try to record your experiences and what happens as a result.

1. **Watch your language**
For a full day, or for as long as you can, heighten your awareness and listen to your own language and the language of people around you. How often do you hear reactive phrases such as 'There's nothing I can do', 'I have to do xxx' or 'That's just the way I am'. Try re-scripting these to more proactive language, such as 'I have lots of different options', 'I choose to xxx', or 'I can use a different approach and see what happens'.

2 Commit to being proactive

Think of something you have coming up where you might normally behave reactively, or where you might normally not consider taking the initiative. This might be something at work or it may be a personal situation. What might be a proactive way to respond? Remember the gap between stimulus and response and make a commitment to choosing your response.

Write down your reflections and ideas here:

_____

_____

_____

3 Take stock

Think about what is happening at the moment at work or home. Are things how you want them to be? What are some things where you can initiate changes? If you're not working and want to, what changes can you make to your skills and experience to help you find fulfilling, interesting and rewarding work? Do different things or do things differently if something isn't working. If you wait for it to change by itself, it won't happen! Scan for opportunities as much as you can. And when those opportunities come, grab 'em!

Try completing a wheel of life exercise to help you – you can download one here:

https://unimenta.com/being-proactive/

_____

_____

_____

4 Learn something new

If there is something you've always wanted to try, now is the time! Want to learn to sing? Go for it. Travel to an exotic place? Volunteer in a disadvantaged community? Learn to bake? We have so much capacity in us for learning. If you particularly go for learning something you previously thought you would not be able to do, taking steps to reach that goal will significantly develop your ability to be proactive. I love baking but there was a time when I was hopeless at it and didn't even enjoy it. I taught myself to bake and I did this quite deliberately. It helps me focus on detail and precision, which I don't find natural since I prefer to look at the big picture. What is funny now, though, is that others perceive me as being a great baker and being good at it, when actually I find it quite difficult!

What new thing do I want to try?

_____

_____

_____

If it is a new skill, where or how can I go and learn it?

_____

_____

_____

Which countries do I want to visit most?

_____

_____

_____

5 **Start something in your community**

When I first moved to the town where I now live, I dreamed of starting a community gospel choir. I decided to do it and, despite initial rejection and personal misgivings as to whether I could do it or not, I moved forward with it and we now have a strong, powerful choir with 80+ members, from which I get extraordinary satisfaction and fulfilment. Running it is hard work and not always easy, but nothing can beat what you get from knowing you've started something yourself.

Look for opportunities to start something. And if there is something you have always wanted to do or be part of in your community – if it does not exist already, make it happen! Instead of saying 'why me', say 'why not me?'.

What do I want to start?

_____

_____

_____

⑥ Whatever it is, begin it

Goethe said that 'boldness has magic and genius in it', referring to following a goal or dream by taking the first step towards it. Take action. Don't stop at the idea stage. You may have to first define what that goal is, but once you have, start. You are the only one who can!

What goal/dream/project or ambition could I take the first step towards starting right now?

_____

_____

_____

What is the first step I could take towards it? It might be researching something, it might be making a call or asking a question. Try to identify at least three initial first steps you could take in the next couple of days:

_____

_____

_____

What other action steps can I identify that will help me move towards this goal? Remember that writing these down here and now can be very powerful and it's quite likely you'll actually go and do them!

_____

_____

_____

7 Light up the room

For one day try to be a light, not a judge; a model, not a critic.
Choose to be part of the solution, not the problem. Try this
in your relationship, in your family, in your work. Try it the
next time you are in a meeting or having a conversation. Try
it both online and offline. Don't engage in moaning, gossip or
blaming. Work on the one thing you have control over – you!

Try it – what happened as a result?

_____

_____

_____

A day in the life of. . .

Let's take a magnifying glass to the skill of being proactive
through a day in the life of Mark. We'll start with a brief
introduction to Mark, to give a quick snapshot of his life.

About Mark

_Mark is an undergraduate studying media and arts. He isn't sure
what he wants to do when he graduates and hasn't really thought
about it much. He enjoys his media studies and considers himself
lucky to be studying something that is a genuine and strong
interest of his. He's good at his studies and works hard, getting
good grades (he's headed for a First) and is a great communicator,
whether that's giving presentations, managing a team project or
preparing a report. Mark has an active social life and takes full
advantage of everything student life has to offer. He has a steady_

girlfriend, a great relationship with his family and generally life is good. He's done a little bit of work experience but not very much. The long summer break is looming ahead and, as yet, Mark has nothing planned. He might work part-time at the local supermarket and use the money to travel. He knows the job market is potentially tough but he is a confident young man, very likeable and gets great feedback on all his work and team projects. He thinks he will have no problems finding well-paid work on graduation, although he hasn't put much work into updating his CV. Mark lives in a house share. His parents have already told him that when he graduates, he is welcome to move back home and that there is no rush to move out given the economic climate.

Let's have a closer look at a typical day in Mark's life and how building the skill of being proactive can help him.

Mark's typical day

Mark is just finishing his second year of studies. He gets up fairly late as he has no lectures today. He meets up with his girlfriend for coffee and they chat about what they are going to do this weekend. Mark goes to the library at lunch to finish an essay he needs to hand in. He thinks about doing some work on his dissertation topic for next year but decides to put it off – it's such a long time off and he's sure he'll come up with a good topic over the summer. In the afternoon Mark takes part in a student debate on the cost of studying. He thinks himself lucky as he started his degree before tuition fees increased. He's not really affected by the increases but thinks he should support the cause anyway. He then attends a seminar and contributes actively to the discussion related to a lecture earlier that week. Later that day he ambles off to the student bar to meet up with some friends and talk about summer plans. The afternoon stretches into the evening, when he goes for a bite to eat with a group of friends, plays a round of pool in the student bar and enjoys a few more drinks. Life could not be better.

What's going on here?

Mark sounds like a lovely young man and he probably is, but he is actually in real trouble here. He is so relaxed and positive that he is not really anticipating change ahead and thinks he is well equipped to handle the upcoming challenge of finding work when he's anything but. The reality is that jobs in the media industry are extremely hard to come by without any experience and, even if a few years ago Mark could have got by on his charm, high grades and enthusiasm, it's not going to be enough in today's job climate. Although Mark is not a reactive person, as such, he still gives the perception of being quite lazy and he's not really taking any responsibility for his life and its direction. He's coasting a bit, and for a while this will work because of his personality and likeability. He is also obviously intelligent, hardworking and has some good skills that he could be making more of.

His parents are not really helping by reassuring Mark that he can move back home. They are, in their own way, feeding into a self-fulfilling prophecy of a 'tough job market for graduates' and, therefore, no jobs. They see all their friends' children moving back home so mean well, but just because it's competitive out there doesn't necessarily mean there aren't any jobs going.

One day, Mark goes to a talk held at his university about the soft skills you need to get ahead. He's curious as he thinks he has quite strong soft skills.

What happens when Mark starts to put some of the ideas about being proactive into practice?

Let's revisit Mark's 'typical day' six months later.

How Mark's life has moved forward

Mark is now in his final year of studies. He decided not to travel over the summer after all and, instead, spent half the time

*working and saving a bit of money, as he reckons this might
be useful for when he graduates, even if he does not have large
debts to pay off. He definitely does not want to move back in with
his parents when he graduates so he is quite motivated. He also
managed to get some work experience with a reputable media
company – it was only for two weeks, unpaid and very basic, but
he has focused on the transferable skills it has given him and he
is making more of these and working on how to best describe his
soft skills in his CV. He also went into the work experience with
a bright attitude, determined to learn and exceed expectations,
even when he didn't feel like it. He made a positive impression
and has started to build his professional network.*

*Today he is up early working on his dissertation. Although the
company he did work experience for did not want to offer any
promise of future work, Mark asked them if there was a particular
project they wanted support with and he is making this part of
his dissertation. Having a focus like this helps him have more
excitement about the dissertation. It's a huge project but he's
broken it down into more manageable chunks and has started
planning his week more effectively to do the work, rather than
waiting till the last minute. He plans to present the results
and his findings to the company next Spring. Mark hopes the
company may offer him more permanent work as a result, but
even if they don't, his dissertation subject is so topical he feels
more confident about using this as a tool to help find work. As
it's Mark's final year he is looking for other opportunities to get
work experience and to do this alongside his studies at weekends
and in the evenings. He has a couple of interesting leads and
is following these up. Mark presents well so he always tries,
wherever possible, to get a face-to-face meeting. He has learned
that just sending out an email isn't going to get anywhere. Mark
is also planning ahead for when he graduates. He's managed to*

get an extension on the house share so will be able to stay there, for an affordable rent, for a further six months after graduating.

That evening Mark goes out for dinner with his girlfriend. She encourages him to set up a debate himself to help other students be more proactive. For Mark this was not easy to do at first, but now thinking more about what he wants to do and planning is starting to become second nature.

Here we see how proactivity is crucial, even to someone who is actually doing quite well. We really need to up our proactivity to get ahead and to lead more rewarding lives. It is the only way to move forward.

Interested in learning more?

I've put together some extra resources for you:

Baumeister, R. and Tierney, J. (2012) *Willpower: Rediscovering Our Greatest Strength.* Allen Lane.

Bell, R. (2017) *How To Be Here: A Guide to Creating a Life Worth Living.* William Collins.

Coulter, A. (2017) *How to Stop Procrastination and Get More Done.* CreateSpace.

Covey, S. (2004) *The 7 Habits of Highly Effective People*: Personal Workbook. Simon & Schuster.

Duckworth, A. (2017) *Grit: Why Passion and Resilience Are the Secrets to Success.* Vermilion.

Dweck, C. (2017) *Mindset: Changing the Way You Think to Fulfil Your Potential.* Robinson.

Steel, P. (2011) *The Procrastination Equation: How to Stop Putting Things Off and Start Getting More Done.* Pearson Education.

Articles and websites

www.goalcast.com – website with lots of tools, resources and ideas for becoming more proactive.

You can also find more tips, ideas, curated video clips and exercises to strengthen your being proactive skills by visiting https://unimenta.com/being-proactive/

Sign up too for daily tips – a daily quote, tip and video clip on one of the seven skills direct to your inbox. https://unimenta.com/seven-skills/

'Success is going from failure to failure without losing enthusiasm.'

Winston Churchill

Chapter 7

RESILIENCE

When the world is stacked against you, do you rise or do you fall? Do you lash out or do you survive? We all know people who've overcome some amazing obstacles and who seem bulletproof when it comes to life's challenges. In the face of adversity, they seem able to easily bounce back quickly and with little damage. We may even think, 'Would I be that strong?' if faced with a similar situation. On the flip side, we all know people who completely go to pieces when life throws them a curve ball: people who just lose it and can't seem to get it together, no matter what. Resilience is the ability to respond well to pressure, deal with setbacks effectively, respond well to change and challenges and, basically, bounce back. Most importantly, it is not a fixed character trait but an ability and a capacity, which means it can be developed. Research suggests that people who are more psychologically resilient have higher levels of emotional stability, gratitude, purpose in life and altruism. Resilience and happiness definitely seem connected.

Resilient people are goal-orientated, which gives them a reason to get back up and keep going in the face of adversity. They don't give up easily, if ever. Resilient people know their own strengths and they know that they can depend on themselves to do what it takes to get the job done, even if this means going it alone. Yet they can also call on support if they recognise they need it. They keep a sense of proportion, knowing what is reasonable and what is impossible.

resilient people get right back up when life deals a setback

What is resilience?

Resiliency is actually built into the human brain as what's known as an 'adaptive survival mechanism'. This is a behaviour, strategy or technique enabling us to survive. This means that some of us are naturally very resilient and will be able to cope well, even with early stressful life events. However, it also means that some of us may not be as resilient, either because we are not naturally as resilient (down to genetics) and/or due to lack of supporting factors in our environment.

How resilient you are comes down to three main areas:

1   **Your personality and individual characteristics:**
    Resilience is seen as an innate ability that forms part of your personality. This is why we perceive some people as just being far better able to handle setbacks than others. Personality traits here include: the extent a person feels in control of their lives, perseverance, emotional awareness, optimism, perspective, sense of humour, self-belief and the ability to problem solve.[1]
    These are also traits you can develop and nurture too.

2   **Your environment:** Resilience is seen as being wholly dependent on your experiences and how you interact with your environment. So, factors external to you will determine how resilient you are, such as how much social or family support there is in place at the time.[2]

3   **You and your environment:** Resilience is a product of a person's personality, in combination with external influences such as family, peers and social environment.[3] What this means is a combination of 1 and 2. Someone with both a personality prone to resilience as well as strong environmental support may well be incredibly well equipped to deal with setbacks and difficulties as they go through their lives. And you

can actively focus on both of these areas to ensure that you too are well equipped.

Consider this

Who would you describe as resilient? (Friend, relative or celebrity!)

_____

_____

_____

_____

You may notice that they share some of these characteristics:

- They tend to have clear and focus-specific goals they are working towards proactively.
- They are self-aware and have a good sense of their strengths and weaknesses.
- They tend to respond to negative events positively and flexibly.
- They take risks and learn from their mistakes.
- They have clear driving values and a distinct sense of purpose in their lives.
- They are often reflective and evaluate situations and events carefully.
- They have a strong personal and professional support network around them.

We can also build resilience simply by going through adversity. We all know of people who have suffered enormous hardship while growing up, and yet emerge from this as powerful human beings making a great success of their lives. We also see the opposite. This is where the personality and environment issues mentioned come into play. The extent to which they are there or are nurtured and developed is what determines just how resilient someone may be.

I believe I probably am naturally resilient, but also that I have built up my resilience by experiencing difficult times growing up. Part of that included having very broken schooling, which meant I had to gain my education as a mature student in my twenties as a single parent. But not having ever studied mathematics properly and a fear of numbers meant that it was extremely difficult for me to get into the leading business school of my choice to do an MBA in my thirties. I failed on the first two attempts because of my lack of numeracy skills and was told in a personal phone call from the subject Head of Finance that I should apply somewhere else. Most people probably would have accepted that but I believed I could somehow learn those basic maths skills that would enable me to pass the numeracy test. I'd done brilliantly in all the other assessments and the interview. I requested one last go to get in, even though this was not normal policy. This was granted and I spent two weeks with an A-level maths tutor learning all the mathematics skills I should have learned aged 18. I passed the test, got into Cranfield and ended up taking Finance electives in my second year and doing very well. And the Head of Finance later admitted he had been wrong about me! My resilience skills, in this case, changed my life.

I know that resilience is something that we **can** learn and develop (and need to), even though some of us may be more naturally disposed to being resilient than others. This is not to say, though, that we need deliberately to seek out adversity in order to build better resilience.

Adversity **can** develop resilience. A study, which focused on studying people's resilience in connection with economic recession, showed that capacity to be resilient **increased most** during the toughest of times and was not worn down by all the uncertainty and rapid change.[4] This proves, then, that we do have far more capacity to cope than we think.

Resilient people tend to view life's difficulties, regardless of how many there are of them, as challenges and respond with action. What I mean by this is that they are almost accepting of the fact that there will be setbacks and challenges in life or in a specific endeavour but feel in control enough to respond, rather than be reactive. Setbacks force us to take risks, learn and grow. There are unlimited opportunities for us to develop our capacity for resilience. In fact, you may be far more resilient than you think. Everyone has experienced setbacks – it is part of life. We often resist setbacks or waste energy, more

> accept setbacks, embrace them, look for the opportunity in them

than is needed, on denial, anger, endless discussion with friends and family. It's ok to experience some emotion when dealing with a setback – what's not ok is allowing it to continue for too long. Resilient people focus fast on taking action in the face of setback. They do that first through acceptance.

Optimism is strongly linked with being resilient – choosing to focus on maximising strengths and accomplishments and choosing to look at the positives in a situation. The word 'choosing' to look at the positives is deliberate – we really do choose what we decide to think about or expend energy on. The ability to do this and to learn from adversity is dependent on whether you interpret setbacks or problems as triggered by personal choice or by the choices of others. There are two classic ways of responding to adversity, both of which have a connection with optimism and positive psychology (see also the chapter on optimism). The first is to assess a situation critically and the second is to take it personally. An example of this is, let's say you did badly on a piece of work or a project that you worked very hard on. Your response to this can be to tell yourself: 'I have been under a lot of pressure lately and haven't been sleeping well. Even though I worked hard, I know my mind wasn't really focused and I wasn't able to give this my best shot' – critically assessed. The second way of dealing with this setback is to say to yourself: 'I did badly because I am just not good at this. I'm obviously not the right person for this kind of project'. Positive psychology suggests that the healthier way of viewing adversity is the first one. The more you personalise a setback, the harder it is to bounce back from it because the second method suggests something more permanent that you cannot easily change: 'I am just no good at this kind of work', which, of course, may or may not be true.

Try this

Face your fears – We tend to avoid whatever makes us uncomfortable but if you don't face your fears, it restricts your life and you never extinguish what is making you afraid. Try to think of fear as a friend – learn as much as you can about it and see it as an opportunity to develop any specific skills that might help you face it more effectively.

Embrace change – Change isn't easy but it is inevitable so why fight it? To build resilience, you must come to terms with the fact that you cannot control all of the circumstances surrounding you, but you can control the way you react towards them. Tackle problems head-on and choose to be optimistic regarding the ultimate outcome.

Be vulnerable – Sometimes being resilient is being willing to be vulnerable in potentially difficult situations. It is easy to avoid people who voice different opinions or viewpoints, for example, especially if you are a natural introvert like me! Use listening skills – really totally and utterly LISTEN and look for an opportunity to support or build on someone else's viewpoint and to then include your own.

Make mistakes – The more mistakes you make, the more resilient you'll be. Sometimes that simply means taking risks – going for that new project, taking on the presentation, saying 'yes' to opportunities. Yes, you may make mistakes but this is how we learn and develop the most.

Think about this like exercising a muscle – the more you consciously practise these things, the stronger the skill becomes. Speaking of exercising, this is correlated with strong levels of resilience, maybe due to the endorphins produced and feeling physically stronger, or both. If we believe there is a connection between body and mind, then exercising and being fit and strong physically and building that strength may also help increase resilience skills. Exercise contributes to both physical and mental resilience because it helps you respond in more adaptive ways. So going to the gym may be even better for us than we think, although it doesn't matter if it's walking, swimming, playing golf or scuba diving – any type of movement can help.

How mindfulness boosts resilience: There is a substantial body of research that links mindfulness practice to resilience including:

- Making it easier to cope with difficult thoughts and manage stress effectively
- Increasing ability to see the bigger picture with calm and with clarity
- Encouraging being in the present moment more – being with what *is*
- Helping with practising acceptance
- Building stronger self-awareness
- Avoiding getting stuck in an emotionally unhealthy story
- Slowing you down so that you are more effective
- Encouraging true reflective practice!

It's also about *doing* things mindfully – e.g. having that cup of tea without scrolling at the same time!

Practising mindfulness also gives your productivity levels a boost and plays a big role in empathy skills too!

Refer to the empathy chapter for more on mindfulness exercises. You can download some mindfulness here:

https://unimenta.com/empathy/

'Our greatest glory is not in never falling, but in rising every time we fall.'

Confucius, 5th-century Chinese educator and philosopher

Why resilience is a must-have skill

Your resilience skills are what enable you to not only respond to challenges and change well but to also become happier and more confident knowing you have the resources to handle anything life throws at you. Your resilience skills help you to become happier and more comfortable with taking risks and with failing so that you learn faster and simply become better at coping with the present and building yourself a better future.

If you have just lost your job, you can't afford to not bounce back quickly. But resilience is also important simply because the dynamic conditions we live in mean that we need to be willing to try new things and venture into places we have not been, or maybe where no one has been before. It's far easier (and comfortable) to do things the way they have always been done but that will not necessarily give you what you need or want. Taking risks and trying new things inevitably means you will make mistakes, and that is where resilience comes in: knowing that it is ok to make mistakes, learn and move on applying that learning.

I think being resilient can also buffer you against what may feel like risky behaviour. I believe that to thrive in this life you probably have to take more risks than ever. My husband, for example, changed his work voluntarily and purposefully a few years ago to pre-empt a work situation that he felt could otherwise, in the next few years, change dramatically and not in his favour. Although things were going really quite well in his current employment, he felt that the nature and corporate culture of his firm would not help him to develop the long-term value needed. Instead, he decided to join forces with a trusted colleague to help set up and run a boutique consultancy firm – more risk but also potentially more reward, both emotionally and potentially

> **Never be afraid to let go of the good so you can go for the great**

monetarily, and certainly better in terms of work–life balance. It also gives the opportunity to present the very best of himself, up his game and sharpen his skills. It's exciting, and we now know that it was the best career move he could have made. It's going well and he seems much happier with this decision, even though there are also huge challenges ahead of him. Being resilient is also being more aware of opportunities and actively seeking those out, **ahead** of any potential adversity or problems. Resilience is, therefore, also about taking control.

Try this

Identifying thinking errors: *These are simply ways that our brain tries to make sense of a situation internally. You can train your brain to 'reframe' the way you see something simply by noticing when you do one of these classic 'thinking errors'. Remember, we are all prone to them!*

- All or nothing thinking – *'This happens to me every time!'*
- Overgeneralising – *'This always happens.'*
- Mental filter – everything is negative – *'Everyone has it in for me at the moment' or 'This is an absolute catastrophe.'*
- Jumping to conclusions – *'Obviously they thought I was not up to the task.'*
- Mindreading – *'She things I'm not very organised.'*
- Magnification – *'This is a disaster.'*
- Emotional reasoning – *'If X does not happen I'll feel utterly hopeless.'*
- Should, must, ought to statements – *'I should have done XYZ.'*
- Labelling and mislabelling – *'I'm bad at technical stuff.'*

We use this exercise on our workshops and it really heightens awareness of just how much we engage in this kind of thinking.

As well as increasing individual resilience, it is important to actively seek out formal and informal support networks, both face-to-face and virtual, to buffer against the changing dynamics of the workplace and society in general. We see this happening more and more with sites such as LinkedIn, and other social media that have become the 'after-work economy' of informal drinks and dinners, where relationships, networking and your personal credibility really matter.[5] Resilient individuals tend to have strong social networks both online and offline.

Top tip

Build a strong social and professional network

Who is in your network? Make sure you have a group of friends and family who are there for you. In the workplace look for colleagues, mentors and role models you trust. One of the single and most important things when it comes to resilience, is having a strong, supportive community on whom you can rely and who can rely on you. Being around people you trust makes you more likely to use active coping techniques such as gathering information and problem solving rather than passive coping ones like avoidance and denial.

Who are the most important people in your network?

_____

_____

_____

How resilience helps us at work

The modern workplace can be very stressful. At work, resilient people are better able to deal with the demands placed upon them, especially where those demands might require them to be dealing with constantly changing priorities and a heavy workload.

Resilience is not something passive – it is an active process. Think of it as being simply that resilient people engage in more behaviours that help them respond better to stress and pressures.

> 'Why is it that some people thrive in the face of challenge and adversity at work, while others panic and withdraw into themselves? And why is it these same people who appear to get ahead while others tread water, or slowly drown in turbulent waters of life?
>
> Most people think that a combination of intelligence, long working hours and lots of experience allows people to thrive in potentially hostile working environments. In fact, it is those with resilience who cope best with challenges like constant organisational change and upheaval, impending staff cutbacks, looming deadlines, argumentative meetings and incessant competition from business rivals.
>
> The good news is that although some people seem to be born with more resilience than others, those whose resilience is lower can learn how to boost their ability to cope, thrive and flourish when the going gets tough.' (Centre for Confidence and Well-Being 2006)

Here are some simple ways to actively increase your resilience skills in the workplace:

- **Try to treat problems as a learning process.** This can be challenging, especially if you are new in the workplace or in a new position. Use these challenges as opportunities for you to develop whether that is by mastering new skills or developing your self-awareness and becoming more reflective. Ask for feedback, be open and willing to learn from every single experience. It's also important to train your mind to look for the positives – review your day and work out what went well and why.

- **Allow small stresses and strains to wash over you.** If you react to every single daily stressor from your train being late to an overload of emails you will quickly create more stress. Become more aware of how you interpret and respond to events.

- **Develop realistic goals for yourself.** Cultivate the attitude of constantly learning and moving towards these goals in small steps. Positive action brings a sense of control and achievement

- **Compartmentalise your cognitive load.** We receive millions of bits of information every single second, yet our brains can only effectively process a tiny percentage of that. Although you may not be able to control the vast amount of information you are hit with, you can boost the way you process it by compartmentalising some of your tasks. This means grouping things together into chunks like having a specific time for checking email, using certain times of the day for big writing tasks or projects and trying things like having some of your meetings outdoors or even during a walk. For example, the days that I blocked out two to three hours for writing this text, saving email or meetings for later in the day I definitely achieved more and felt more in control.

Perseverance and resilience

A key facet of being resilient is the ability and willingness to stick at something for a period of time. Why is it difficult for some people to persevere? It's because perseverance is about sustaining effort and interest. These days we lose interest far more quickly than ever before because we have so many options available to us in the first place. Technology and speed also mean that we expect an immediate return for our efforts. We lose interest quickly and so we are quite capable of getting excited about multiple projects and achieving none.

Another important facet of resilience is mindset. Dr Carol Dweck, a leading researcher in the field of motivation, has conducted numerous studies into the link between achievement and success. In a fixed mindset, people believe that qualities like intelligence or talent are fixed traits. In a growth mindset, people believe that their most basic abilities can be developed through dedication and hard work and that brains and talent are just the starting point. This growth view creates a love of learning and a resilience that is essential for great accomplishment.

Top tip – Find a sense of purpose

Having a well-defined purpose in life can not only lead to superior cognitive functioning but can also make you more likely to roll with the punches. People with a purpose or mission in life tend to be more resilient. How? Start developing a positive outlook for your future. Try creating a vision board to help you achieve your goals. Living with purpose will afford you a better understanding of why certain things happen and you'll be better equipped to handle what comes your way. Download the free worksheet for creating your own vision board: https://unimenta.com/resilience/

How to become more resilient

TED conferences bring together talented and successful people from across the globe from the fields of technology, entertainment and design to give 10- to 15-minute presentations on a topic.[6] Richard St John gives a great TED talk about success and he mentions eight key points, one of which is the acronym C.R.A.P.[7] You have to be able to deal with C.R.A.P. to be truly successful and I think this applies to anyone who is trying out new things whether it's a new business, reinventing themselves or striving to stand out in a competitive market. The acronym stands for the following, and sums up resilience really well:

- **Criticism** – If you are going to take risks, grab opportunities, make changes in your life or indeed for any type of new initiative you take on, you will face criticism. You have to be able to handle and deal with criticism without becoming defensive and willing to look at it constructively.

- **Rejection** – We know this is going to happen more than once in life. If you can't bounce back fast, you will have problems. Funnily enough, this actually becomes easier and quicker to do the more you are rejected! So go for lots of things and take more risks!

- **Assholes** – Everywhere in life we are going to encounter people who are aggressive, drain our energy, want to take credit or want to exert power and influence over us; it's unavoidable and you have to be able to deal with them! Choose your battles and let things that do not matter wash over you.

- **Pressure** – We are under more pressure than ever before and there will always be pressures and deadlines. We have to be able to manage ourselves effectively to handle these pressures with grace and ease. Otherwise they will handle us.

The best way to handle C.R.A.P. is by accepting that you will face these elements and have strategies in place to deal with them rather than wasting your energy on avoiding or reacting. It's almost like a boxer in the ring – if you're rejected, how long do you really want to be on the ground for? If you're dealing with someone who is aggressive, what are better ways of responding to this that don't ruin your day or zap your own positive energy? Empathy is quite handy here as well! How can you plan and manage your time to handle the pressures?

Try this

Think of a project or venture you are currently working on:

What sort of criticism or 'nay-sayers' are you likely to face? Write down typical criticism you may experience. If you find it hard to think of something specific, imagine a little nay-sayer on your shoulder (we all have them). What might they be saying?

_____

_____

_____

Now decide how you are going to deal with this criticism. First decide if there is anything valid or constructive in it. If there is then take this on board. If there isn't then think about what you can do to respond to this. Write down your responses here:

_____

_____

_____

How do you typically handle rejection? What are some more positive ways of handling it? If a proposal is rejected or someone is not in favour of your idea, there are some positive ways of handling this. Perhaps the timing was not right, perhaps you missed out some important points that were in their criteria, perhaps you are not the right fit. What are some positives that you can take from this and move on constructively?

_____

_____

_____

Equipping yourself to respond to adversity

Why is one person able to bounce back more easily than another? Take two different people who have lost their jobs. Let's call them Jack and Kyle. Both of them respond by being sad, listless, anxious about the future and indecisive. Jack gets his head together after a few weeks of this, tells himself the economy is going through a bad patch and that he has marketable skills. He updates his CV, sends it out to dozens of companies in his network and gets rejected by them all. He then tries six more companies, using a more thoughtful and focused approach and eventually lands a position. The position may well be in a different field and applying his skills in a different way.

Kyle, on the other hand, spirals into a kind of self-perceived hopelessness, believing he got fired because he can't perform under pressure, and does not try again because of a paralysing fear of failure. He begins drinking in the evenings because he feels depressed. He makes a few half-hearted attempts at brushing up his CV but after being rejected twice he tells himself he just 'doesn't have what it takes' to compete in this fierce economy and that there are therefore no jobs out there for him.

> *'Only those who dare to fail greatly, can ever achieve greatly.'*
>
> Robert F. Kennedy, former United States Attorney General

The speed at which you are able to bounce back and move forward positively comes back to the classic ways in which we tend to respond to adversity based on that combination of natural characteristics and personality traits, together with the type of support network we have (or have had in the past) around us. In Jack's case, he may naturally be more resilient and also have the strong support of family and friends. Kyle, on the other hand, may be less resilient naturally and may not have strong family or social support. He may possibly also have other issues going on in his life that means he is more vulnerable to pressure.

Resilience can be developed, and in fact does develop, without intervention through life experiences. We don't necessarily have to go through repeated experiences of adversity.

Try this simple awareness-raising exercise here to understand how you tend to respond to difficult experiences. You may discover that you are more resilient than you think! You can download it here:

https://unimenta.com/resilience/

Learn optimism

Martin Seligman says, in his book *Flourish*, that the key to building resistance is learned optimism. His research shows that people who don't give up and are resilient have a habit of interpreting setbacks as temporary and changeable and suggests that people can be taught how to think like optimists.

The Penn Resiliency Program, designed by Jane Gillham, PhD, and Karen Reivich, PhD, has created an innovative set of lessons for young people.[8] Based on cognitive–behavioural theory, the program teaches resilience skills by introducing resilience concepts through role-play, short stories and cartoons.[9] These are then practised using a variety of tools for solving problems and difficult situations, which are based on real-life situations. The skills practised are assertiveness, negotiation, decision making, social problem solving and relaxation. These projects are now being taught to teachers in Australia and the UK to train them in how to deliver resilience skills. The same type of training has also been developed and is being successfully used in the US Army. Such projects are now starting to become more mainstream as the growing awareness for resilience skills increases.

Case study – delivering our Resilience workshop to National Health Service (NHS) doctors and nurses in the UK:

'So I tried to free up an airway – didn't work. I then went through 5 more avenues to get an airway to the patient. None of them worked and he died right there on the operating table. I then had to go home and be "normal" with my family.' – Trainee anaesthetist in response to Resilience context setting exercise.

We deliver our workshop to a range of different groups – it's always different because the group decides what they want to focus on in relation to adaptability, empathy, critical thinking, integrity, optimism, being proactive and resilience. Delivering this awareness-raising workshop to NHS junior doctors is a privilege and an eye opener. These are people who deal with life and death every single day, who never have time to step back from their work to focus on themselves and on this kind of personal development. For them being resilient is all about doing their job effectively but at the same time being able to achieve some kind of work—life balance in the midst of it all.

Try this

When you are going through a tough experience, it can be helpful to think about the following:

- **How important will this be in 6 months?** – *Often what you may be finding very difficult right now, whether that is a disagreement, a setback or rejection may simply be forgotten or less important in 6 months – in other words, what you are experiencing is temporary and recognising that is a key facet of optimism and resilience.*

- **On a scale of 1–10 how awful is this feeling right now? Might it be different if I asked the same question tomorrow, next week?** – *This can be a useful indicator of the temporary nature of our emotions and feelings. If you really want to test this out, simply keep a journal and write your responses – this may be one of the fastest ways to encourage self-awareness.*

- **Tell yourself 'I am having a difficult day – it will pass'** – *Just voicing this can be very powerful as can be recognising that you need to take care of yourself when you are feeling like this.*

- **Learning from the past** – *When have there been other times when I have felt like this? What happened? What helped me most? Can I try any of that to help me now?*

Strengthen your self-awareness

In writing this text I was interested to learn that there are stress inoculation training programmes, known as SIT.[10] Essentially, this is a cognitive–behavioural treatment that is used to help a person gain confidence in their ability to cope with stress and anxiety related to a trauma of some kind. The way it works is that a therapist helps a client become more aware of what triggers stress and helps them come up with coping strategies, which are often simple things such as relaxation and deep breathing. This is resilience training of a kind, as these methods develop self-awareness. Self-awareness is the cornerstone of making any kind of behavioural change – it means you know your strengths and weaknesses and you understand underlying patterns of why you do things a certain way. It also means you understand what can make you stressed, angry or irritated and can start to develop strategies and responses that are more effective than lashing out at others or becoming debilitated by stress.

Get to know your strengths by trying this simple exercise that you can download here:

https://unimenta.com/resilience/

Develop grit

There is considerable evidence that educational interventions in young people can increase their resilience. 'Grit', in psychology, is a person's perseverance and passion for long-term goals and their innate ability to overcome obstacles to reach them (Duckworth et al. 2006).[11] Gritty people are simply more likely to overcome adversity and push themselves towards success. Grit is closely linked to perseverance, purpose and passion but can also be dampened if we have an underlying need for things to be more immediate meaning that if something doesn't happen quickly we may justify why we give up.

Try this

How to develop grit

1 **Pursue what interests you** – The first step is to find something that you are passionate about. No need for introspection – get out there and try different things till you find something perfect for you.

2 **Practice, practice, practice** – You're more likely to stick at something you are good at and you get good by hard work and ironing out weaknesses.

3 **Find purpose** – The difference between someone who is just a hard worker and somebody who has real grit is that the latter finds meaning in what they do.

4 **Have hope** – You need to believe that things can improve and you are going to improve them. Research shows people without hope avoid bigger challenges, quit earlier and act helpless. Remember a growth mindset is the attitude that your abilities aren't fixed. Don't focus on innate talent. Believe you can get smarter and better at anything if you work hard.

Take control

A lot of resilience is about feeling in control of your life and of your decisions and choices. Unfortunately, feeling in control can be significantly influenced by holding on to unhelpful beliefs about ourselves. These are types of 'drag anchors' and a bit like the 'all or nothing' thinking mentioned earlier in this chapter. Resilient people believe they can make a difference and be successful.

Try this

Here are six of the most common types of 'drag anchors'. It's easy to get stuck in these unhealthy thoughts, so cultivate awareness of when you tend to do this.

- **I am the victim of my personal history** – Your past does have an impact, but it is no excuse for not improving yourself now and making positive change.

- **There's so much to do it's not even worth trying** – Life is complex, and you now probably have to do more with less. As a result, you may come to believe there are simply so many imperatives that you can't see where to start. Psychologists call this 'agglomeration' – feeling overwhelmed by the volume and complexity of the issues. Break the problem down, establish priorities and take first things first. Action creates an immediate sense of control and positivity.

- **You only get one shot** – Occasionally this may be the case, but not often – especially in circumstances where even the experts can't predict the right way to go. It then becomes a question of trial and error, being willing to make mistakes and learn and take more risks.

- **There's a right answer to everything** – Analysts dream that by scrutinising data hard enough, the 'correct' answer will emerge. This rarely happens in real life. The danger is that analysis becomes a substitute for, rather than a prelude to, action.

- **I'm on my own** – It's easy to believe that you are the only one suffering and that you have to weather the storm alone. The old adage 'a problem shared is a problem halved' works well in these circumstances; talking things through is a source of strength, not a sign of weakness.

- **This isn't fair** – Doctors claim that perpetrators of crimes heal more quickly than their victims. More generally, if you believe you have in some way contributed to a problem, you may feel more motivated to resolve it. If you are not to blame, you tend to dwell on the unfairness of the situation rather than on what can be done.

Get rid of these drag anchors by **reframing**. Recognise when your thinking is negative and immediately turn it around so that it becomes positive.

Seven steps to resilience skills

You can develop your ability to be more resilient – try these seven simple steps to build buffers and become stronger emotionally, psychologically and physically. Try these out as soon as you can in your next meeting or your next conversation. The exercises will have more impact if you record what happened.

1 **Get some perspective**

   Think about something that you are struggling with right now. Ask yourself these questions:

   Tip: Life is always going to have challenges, setbacks and some adversity. One of my favourite quotes is from James Taylor's song 'Shower the People', in which he sings, 'into each life some rain must fall'. Ultimately, we CAN choose the way we think, feel and act in response to circumstances. It may feel very hard to do that sometimes, but we each have the capacity to do this. And, quite simply, the more you do this, the better you will become at it.

   'How can I learn from this experience?'

   _____

   _____

   _____

   'What is the most important thing in this situation?'

   _____

   _____

   _____

   'What are some other ways I can choose to look at this?'

   _____

   _____

   _____

'How can I make a difference in this situation?'

_____

_____

_____

The better the questions we ask, the better answers there will be. Use questions to get the right perspective to tackle the situation. Make the effort and find time to do this.
Be thoughtful about what you do and the decisions you make.

2 **Know how to manage stress**

Psychologists see stress as an energising force – up to a point, beyond which it becomes debilitating. Highly resilient people have a higher tipping point and, when things threaten to get them down, they know how to deal with it. Sources of stress are unique to you: to boost your resilience, you need to identify what your stressors are and how to counteract them. Become more aware of any stress factors in your day. If you know when you are prone to stress, take care of this by building in time for yourself, or reflection space.

What sorts of things trigger stress for me? _Tip: These may tend to happen at a particular time of day, when you are juggling tasks or when you've had a demanding time at work._

_____

_____

_____

How do I respond when I am stressed?

_____

_____

_____

There are also **personality traits** that make some individuals more stress-prone. Look at the list below. If you

tend towards any of these, discipline yourself to reduce or
eliminate them:

- *Displaying hostility*
- *Hiding feelings*
- *Being unable to listen properly*
- *Being over-perfectionist*
- *Having difficulty relaxing*
- *Being generally critical*

Stress management falls into two categories – distraction and
resolution.

Distraction techniques include exercise, breathing deeply,
walking or extracting yourself from the situation. Resolution is
focused on solving the problem.

3   **Know your strengths – trust and use them**

If you are not sure what you're good at, then find out! Try new
things. Think about what you are good at and excel in and
write those down. Then reflect on how much you are using
these strengths in your life and work. The best person to get to
know is always yourself!

What are my signature strengths?

Tip: Think about them in terms of:

- *problem solving*
- *interacting with others*
- *staying motivated and committed*

_____

_____

_____

How can I further develop and use these strengths?

_____

_____

_____

How can I strengthen weaker areas?

_____

_____

_____

Who do I know who has strengths to help with my development areas?

_____

_____

_____

4   **Build proactivity into your life**

If you're proactive, then you're going to pre-empt adversity to some extent, by your actions – that is, asking for help when you need it or making some changes in your work, like my husband did or learning from a mistake and doing something differently next time. Being proactive also means you are more likely to focus on things you can actually control: your thoughts and actions. Practise interpreting events in an upbeat way and focusing on positive action that you can take to improve or change the situation, whatever it is.

What are some things in my life that I want to change or that worry me?

_____

_____

_____

What are some great things about this situation?

_____

_____

_____

What are some positive actions/steps I can take?

_____

5 Look after yourself

This means taking responsibility for your mental and physical health. Get enough sleep, build in balance, exercise regularly, have a massage or acupuncture so that you are physically resilient and alert – there is a strong connection between body and mind. Eat nutritionally balanced meals. Think about practising meditation and Yoga too. General Casey, former commander of multinational forces in Iraq and former Delta Force hero, said: 'The key to psychological fitness is resilience'. Physical fitness is the other half of psychological fitness.

Revisit the 'self-care' exercise in the Empathy chapter.

How well am I sleeping? What can I do to ensure you are getting regular sleep and rest?

Do I exercise regularly? If not, what are some easy ways I might include this in your day – maybe walking more, taking the stairs or going for a swim after work.

How can I build more relaxation and reflection into my day?

---

6 Manage conflict

Conflict occurs when our views differ from those of another person – so we have to deal with conflict every day. The ability to handle it constructively is an important part of resilience – ensuring that the style of resolution is appropriate, given the nature of the conflict and the other party. The 'Conflict Resolution' panel below gives examples and suggested tactics.

Nature of problem	Possible approach
Although I'm annoyed, it's a trivial matter.	This is one to let drop – get over it.
My solution is better than the other person's but their approach could work.	It's not worth fighting over. Win credit for your flexibility.
This is important, something that requires a well-thought-through solution. I have strong views but so does the other person.	Honest, constructive talking and listening. Collaborate to find a solution acceptable to both parties.
I'm convinced I'm right and the other person is wrong.	Use your powers of influence and persuasion. Sell the benefits of your idea or say it's the way it has to be – but in a way that preserves your relationship.

7 Take more risks

Yes, that's right, more risks! In a world that's changing as fast as ours is, the riskiest thing you can do is be stable and take no risks at all. Remember that making mistakes builds your resistance. Remember the movie *The Yes Man*? In it, Jim Carrey plays the role of a guy playing it safe and ends up lonely, bored and without a job or relationship. He decides to say 'yes' to everything that comes his way, with life-changing consequences.

Try saying 'yes' to the next opportunity and challenge that comes your way. Don't overthink – just say 'yes' and see what happens!

_____

_____

_____

Tip: You can learn to take risks, and doing so builds confidence. Start with 'low-stake' risks, such as trying a new route to work or saying 'yes' to an invite to coffee, and build from there. Try to plan risk into each day and week and build it up.

What 'low-stake' risks can I take in the next week?

_____

_____

_____

What other risks can I take? *Try things like asking to be considered for a new project or pitching for a new piece of work or asking someone out on a date*

_____

_____

_____

A day in the life of. . .

Let's take a magnifying glass to the skill of resilience through a day in the life of Andrew. We'll start with a brief introduction to Andrew, to give a quick snapshot of his life.

About Andrew

Andrew is in his late fifties. He's close to the official retirement age but he knows he will probably, very likely, have to keep working because his pension is not going to be enough to live on. He's a financial analyst for a large company and his job has been becoming more and more demanding in recent years. Projects have been short term with less repeat business. The company has made some cuts and bonuses have become very inconsistent. Luckily, Andrew made quite a bit of money during his earlier career and has managed to save. In the good old days he had a personal assistant too, but that stopped a while back, as did any business-class travel on overseas trips.

He's married and his wife is successful in her own right. The children are grown up but their youngest son, who graduated recently, has moved back home as he can't find work. Andrew and his wife also have three young grandchildren, whom they see regularly. They live in a large, bustling city.

Andrew is generally quite easy-going, though he does have a natural tendency to worry and wants to please. He's always focused on working so, although he has a small social circle, these tend to be other couples he and his wife have known for some years. He is interested in theatre, fine wine and cooking but never seems to find any time for these. He's also aware that he does not get much exercise and often sleeps badly due to a constant feeling of unease about his work.

Let's have a closer look at a typical day in Andrew's life and how building the skill of resilience can help him.

Andrew's typical day

Andrew gets up at 7 am and heads for work on public transport. He tends not to have breakfast as he is in a rush and doesn't normally feel that hungry in the mornings. He grabs a cappuccino at the station café. The rush hour is, as always, very bad, and today he manages to spill coffee on his suit, which really irritates him.

Andrew arrives at work, where he's working on an exciting project with a new team who are all quite young. They are very on top of social media and networking and they see this as a key way to start to win new business and projects. They are always coming *up with new ideas and are full of energy. Andrew doesn't really understand social media and thinks he is just not the sort of person who would find it easy to use. Most of the time he ignores it because he just doesn't have the time and he typically has far too many emails to respond to anyway. The team's enthusiasm sometimes makes him feel a bit sluggish and 'past it' even though he does have some ideas for the project.*

The morning tends to zoom by in a flurry of meetings and dealing with correspondence and, before you know it, it's time for lunch. Andrew pops out for a quick sandwich at lunchtime but doesn't really take a break as there's so much to do. He comes back from lunch but tends to feel quite demotivated by this time of the day, the reason for which he can't put his finger on. Consequently, his afternoon is not very productive and when he runs into his boss at the water cooler, he doesn't feel on top of any new projects and believes he came across poorly, although actually his boss was in a terrible rush and just didn't have time to talk to him.

Andrew decides to work late that evening to try and make up for wasting time in the afternoon. He manages to get through his inbox and notes that the new team are setting up a discussion forum on the company's intranet to put together a social media strategy. He idly wonders if he should attend but quickly decides this is something best left to the younger generation.

Andrew gets home quite late and eats a reheated dinner his wife has cooked. They have a quick glass of wine and a catch-up before watching some news and going to bed. As Andrew tries to drop off to sleep, he keeps thinking about the day and wishing things could have gone differently.

What's going on here?

Now, on the face of it, Andrew's life seems fairly run-of-the-mill. Things are ticking over OK, he has a job and nothing too awful has happened. Is he even in need of any resilience skills? Of course he is, and he knows at the back of his mind he has a need. There is a danger that Andrew might get left behind in terms of his work and that he is not protecting himself sufficiently from adversity nor building the resilience skills he will need if, for example, he were to lose his job. He's also not contributing to projects in a proactive way. His company has been making cutbacks but it is also in debt and is not planning on paying out any bonuses in the medium- to long-term future. He hasn't been pulling in any lucrative projects and isn't on top of things at all regarding social media. He's clearly under pressure but doesn't seem to be handling it that well. He's also not looking after himself – he doesn't eat meals regularly and those he eats are not necessarily freshly prepared. He doesn't appear to do much exercise either and sleeps badly. It's easy to not take a lunch break and to work late in the evenings, telling yourself that you're being productive, but the question is are you really being effective at this time? It's also a common side of pressure to take things personally, such as when he encountered his boss at the water cooler. But part of that was also connected with Andrew's own awareness that he isn't being very productive and he probably knows he isn't bringing in enough meaningful projects to the company or contributing any new ideas.

He dismisses the idea of getting to grips with social media by attending the discussion forum, when this might be the very thing to help him get started and he fails to contribute his ideas because he holds a limiting belief that he is 'past it'. The fact is that, even though he stayed late, it probably didn't make that much difference to what he achieved that day.

What would happen if Andrew focused on building his resilience skills?

Let's revisit Andrew's 'typical day' six months later.

How Andrew's life has moved forward

Andrew is healthier these days and looking after himself more. He's started walking part of his way to work and makes sure he eats a little breakfast in the mornings, even if it's only a banana or muesli bar. He also gets to miss some of that rush hour and takes the bus instead. Because his company has been embracing flexible work, he has explored this with them and on two days a week he comes into work later. Andrew spends an hour at home catching up with emails before leaving for work, and so misses the rush hour completely on those days. He finds this makes him more productive. He decided to be more proactive at work and now has regular check-ins with his boss to discuss new projects and ideas, having put together a clearer strategy for himself. He did this by taking some time to take stock of his life and where he wanted to be with this work. Andrew eventually stopped putting it off and decided to dip his toe into social media, and this was a good thing, given that the company generally is now starting to become far more active on industry platforms. What Andrew has discovered, to his delight, is that social media has proved to be a really useful tool for understanding more about his industry and the marketplace and, although he doesn't post regularly, he is certainly looking at it more and is starting to contribute some articles related to his area of expertise. He's even started writing a blog. Social media generally has also given him an unexpected bonus of a stronger communication channel with his children. He's also keeping an eye out for other work opportunities, and both he and his son are working on improving their LinkedIn profiles. Through this he has started to keep in touch with other colleagues who are now working elsewhere and has even rekindled several personal connections too.

When Andrew was asking himself those questions, he also thought about his strengths generally. He realised that he had perhaps, to some extent, pigeonholed himself at work and, although he is not ready to make any drastic changes, he is becoming far more aware of where he can contribute most and this is giving him confidence in what projects to put forward along with ideas for existing ones. He also remembered that he used to be quite good at computer games and loved playing them with his kids when they were younger. This makes the step into social media less daunting and something that he may start to also get quite good at. He has also rediscovered his love of music and theatre – this was something that he shared with his wife and they used to go to many concerts together. So, now they have started to go to concerts again after work, which gives them both a lot of pleasure and much-needed relaxation time.

Andrew still tends to worry. But he is calmer these days and feels more in control. He's more likely now, for example, to understand that something like the water cooler incident is down to how he himself is responding, and the stronger and more secure he feels the less likely he is to take this sort of encounter personally. He is more likely to cope better with ongoing pressures and, in the longer term, is equipping himself with stronger resilience skills. Andrew is definitely sleeping better at night too!

You need resilience skills to cope in the times we now live in. If you're not naturally resilient (and even if you are), there really are simple things you can do to become more resilient day-to-day that help you to not only deal with setbacks and rapid change but also pre-empt potential difficulties and challenges.

Interested in learning more?

I've put together some extra resources here:

Clarke, J. and Nicholson, J. (2010) *Resilience: Bounce Back from Whatever Life Throws at You.* Crimson Publishing.

Duckworth, A. (2017) *Grit: Why Passion and Resilience Are the Secrets to Success.* Vermilion.

Gladwell, M. (2009) *Outliers: The Story of Success.* Penguin Books.

Hanson, R. (2018) *Resilient: 12 Tools for Transforming Everyday Experiences into Lasting Happiness.* Rider.

Huffington, A. (2018) *The Sleep Revolution: Transforming Your Life One Night at a Time.* WH Allen.

Reivich, K. and Shatté, A. (2002) *The Resilience Factor: 7 Keys to Finding Your Inner Strength and Overcoming Life's Hurdles.* Three Rivers Press.

Seligman, M. (2006) *Learned Optimism: How to Change Your Mind and Your Life.* Vintage Books USA.

Seligman, M. (2012) *Flourish: A Visionary New Understanding of Happiness and Well-being.* Simon & Schuster.

Williams, S. (2016) *Rise: A First-aid Kit for Getting through Tough Times.* W&N.

Zolli, A. and Healy, A.M. (2012) *Resilience: Why Things Bounce Back.* Business Plus.

Articles and websites:

https://ppc.sas.upenn.edu/services/penn-resilience-training The Penn Resilience Program (PRP) and PERMA™ Workshops are evidence-based training programmes that have been demonstrated to build resilience, well-being and optimism.

https://assets.publishing.service.gov.uk/government/uploads/
system/uploads/attachment_data/file/182419/DFE-RR097.pdf

Interesting evaluation report on resiliency programmes that have
been run in the last decade or so in UK education.

You can also find more tips, ideas, curated video clips and exercises to strengthen your resilience skills by visiting https://
unimenta.com/resilience/

Sign up too for daily tips – a daily quote, tip and video clip on one
of the seven skills direct to your inbox. https://unimenta.com/seven-
skills/

THE
BEGINNING

You've reached the end of this book but it's actually only the beginning – the beginning of your own journey into tapping into and developing these inner resources that we all have.

What I wanted to do in *7 Skills for the Future* in both the first and this new edition is to emphasise and set out clearly just why a determined focus on key personal skills is so vital in today's world. Being adaptable, thinking critically, living with empathy and integrity and being proactive, optimistic and resilient are all about developing your individual competences and skills and doing this will give you so much more than the 'traditional' team-building or leadership skills. By working on developing the seven skills, you will be *so* much more effective in your own role and when you are in a situation where you might be leading people, you'll have the resources you need to do so. If you suffer disappointments, you'll be better equipped to handle them. If you are anxious or worried, you'll become so much stronger and able to cope. You will be more productive, happier and relaxed, with strong healthy relationships and live a life filled with meaning and purpose.

It is, however, about application, work and a daily focus on self-awareness. There is no quick fix. I continue to work on these skills each and every day; and even more so as a result of writing this book. Much of what I write about may seem so obvious, but if it is obvious, then why are so many of us either not even aware of these things or not as good as we could be at these skills? Why are so many of us looking for an easy answer and an instant solution rather than tapping into the richest resource we can possibly have – ourselves?

Everything I have written about begins with self-awareness. It is the cornerstone of emotional intelligence and starts with understanding who we are, why we think the way that we do and how we tend to respond to change and difficulties, as well as opportunities and unexpected surprises.

It's about taking the time to really think about what you say and why; what you do and why you do it. And then think about what you will say or do before acting; being truly in control. It's about really knowing your strengths and weaknesses and harnessing and managing these to be truly effective and to fulfil your potential.

We are all fearful, to varying degrees, of change and of putting ourselves in new situations but it's so important to get comfortable with embracing change. The only way to do this is to start with small steps, repeat them and build on them each and every day. Start now!

The seven skills naturally overlap. There is a connection between all seven of them and particularly between the three skills of being optimistic, proactive and resilient. Developing all seven is the key. In the 'A day in the life of' sections at the end of each chapter, I magnify one particular skill but actually we need to develop all seven consistently and apply them holistically, not just to specific situations and circumstances but to our whole life each and every day. This means thinking before responding and having a purpose to everything that you do and say. That purpose is to be the best you can be, with these skills underpinning everything you do.

We are gradually moving towards a place where there is far greater awareness for the need for these skills. There is more training available to help people develop, schools and colleges are starting to include more experiential learning and help people to be more equipped. But the best person to start this change is you.

Now is the time. . .

- to take ownership of your life
- to be the best version of yourself that there is

'Life isn't about finding yourself. Life is about creating yourself.'

George Bernard Shaw, Irish playwright

The unexpected bonus of happiness. . .

One thing I have discovered since writing the first edition of this book and running so many workshops with different people is how much happier I genuinely am as a result of focusing on these skills on a daily basis. I know that when I do that I am happier and that when I don't, perhaps the day does not go so well or challenging situations become worse. I've said before and I tell everyone this: I fall short of all seven every day but that is also why I love building my own awareness of them – time and time again I am taught that it is the simplest of situations and connections that provide you with the most opportunity to practise! By practising we become more proficient and then, in the really high-stake situations we are far better equipped to handle major setbacks, new challenges or difficult people. My teachers are my family, friends, colleagues, people I don't get on with (the best teachers!), new challenges and new experiences.

Advice on how to be happy is everywhere: At the time of writing, a Google search for 'happiness' yields 75 million results, and you can find nearly 40,000 books on or related to the topic on Amazon.

For me, and perhaps for you too, happiness is about living your life well, with purpose and meaning, finding joy in everyday experiences, doing work you love and nurturing strong and healthy relationships with friends and family.[1]

'The actions you take directly impact your levels of happiness.'

Dalai Lama, Spiritual Leader of the Tibetan people

Here's my take on how nurturing each skill makes you happier

Adaptability: Being adaptable is all about saying 'yes' to life and embracing change. You get better and better at this the more you practise and recognise 'ah, now that is an opportunity for me to flex my adaptability skills'. Whether that is being gracious about a last-minute change or about practising acceptance of something not working out as you wanted it to. Being gracious is about how you word that email, how you express yourself to others. Trust me, when you respond to situations beyond your control with adaptability, you have a much easier time. Although a default reaction may be to complain or be upset or to 'make a point', rarely does it actually get you anywhere beyond a momentary good feeling and being labelled as a 'difficult' person!

When you choose to expand your comfort zone, life immediately opens up a whole host of opportunity to you. Breaking out beyond limiting beliefs and mental scripts is hugely freeing – you get a big confidence boost by doing so and you will keep discovering what you are capable of and more of what your true potential is. All the most exciting things I have done have come from operating in my stretch zone. Even choosing to develop an experiential learning workshop to raise awareness of these seven skills has been risky and has definitely put me in my stretch zone. Yet I can honestly say from my heart that never has my work been so rewarding and never have I felt closer to my true life's purpose. It's an incredible feeling.

One big limiting belief I held from childhood was connected with a fear of dogs because I was bitten by one as a child. We moved to a beautiful village in the countryside three years ago. My husband wanted a dog. I didn't and was very closed to the idea – until I realised that it was a limiting belief and questioned it. I recognised that here was a great opportunity for me to be adaptable! That is how Oscar, our Golden Retriever came into our lives as an 8-week-old puppy. I learned how to take care of a puppy and how to be a dog owner. To say Oscar has changed my life is an understatement. To think that I could have missed out on the joys of owning a dog because of a life-long fear. Choosing to rise above that belief and own a dog was incredibly liberating and Oscar has made me happier generally (which is of course a dog's purpose).

Perhaps I shouldn't be surprised as Oscar is the best dog in the whole world! (Check him out on Instagram at oscar.the.goldens_ world)

Critical thinking: Perhaps this is not a skill you might immediately connect with being happier but I think it really does boost happiness levels in unexpected ways. By using this skill to the full, you are far less prone to making assumptions and quick judgements about things and you will, at the very least, start questioning those judgements and assumptions more. This will make you much better at decision making and problem solving as well as tapping into your natural creativity. Critical thinking will help you handle the huge overload of information we are all bombarded with on a continual basis because you will find better ways of using your brain's resources that will help you to be more productive and you'll become more discerning over the information you choose to expose yourself to. You're less likely to be swayed by what you see online or what you are sent by others and you'll be far more effective when it comes to reading and responding to email. I think all of this simply means that you are less likely to be operating in a more or less constant state of alert which so many of us are. You'll be using your brain in a more optimum way, having more creative ideas, being more productive and resourceful and feeling more in control.

Empathy: Empathy makes you happier for so many reasons! As a number of studies have shown, including the Harvard-Grant Study, a 75-year longitudinal investigation into what accounts for a fulfilling life[2] – strong relationships are consistently the strongest predictor of happiness. The best way to build strong relationships with others is through practising empathy. The huge value of simply giving others the gift of your attention by actively listening gives all your relationships, whether personal or professional, the X-factor. Being present enough to do that though requires reflection, mindfulness and the ability to look up from your smartphone on a regular basis. I emphasise the regular practice of mindfulness because mindfulness helps you to be more present, calmer and less reactive. It also activates the parts of your brain that are naturally hardwired to be empathetic.

Experiencing empathy also means you having more compassion for yourself as well as positive self-care – both of these are important for boosting happiness levels. You're more likely to be getting more sleep, achieving work–life balance, getting optimum amounts of exercise and nutrition as a result of self-care – all of these boost happiness levels. You are also going to be in a better place for finding a rewarding and fulfilling romantic partner, if this is something you desire.

Integrity: If you live your life with integrity, you are very likely being authentic, living aligned to your values and attuned to your life purpose. You keep your promises, you do what you say you are going to and you generate trust. Integrity is also about knowing yourself and understanding yourself. Knowing yourself requires honest self-reflection. The more honest you are with yourself, the greater happiness you will experience. Being truthful brings about an inner ease and happiness flourishes when, as John O'Donohue writes, 'we feel at home in our life.'

Optimism: Almost goes without saying why using this skill connects you with being happy! If you follow the exercises and ideas outlined in this chapter, you will be practising positive psychology rather than simply telling yourself that you are optimistic or relying on your moods. When you strengthen optimism, you are also less likely to complain and be vocally upset when things don't go as you had hoped because you are focusing on solutions instead.

You will personalise events and circumstances less and be more aware of how you respond to events in your life, choosing to look for the opportunities and rising up fast from setbacks. Optimism is interlinked with being proactive and resilient – if you strengthen any one of these, you are also strengthening the other two. If I wake up in the morning and feel a bit 'out of sorts', I now have the awareness to work out where that feeling might be coming from and to take action to change the feeling. Practising gratitude, one of the exercises I advocate both in this book and on our workshops, is strongly linked with happiness levels because it gives us perspective and it helps us to savour life's positive experiences, even in the middle of a challenging time. Numerous studies in recent years support this.

Being proactive: When you're proactive, you are back in control of your life. People who are happy focus their energy and efforts only on things that are truly important and within their control. Getting consumed by the things that you have absolutely no control over is a waste of time and leads to unhappiness. When you're proactive, you are deciding what you give your energy to and you're also deciding how your day will go in terms of managing your time.

Proactive people take positive action towards goals and life changes they might want to make. You are more likely to persevere when you're proactive and seek out different approaches if one does not work. Perhaps the best way to illustrate how being proactive links to being happy is this:

- If you have an **internal locus of control,** you believe that the quality of your life is largely determined by your own choices and actions. You believe that *you* are responsible for who you are and what you are.

- If you have an **external locus of control,** you believe that the quality of your life is largely determined by your environment, by luck, by fate. You believe that *others* are responsible for who you are and what you are.

Proactive people operate from an **internal locus of control** knowing they are in control over their lives and how they respond to events around them. Because they are proactive their actions will also often influence the situation or circumstances in a positive way too.

Resilience: Being resilient is all about developing the ability to bounce back quickly from setbacks and rejection. This happens faster the more you develop your mental, physical and emotional strength.

In this sense, resilience is linked with every other skill but especially with optimism and being proactive. Positive emotions play a large role in resilience helping us recover faster from trauma and find opportunities for growth from stressful experiences. Living with resilience is more than just 'bouncing back'; it is about shifting our perceptions, changing our responses and experiencing real growth. The only thing we have control over is that we have the ability to definitively and consciously change how we respond to what life throws at us at any given moment. We all endure challenges, big and small, which are meaningful opportunities for learning and building strength.

> *'The most important thing is to enjoy your life – to be happy – it's all that matters.'*
>
> Audrey Hepburn, British actress

Beyond this book you can get more tips, tools, articles and exercises to help you with developing and using these skills day-to-day by visiting https://unimenta.com/seven-skills/

For trainers and teachers, you can get further support for materials, programme design, soft skills and experiential learning activities at www.unimenta.com. Membership is free. If you are interested in becoming licensed to deliver workshops to raise awareness of the seven skills, find out more here: https://unimenta.com/advantage-licensed-trainers/

If you are interested in coming along to one of our workshops or having us run one at your organisation follow this link: https://unimenta.com/advantage-workshop/

We deliver these workshops to a wide range of clients and I am always interested to hear from trainers and teachers who might like to join our team.

And if you want to write to me directly, I'd love to hear from you!

emmasueprince@unimenta.com

> *'Extend your arms in welcome to the future. The best is yet to come!'*
>
> Anthony de Mello, Indian Jesuit Priest

Notes

The World We Are Living In

1 *Front Psychol.* 2017; 8: 605. Published online 2017 Apr 25. doi: 10.3389/fpsyg.2017.00605 PMCID: PMC5403814. PMID: 28487665. Smartphones and cognition: a review of research exploring the links between mobile technology habits and cognitive functioning

2 Appl Neuropsychol Child. 2014;3(3):173-81. doi: 10.1080/21622965.2013.875296. Breaking through barriers: using technology to address executive function weaknesses and improve student achievement.

3 Nesta, Pearson, Martin Oxford School: The future of skills: employment in 2030

4 Workforce of the future: The competing forces shaping 2030

5 https://www.britishcouncil.org/organisation/press/'-uk-must-go-india'-new-british-council-report-urges

6 www.telegraph.co.uk/education/expateducation/9020560/University-to-open-first-UK-campus-in-Thailand.html Hyslop, L. (January 2012) 'University to open first UK campus in Thailand', *The Telegraph*

7 www.wonkhe.com/2011/06/27/globalisation-where-on-earth-does-he-start/ Hughes, M. (June 2011) 'Globalisation: Where on Earth Does He Start?', Wonkhe – blog for Higher Education sector

8 Autor, D. (April 2010) in 'The polarization of job opportunities in the US Labor Market', Page, S. E. (2008) *The Difference: How the Power of Diversity Creates Better Groups, Firms, Schools and Societies.* Princeton University Press

9 'Economic Views BRICS', www.economics.pwc.com, February 2012

10 https://www.pwc.com/gx/en/services/people-organisation/workforce-of-the-future/workforce-of-the-future-the-competing-forces-shaping-2030-pwc.pdf

11 www.peopleandplanet.net/?lid=25995&section=33&topic=26 'The Ageing World', (January 2008), People & the Planet

12 www.cbi.org.uk/business-issues/education-and-skills/in-focus/ education-and-skills-survey/ CBI Education and Skills Survey 2012

13 www.economist.com/node/15640999 'Much to Learn – German's Education System is a Work in Progress', (March 2010), *The Economist*

14 online.wsj.com/article/SB10001424052702303666590457745252145 4725242.html?mod=WSJ_business_whatsNews Fuhrmans, V. (June 2012) 'Germany's New Export: Jobs Training', *The Wall Street Journal*

15 www.guardian.co.uk/science/2012/jun/30/self-help-positive-thinking Wiseman, R. (June 2012) 'Self-Help: forget positive thinking, try positive action', *The Guardian*

Chapter 1

1   Buch, K. (2009) 'Adaptability – Leading Through Focused Conversations', The Public Manager

2   https://learning.linkedin.com/content/dam/me/learning/en-us/pdfs/ linkedin-learning-workplace-learning-report-2018.pdf

3   www.clarionenterprises.com/assessments-eq.php#eci

4   Barnett, D.; Bauer, A.; Bell, S.; Elliott, N.; Haski, H.; Barkley, E.; Baker, D.; Mackiewicz, K. (22 June 2007) 'Preschool Intervention Scripts: Lessons from 20 years of Research and Practice', *The Journal of Speech-Language Pathology and Applied Behavior Analysis*

5   psychology.about.com/od/crisiscounseling/tp/become-more-resilient. htm Cherry, K. (2012) *10 Ways to Become More Resilient*

6   www.telegraph.co.uk/health/healthnews/9173552/Learning-another- language-could-protect-against-dementia.html Adams, S. (March 2012) 'Learning Another Language Could Protect Against Dementia', *The Telegraph*

7   www.trainingzone.co.uk/topic/role-play-real-play/174137 Holmes, S. (May 2012) 'From role play to real play', The Training Zone

8   Jon Wilkerson – www.internationalfunnybusiness.com

9   Calarco, A., Gurvis, J. (2006) *Adaptability : Responding Effectively to Change*. USA: Center for Creative Leadership, p. 12

Chapter 2

1 donaldclarkplanb.blogspot.co.uk/2011/01/huge-study-do-universities-really-teach.html Clark, D. (2012) 'Do Universities Really Teach Critical Thinking? Apparently Not', Donald Clark Plan B blog

2 cart.critical-thinking.com/critical-thinking-an-interview-part-i 'Critical Thinking' (2012) an interview with Richard C. Wells, BPI's VP of R&D

3 IBM, 'What Is Big Data?', Nov. '16.

4 www.criticalthinking.org/pages/dr-linda-elder/819 'The Critical Thinking Community', profile of Dr Linda Elder

5 www.sciencedirect.com/science/article/pii/S0160289610001303 Nusbaum and Silvia (2010) 'Study: Are intelligence and creativity really so different?', *Science Direct*

6 blogs.hbr.org/baldoni/2010/01/how_leaders_should_think_criti.html Baldoni, J. (January 2010) 'How Leaders Should Think Critically', *Harvard Business Review*

7 www.stanleymilgram.com/milgram.php Stanley Milgram profile

8 Winner, M.G. (2007) *Thinking About You, Thinking About Me*. Think Social Publishing

9 '*For learners to develop cognitively flexible processing skills and to acquire contentive knowledge structures which can support flexible cognitive processing, flexible learning environments are required which permit the same items of knowledge to be presented and learned in a variety of different ways and for a variety of different purposes (commensurate with their complex and irregular nature).*' Spiro (1996)

10 Winner, M.G. (2005) *Social Behaviour Mapping*. Think Social Publishing

11 www.wired.com/science/discoveries/news/2008/04/smart_software Madrigal, A. (April 2008) 'Forget Brain Age: Researchers Develop Software That Makes You Smarter'

Chapter 3

1 Daniel Pink, author of *A Whole New Mind* argues that empathy is one of six areas vital to success today.

2 A key example from *Wired to Care*

3   https://media.nesta.org.uk/documents/the_future_of_skills_ employment_in_2030_0.pdfs

4   www.myiris.com/newsCentre/storyShow.php?fileR=20120711102309 717&dir=2012/07/11 MyIris news site (2010) 'Rising Talent Management Challenges for Rapid Growth', Ernst &Young Survey

5   www.forbes.com/sites/sap/2011/08/22/social-media-success-is-just-about-one-thing-empathy/ Wilms, T. (August 2011) 'Social Media Success is Just About One Thing: Empathy', *Forbes Magazine*

6   https://www.telegraph.co.uk/science/2018/03/12/ empathetic-people-made-not-born-new-research-suggest

7   Singer, T. and Lamm, C. (2009) *The Social Neuroscience of Empathy.* University of Zurich

8   www.livescience.com/220-scientists-read-minds.html Than, K. (April 2005) 'Scientists Say Everyone Can Read Minds', Live Science

9   www.psychologytoday.com/basics/neuroscience Neuroscience description in *Psychology Today*

10 www.washingtonpost.com/wpdyn/content/article/2007/05/27/ AR20070527010.html

11 www.psychologytoday.com/basics/altruism Altruism, Understanding Altruism description from *Psychology Today*

12 www.psychologytoday.com/basics/cognition Description of Cognition from *Psychology Today*

13 www.danpink.com/whole-new-mind Pink, D. (2011) A Whole New Mind. Marshall Cavendish

14 www.paulekman.com/ Paul Ekman

15   en.wikipedia.org/wiki/Forum_theatre Definition of Forum theatre

16 www.guardian.co.uk/lifeandstyle/2008/mar/18/healthandwellbeing. features1 Darling, A. (March 2008) 'Mind over Matter', *The Guardian*

17 Langer, E. (1990) *Mindfulness.* Westview Press

18 Anna Ridderinkhof, Esther I. de Bruin, Eddie Brummelman & Susan M. Bögels. 'Does mindfulness meditation increase empathy? An experiment.' Pp. 251–269. Received 24 Feb 2016, Accepted 04 Dec 2016, Published online: 02 Jan 2017.

19 For example, Feldman, C. & Kuyken, W. (2011). 'Compassion in the landscape of suffering.' *Contemporary Buddhism, 12,* 143–155. doi:10.

1080/14639947.2011.564831[Taylor & Francis Online] [Web of Science ®], [Google Scholar]; Kabat-Zinn, J. (2011). 'Some reflections on the origins of MBSR, skilful means, and the trouble with maps.' *Contemporary Buddhism, 12,* 281–306.

Chapter 4

1   'Integrity', *The American Heritage Dictionary of the English Language* (4th ed.). El-shaddai. 2000. Retrieved 2009-05-13 from integer, whole, complete.

2   'Perspective Leadership Moments', *FBI Law Enforcement Bulletin* (October 2011).

3   www.stephencovey.com/blog/?tag=integrity Covey, S.R. (October 2008) website, extract from interview: 'Crisis Creates Humility'

4   www.ame.org/target/articles/1998/07/ best-companies-have-most-integrity Park, D. and Huge, E. (July 1998) 'The Best Companies Have the Most Integrity', Association for Manufacturing Excellence

5   www.brandmovers.com/blog/so-what-is-monochronic-vs-polychronic-behavior/ Brandmovers Blog (2011) 'What is Monochromic vs Polychronic Behaviour?'

Chapter 5

1   www.time.com/time/health/article/0,8599,2074067,00. html#ixzz20QwcyQW1 Sharot, T. (May 2011) 'The Optimism Bias', *Time, Health & Family*

2   en.wikipedia.org/wiki/Law_of_attraction Description of the Law of Attraction

3   www.oliverburkeman.com/books

4   www.guardian.co.uk/science/2011/may/15/flourish-science-of-happiness-psychology-review Layard, R. (May 2011) 'Flourish: A New Understanding of Happiness and Well-Being and How to Achieve Them', *The Guardian*

5   Seligman – PERMA model.

6   'Optimism and self-esteem are related to sleep. Results from a large community-based sample.' *International Journal of Behavioral Medicine.* Volume 20, Issue 4, pp 567–571.

7   The Losada ratio is the sum of the positivity in a system divided by the sum of its negativity. A ratio of 3.0 to 6.0 has been found to be highly correlated with high performance.

8   Ben-Ze'ev, A. (2000) *The Subtlety of Emotions.* Bradford Books

9   Taylor, S.E. and Brown, J.D. (1994) 'Positive Illusions and Well-Being Revisited, Separating Fact from Fiction,' *Psychological Bulletin,* Vol. 116, No 1, 21–7 (as cited in Taylor and Gollwitzer, 1995).

10 Taylor, S. and Armor, D. (December 1996), 'Positive Illusions and Coping with Adversity,' *Journal of Personality,* 64(4), 873–98.

11 Marshall, G.N.,Wortman, C.B., Kusulas, J.W., Hervig, L.K., and Vickers, R.R. (1992) 'Distinguishing Optimism From Pessimism: Relations to Fundamental Dimensions of Mood and Personality' *Journal of Personality and Social Psychology,* 62(6), 1067–74.

12 http://labs.psychology.illinois.edu/~ediener/discoveries.html; Ed Diener, Psychology Professor advises Gallup on research in psychological well-being. His current research focuses on the theories and measurement of well-being; temperament and personality influences on well-being; income on well-being; and cultural influences on well-being; and how employee well-being enhances organisational performance.

13 Oettingen, G. (2002) 'The Motivating Function of Thinking About the Future: Expectations vs Fantasies,' *Journal of Personality and Social Psychology,* 83, 1198–1212.

14 Pham, L. B. (1999) 'From Thought To Action: Effects of Process versus Outcome-based Mental Simulations on Performance' *Personality and Social Psychology Bulletin,* 25(2), 250–60.

15 www.trackyourhappiness.com

16 www.hup.harvard.edu/collection.php?cpk=1162 The work of William James, Harvard University Press

17 www.guardian.co.uk/science/2012/jun/30/self-help-positive-thinking?INTCMP=SRCH Wiseman, R. (June 2012) 'Self help: Forget positive thinking, try positive action', *The Guardian*

18 www.clarku.edu/faculty/jlaird/Publications.htm About James Laird – research into the perception of self

19 Seligman, M. *Learned Optimism: How to Change Your Mind and Your Life.* Vintage Books USA

20 www.forbes.com/2009/01/15/self-help-industry-ent-sales-cx_ml_0115selfhelp.html

Chapter 6

1   Covey, S.R. (2004) *The 7 Habits of Highly Effective People: Personal Workbook.* Simon & Schuster

2   www.lifehack.org/articles/productivity/are-you-proactive-or-reactive.html

3   Grant, A.M. and Ashford, S.J. (2008) 'The dynamics of proactivity at work,' *Research in Organizational Behaviour,* 28, 3–34.

4   Bindl, U. and Parker, S. (2010) 'Proactive Work Behaviour: Forward-Thinking and Change-Oriented Action in Organizations,' Institute of Work Psychology, University of Sheffield

5   *Journal of Leadership and Organisational Studies* (August 2009)

6   www.linkedin.com

7   Crant, M. (July 1996) 'The proactive personality scale as a predictor of entrepreneurial intentions' *Journal of Small Business Management,* 34(3) 42, 2 charts.

8   Dweck, C.S. (1999) *Self-Theories: Their Role in Motivation, Personality, and Development.* The Psychology Press.

9   Steel, P. (2011) *The Procrastination Equation: How to Stop Putting Things Off and Start Getting More Done.* Pearson Education.

10 Viktor Emil Frankl, MD, PhD was an Austrian neurologist and psychiatrist as well as a Holocaust survivor. Frankl was the founder of logotherapy, which is a form of existential analysis, the 'Third Viennese School of Psychotherapy.'

11 Kirby, E.G., Kirby, S.L., Lewis, M.A. (July 2002) 'A Study of the Effectiveness of Training Proactive Thinking,' *Journal of Applied Social Psychology,* 32(7), 1538–49, Southwest Texas State University.

Chapter 7

1   Kelly, R. (2005) '*innate psychological human immune capacity*' in 'Developing resilience', Affinity Health at Work (2011)

2   Greef (2002) '*a multi-faceted process from which people draw and learn from the best they can find in their environment, which can include family, school or the community*' in 'Developing resilience', Affinity Health at Work (2011)

3   Richardson (2002) '*categories that promote resilience, namely individual dispositional attributes, family support and cohesion and external support systems*' in 'Developing resilience', Affinity Health at Work (2011)

4   Jessica Pryce-Jones, CEO of iOPener, a human asset management consultancy and author of *Happiness at Work*

5   Hinsliff, G. (2012) *'Half a Wife', The Working Family's Guide to Getting a Life Back*. Chatto & Windus

6   www.ted.com/pages/about About TED

7   www.ted.com/talks/lang/en/richard_st_john_s_8_secrets_of_success. html TED talk, Richard St John – '8 Secrets of Success'

8   www.ppc.sas.upenn.edu/prpsum.htm University of Pennsylvania, Positive Psychology Center

9   The curriculum teaches cognitive-behavioural and social problem-solving skills and is based in part on cognitive-behavioural theories of depression by Aaron Beck, Albert Ellis and Martin Seligman (Abramson, Seligman, & Teasdale, 1978; Beck, 1967, 1976; Ellis, 1962). Central to PRP is Ellis' Adversity-Consequences-Beliefs (ABC) model, the notion that our beliefs about events mediate their impact on our emotions and behaviour.

10 SIT is a form of cognitive restructuring as it is a method of changing an individual's thinking patterns about themselves and their lives. The aim is to change their emotional responses and their behaviour, ideally before the individual becomes very anxious or depressed as a result of stress. 'Stress Inoculation Training: A preventative and treatment approach.' Dr Donald Meichenbaum, chapter in Lehrer, P. M., Woolfolk, R. L. and Sime, W. S., (2007) *Principles and Practice of Stress Management* (3rd edition), Guilford Press.

11 Duckworth, A.L., Peterson, C., Matthews, M.D. and Kelly, D.R. (2006) 'Grit, perseverance and passion for long-term goals,' *Journal of Personality and Social Psychology*, 92(6), 1087–101.

The Beginning

1   There are 5 elements essential to lasting contentment. These are positive emotions and the extent to which you experience them, levels of engagement with your work and the world, relationships, meaning/purpose and sense of accomplishment and we need each of them to feel contented and happy – Seligman PERMA model.

2   https://www.huffingtonpost.co.uk/entry/ how-this-harvard-psycholo_n_3727229

Index